PRAISE FOR *THE WILDES*

Poachers beware! Randy Nelson takes us on a storyteller's roller-coaster ride, up, down and around the ofttimes humorous, sometimes sad, but always poignant tales from the poacher's underworld. Fun to read, entertaining and brilliantly told, there are serious messages underlying Nelson's narrative: "Poaching would be worse if observant, honest hunters weren't out there."

— **Jim Shockey**, producer and host of *Uncharted*

Poaching never paints a pretty picture. In this wide-ranging and entertaining volume, Randy Nelson provides experienced insight into a world very few of us see, that of illegal wildlife takings and the heroic efforts of enforcement officers and their families to curb this corrosive and frequently violent activity. With its short, crisp chapters and accessible writing style, the book takes the reader into a massive corruption culture that has a startling range of players and an extraordinary diversity of wildlife species. For the general reader and the seasoned wildlife professional alike, this book is a disturbing reminder of why poaching should matter to us all.

— **Shane Mahoney**, president and CEO of Conservation Visions

Randy Nelson's book is required reading for all conservationists and hunters. It portrays our passion for everything that walks, swims and flies. Focused on real stories from all over North America, all future writing regarding game wardens and poachers will pale in comparison. The "Hunting for Dummies" vignettes sparkle with humour and relevance. I highly recommend this book.

— **Chuck Zuckerman**, president of BC Wildlife Federation

I was immediately sucked in by *The Wildest Hunt*. Randy Nelson has presented us with snapshots of wildlife crimes from all over North America, highlighting the threats of poaching, while also pointing out the humor and irony in many of these cases. As an officer in the field of wildlife law enforcement for 29 years, this book has made me even more appreciative of the job our wildlife officers do every day.

— **Rick Langley**, president of North American Wildlife Enforcement Officers Association

THE WILDEST HUNT

THE
WILDEST
HUNT

TRUE STORIES
OF GAME WARDENS
AND POACHERS

Randy Nelson

**HARBOUR
PUBLISHING**

HARBOUR PUBLISHING CO. LTD.
P.O. Box 219, Madeira Park, BC, VON 2HO
www.harbourpublishing.com

EDITED by Arlene Prunkl
COVER DESIGN by Anna Comfort O'Keeffe
TEXT DESIGN by Libris Simas Ferraz / Onça Publishing
PRINTED AND BOUND in Canada

Harbour Publishing acknowledges the support of the Canada Council for the Arts,
the Government of Canada, and the Province of British Columbia through the BC
Arts Council.

LIBRARY AND ARCHIVES CANADA CATALOGUING IN PUBLICATION
Title: The wildest hunt : true stories of game wardens and poachers / Randy Nelson.
Names: Nelson, Randy, 1956- author.
Identifiers: Canadiana (print) 20220231435 | Canadiana (ebook) 20220231443 |
   ISBN 9781550179989 (softcover) | ISBN 9781550179996 (EPUB)
Subjects: LCSH: Game wardens—Canada—Anecdotes. | LCSH: Game wardens—
   United States—Anecdotes. | LCSH: Poaching—Canada—Anecdotes. |
   LCSH: Poaching—United States—Anecdotes. | LCSH: Wildlife crime
   investigation—Canada—Anecdotes. | LCSH: Wildlife crime investigation—
   United States—Anecdotes. | LCSH: Wildlife conservation—Canada—Anecdotes.
   | LCSH: Wildlife conservation—United States—Anecdotes.
Classification: LCC SK361 .N55 2022 | DDC 364.16/2859—dc23

This book is dedicated to the spouses and families of fish and wildlife officers. They often stay up late, waiting and not knowing if or when the officer will safely return. Will they drag home some wounded critter? Will they reek of some dead animal they have dealt with? They could share another horror story or maybe one that will make them laugh. To those spouses and families who don't realize it—you are the most important part of any officer's career. Thanks!

TABLE OF CONTENTS

INTRODUCTION

GET READY TO READ ABOUT SOME OF THE WILDEST POACHING stories imaginable. The following pages contain at least one fish and wildlife poaching story from every province and territory in Canada and every state in the United States. Poaching is an international disgrace, and it is likely happening in your own neighbourhood.

These stories range from absolutely disgusting to hysterically hilarious. I think it's important to maintain a sense of humour in what could often otherwise be depressing, grisly accounts. Every poacher in these stories has been given a pseudonym because I don't want to bring any (further) notoriety upon them. Through thousands of phone calls and emails I contacted hundreds of investigating officers—at least one involved in nearly every poaching story—to help provide some insights that have never been heard before.

You will quickly learn that I don't care much for poachers. I hunted them for thirty-five years and never met one I liked. But a few changed and I liked them after that. I stalked them, tracked them, tricked them and bagged and tagged them. I quite literally ran them down. I chased hundreds of poachers on foot and never had one get away. I was an elite long-distance runner and just trotted behind them until they collapsed. That was fun!

After retiring in 2012, I wrote a book about my career as a fishery officer with the Department of Fisheries and Oceans (DFO) in British Columbia titled *Poachers, Polluters and Politics*. The book sheds light on the vast world of salmon poaching in BC. The feedback was so positive that I decided to write another book about poaching all over North America. In the process, I discovered poaching extremes that shocked even me. This book is a collection of over one hundred North American fish and wildlife officers' stories. Enjoy!

1

Note: In this book, I generally refer to these professionals as fish and wildlife officers or game wardens to cover the full range of agency titles such as game warden, wildlife officer, conservation officer, environmental conservation officer, fishery officer, fish and game officer, detective, police, and in some states, state trooper.

As well, because I'm a Canadian and this book was published in Canada, I have chosen to use metric measurements rather than imperial in most cases.

POACHING IS OUT
OF CONTROL

I ALWAYS LIKE TO BE OPTIMISTIC AND I'M USUALLY CRITICAL OF doomsayers, so I struggled to write this section. I lost my sense of humour for a couple of pages. Being a Canadian, I will say sorry for that. But I battled poachers for thirty-five years, and the truth is that it only grew more out of control during that time. Eight years after retiring, I still want to do something to help fish and wildlife. I want everyone to think about wildlife poaching and the impacts it is having on the world and what they can do to help. I don't mean for folks to donate to some alleged conservation group that preys on your compassion for dollars to support their pet project. I mean supporting the fish and wildlife enforcement officers who want to work with you. No one cares more.

There are many reasons poaching is out of control and will continue to grow. The fact that it took only two months to locate poaching stories from every state in the US and every province in Canada indicates how widespread the problem is. Certainly, gains are being made in some areas, but I refer to the overall poaching and trade in fish, wildlife and plant resources. Let's start with the chance of getting caught. You have seventy-five times the chance of encountering a police officer in whatever you do in your everyday life versus being checked by a fish and wildlife officer while you are out poaching in a forest or field or stream. That's a fact, based on our population, police numbers and game warden numbers in North America.

Way back in 1950, Jim Kjelgaard conducted a countrywide survey in the United Sates regarding poaching. He pointed out that the number of wardens was so low that poachers had only a 1 per cent

3

chance of being caught. Thirty-five states responded to the survey. All but three showed increases in poaching, and in some of those states increases were as much as 200 per cent. The estimates in his survey also showed four times as much wildlife was taken through poaching as by legal means.

There are people who have been out hunting and fishing for decades and have never been checked by wildlife officers. One of the most basic and important deterrents for crime reduction is officer presence. What happens when a police patrol car is seen on the highway? Most everyone taps their brakes, even if they aren't speeding. The chance and thought of getting caught equates to compliance. But what would happen if you never saw a patrol car on the highway? The same is true for fish and wildlife users. If people even see an officer, compliance will improve. It doesn't stop poachers but it helps.

Organized criminal groups will trade in whatever form of "currency" they can find. Cocaine, for example, is used as currency in some parts of Colombia. If a certain plant or animal becomes rare and happens to be sought-after, criminals will turn to that form of currency for trade. It's much easier to access and less likely that someone will notice their crimes. If a car thief steals twenty cars there will be twenty very upset owners and twenty complaints to the police. Your car is insured, but wildlife is not. If that same criminal becomes involved in the illegal trade of wildlife, it's more likely no one will notice. There are numerous examples of poachers taking dozens or even hundreds of animals. We're all surprised when they happen to get caught. Most of the public will not even realize the crimes have happened unless they get caught. To catch them takes a caring citizen or game warden or both. And even when they are caught, it can be difficult to gather enough evidence to prove the case in court.

If they do get to court, there has to be an educated prosecutor and judge willing to understand the facts and the impact poaching has on the resource and apply appropriate sentencing. Everyone agrees a drug dealer is bad and should be put away (except maybe the drug dealer himself). You never hear anyone say, "Oh, that nice drug dealer is my neighbour, he's only putting food on the table." Yet many people sympathize with a poacher. Public attitude is improving but we have a long way to go.

Global trade in the world's commodities has opened avenues for illegal trade in wildlife as well. Massive quantities of illicit wildlife products are transported around the world daily with little chance of apprehension. If one load happens to be caught, it's just the cost of doing business for the poachers.

If a highly sought-after animal or animal part or plant is over-exploited in one part of the world, poachers will simply find another country with the animal's population to exploit. The value increases as the population diminishes, making the species even more vulnerable to poachers. Most people think of rhinoceroses, elephants and tigers when they think of poaching. But there's a whole world of poaching of species I didn't even know about in North America. If the animal or plant disappears, criminals will simply move on to the next most lucrative item. It's horrible what's happening in some African countries. It's also horrible what's happening in our own backyards.

Many fish and wildlife agencies in the United States and Canada receive funding from the sale of hunting and fishing licences. As the numbers of legal hunters and fishers decline, so do the budgets for protecting the animals. It's a dangerous cycle if you're a wild animal. Fewer legal hunters and fishers means more room is created for poachers with an even less likely chance of getting caught.

There's constant pressure on all fish and wildlife agencies to stay within budgets. In times of budget cuts, it's also highly likely that fish and wildlife officer numbers will be reduced first. The easiest way to save money is to not fill job vacancies. No one really notices a few fewer officers here or there, much like the resources they protect. It's up to everyone who votes to demand more protection and increase rather than decrease fish and wildlife officer numbers. Fish and plants and wildlife can't talk and they don't vote. We need to vote for them.

A HISTORY OF FISH AND WILDLIFE OFFICERS

BEFORE WE DELVE INTO INDIVIDUAL POACHING STORIES, IT MAY be helpful to briefly look at the history of wildlife officers. Who were the first game wardens and where did they patrol? The first wardens were called gamekeepers and were hired by Danish king Cnut (or Canute) around the year 1010 AD. King Cnut ruled parts of England and current Scandinavian countries during his raid-filled reign. Cnut's grandfather was known as Bluetooth because his teeth were unusually blue. Some think he might have filed them and dyed them. I think it was the wine. Cnut was a somewhat ruthless ruler. He once returned some captives after cutting off their ears and noses. As most kings did, he enjoyed hunting and noticed too many others were partaking in the sport. He passed a law that made unauthorized hunting punishable by death. No repeat offenders back then. They didn't "need no stinkin' badges" either. Gamekeepers have been used throughout the ages to modern times.

Canada hired its first game officers at the time of Confederation in 1867. The east coast cod fishery was being exploited by many European nations, and the first Canadian fishery officers were hired to patrol and enforce fishing quotas on the Atlantic Grand Banks. Fishery officers are part of the oldest wildlife enforcement agency in Canada (and in North America), established six years before the North West Mounted Police (the RCMP today).

Michigan was one of the first states in the US to hire game wardens, in 1887. Fishing and hunting laws had existed for about fifty years, but county sheriffs had done the enforcement until then. Another state to hire a game warden early on was Florida. Guy

Bradley was a guide for fishermen and plume hunters. Visitors would hunt for the many shorebirds in Florida to gather their plumage and sell the feathers for decorative hats. Hunters could make thousands of dollars shooting birds for their feathers. The concentrated shorebird rookeries gradually became decimated and bird populations plummeted. Legislation changed to stop the hunting, but poachers continued to hunt birds. Bradley was hired in 1902 by the American Ornithologists' Union, and in his job he patrolled vast areas of the Florida coast. Sadly, he was shot and killed in 1905 by a father and son poaching shorebirds.

Bradley's killer, "Waldo," had been convicted for shooting birds before. In that previous incident, he vowed to kill Bradley if he ever encountered him again. Waldo was a very wealthy man. In a bizarre sequence of "money talks" events, he hired the local prosecutor as his defence lawyer. The jury was made up of poor locals who empathized with men who shot birds for a living because they could see themselves doing the same thing. It's difficult to understand why that thinking still exists today. People hear of someone selling fish or wildlife illegally and don't regard it as a serious crime. Yet if that same criminal broke into their home and stole a television, they'd be livid. It is getting better, however, and some members of the public are becoming more protective as they realize that wildlife resources belong to everyone and they must become involved to help protect them.

In Waldo's trial, the prosecutor entered very sketchy evidence. The two men claimed self-defence, though Bradley had never fired his gun. They were not convicted and freely walked away. Thirty-five-year-old Warden Bradley left behind a wife and two children. His death sparked a conservation movement that inspired the nation and helped advance future legislation for bird protection.

The job of a fish and wildlife officer is just as dangerous today. The people they encounter are often armed. Patrols are commonly in rural or remote areas where backup support is not readily available.

Poachers are often hardened criminals with a sickened sense of entitlement to pilfer fish and wildlife resources. And it's not just the risk of injury or death from poachers. Travel on remote roads has resulted in officer deaths in vehicle, boating, snowmobile and airplane accidents, as well as deaths from animal attacks, drowning and hypothermia. The chances of being killed on the job as a fish and wildlife officer are three to four times higher than those of a police officer.

A horrible example of this happened nearly sixty years ago, in 1965. Two Saskatchewan conservation officers were driving a purple Bombardier (a large, tracked vehicle for snow) on patrol. A "hunter" forty-five metres away thought the purple vehicle was a moose and shot a number of rounds into the front windshield, killing the driver, Officer Alfred Newland. The hunter was fined $2,000 and given zero jail time.

Despite the dangers, many agencies have numerous applicants when jobs become available. Many officers spend their entire career, often thirty-plus years, doing the job they enjoy. Personally, I was addicted to catching poachers. I spent many sleepless nights scheming up new plans to bag a few more. It's a lot like hunting, but without limits. And the prey is criminals, not innocent creatures.

DEFINITION OF A POACHER

MY DEFINITION OF A POACHER IS AS FOLLOWS: *A PRIMITIVE ORGANism attempting to eliminate any form of life with more intelligence than its own.* Poachers are proof that we are regressing in our ability to live in harmony on this planet.

Humans are fast becoming a race that can't think on its own. Take the COVID-19 pandemic reaction, for example. Someone started a story on social media that everyone should stock up on supplies, and what was the most important supply? Toilet paper! Really? Masses rushed out to buy cartloads of toilet paper. I realized it really happened because if one person coughed, ten more people crapped their pants. What about food? If you don't eat, you don't need toilet paper, right? Maybe it was me who started the next stampede to empty grocery store shelves.

This same reactive thinking often leads us into the poaching world. If a rare plant or animal becomes a symbol of wealth, social status, good luck or sexual potency, a market will develop to exploit that resource. Criminal organizations join in, using the items as another form of currency, a practice commonly associated with the illegal drug trade. Rather than being critical of this "lemming" mentality, perhaps we could use it in the fight against poaching. We'd just have to get a few key people with millions of internet followers to state that noxious weeds or some invasive species will add years to your life, and that eating or owning some rare species causes infertility. Problem solved. Seriously though, poachers are far more prevalent than most would believe. Poachers ignore all boundaries, whether it's a hunting boundary, a park, state or country boundary, even across continents.

Poachers can come from any occupation imaginable. They could be farmers, doctors, lawyers, police officers, teachers, loggers, politicians or even a hunting show host or a family member. Some follow generations of poachers in their family tree. Others may have fallen out of a tree or lacked oxygen at birth. Or it may simply have been the case of having a small appendage.

Hunters are not poachers, though they can turn into poachers. Poachers like to think of themselves as hunters, but they are not. Poachers give the legitimate hunter or fisher the wrong public image that is often eagerly latched on to by those who are against all hunting. I don't consider an occasional fishing trip out with the grandkids without a fishing licence or other minor infraction to be a poaching crime. Some fish and wildlife violators have simply made a mistake. That doesn't make it right, but neither does it put them in the category of a poacher. But people who know poachers or support this international trade through illicit purchases are part of the poaching problem.

The worldwide poaching trade is estimated to be worth billions of dollars. A number of studies rank wildlife poaching next only to firearm, drug and human smuggling in value. Those who buy illegal fish, plants or wildlife are just as guilty as the poachers themselves. If you have ever knowingly purchased illegal fish or wildlife, you are a poacher. You are also part of the problem if you know of someone who is a poacher or someone who has purchased illegally taken fish or wildlife and you have not reported it. If you're still reading, you can become part of the solution.

Poachers disrupt the entire system of wildlife management. Wildlife managers try to allocate numbers for harvest quotas of wildlife using fact-based, population-driven reasons. Occasionally, a decision for harvesting animals may be too liberal and negatively impact a population. That same decision may not harvest enough animals and cause different concerns. It's not easy to manage fish and wildlife. Biologists making the management decisions have to take into account all stakeholders—hunters, fishers, Indigenous people, the public, political pressure, economics, their own biases and the resource itself. Poaching complicates the entire process.

Although I have personally caught hundreds of poachers over my career, I've always known I was only catching a tiny fraction of them. The magnitude of the poaching problem is rarely talked about in political circles; it's easy to ignore because the public (voters) doesn't realize how widespread it is. Hopefully, this book will help to bring awareness to some of those concerns and raise interest in creating worldwide support for enforcing laws to protect our precious wildlife resources.

A 1950 Saskatchewan game code reads: "The best conservation laws are not found in the pages of our statute books, but are engraved on the conscience of the true sportsman."

HUNTING FOR DUMMIES

Mr. "Ego" of North Carolina devised a plan to become the holder of the biggest deer in his state. He purchased a huge set of shed non-typical white-tailed deer antlers from a deer farm in Pennsylvania. He went out and poached a small local buck and posed for pictures with the larger antlers. He was now the proud hunter who owned the new state archery record. Really! He honestly thought he could get away with attaching the giant antlers to a much smaller buck body. Mr. Ego became the joke among hunters for a long time. He lost hunting privileges for two years on top of his fine. I think if I'd caught this guy I would have mailed him a sympathy card for Christmas.

FISH AND WILDLIFE OFFICERS IN NORTH AMERICA

NORTH AMERICA, INCLUDING CANADA AND THE UNITED STATES, has an average of 204 police officers per 100,000 residents. How many fish and wildlife officers? There are 2.7 per 100,000, or 1.3 per cent as many fish and wildlife officers compared with police officers (based on 2017 numbers).

It's not uncommon to encounter outdoor enthusiasts who have never been checked by a fish and wildlife officer. These officers patrol vast areas in both countries. In the US every officer patrols an average area of 1,640 square kilometres. In Canada each officer covers an average of 5,000 square kilometres. How can they do this? They use very good binoculars and have tracking devices on all the animals. I'm only half kidding. Both are partially true. You can see why fish and wildlife officers rely heavily on the public to do their jobs. Although the numbers of officers per capita are higher in Canada, each officer covers a much larger area.

Wildlife officers' duties vary substantially between agencies. Almost every state and province in North America has a fish and wildlife agency. Some separate them into fish and wildlife, while in some states such as Oregon and Alaska, wildlife laws are enforced by a branch of the state troopers. Both Canada and the United States have federal agencies for fish and a separate one for wildlife. Most agencies cross over and assist one another wherever they can.

Some agencies have the authority to enforce all laws in their jurisdictions and some cannot cross over to do police work. This seems like a missing link in areas where fish and wildlife officers aren't allowed to enforce things that they happen across. For example, I worked with the Department of Fisheries and Oceans and had the authority only to enforce the laws under the Fisheries Act. If I happened upon another serious crime while on a fisheries patrol, I could not technically act upon it. Legal opinions varied on what would happen if an officer were forced to act and were injured. Legally, I could not respond—if I had, I might not have been legally covered. Many jurisdictions have corrected this by giving cross designations. Hopefully, all remaining agencies with this issue have it corrected before someone is hurt or killed, only for it to be discovered later that they were acting without authority. Most fish and wildlife officers should not and do not want to do police work; they just want the authority to act should they encounter a serious crime and be forced to act. This would also provide better service and safety to the public.

HUNTING FOR DUMMIES

This is not a poaching story, but wildlife and a warden were involved nonetheless. A young couple drove their vehicle to a remote part of Jasper National Park in Alberta. They left their vehicle and headed to a secluded meadow and began to entertain themselves as best as two can do in the outdoors with only a blanket. They were so in touch with each other that they didn't see a curious black bear approach, looking for a free lunch. The naked couple panicked and ran to their vehicle. A park warden pulled up just as the couple arrived at their car. It seemed the keys were in the pants pocket left behind in the meadow with the bear. Bummer.

PRICKLY POACHERS

CACTI ARE LIKELY ONE OF THE LAST THINGS YOU'D THINK ABOUT when discussing poachers. Sadly, criminals will use anything with a value to pay for their illegal operations. Cactus poachers sell their plants to anyone in the world who is willing to pay.

China and Europe are two of the main buyers of the rarer types of these succulents. In some places they are even considered sacred. The trade of cactus plants is not viewed as a real concern in those parts of the world, thereby allowing the market to flourish. The internet has provided a safer haven for poachers to hide in and advertise their product. A single rare plant can bring thousands of dollars when it's smuggled into a country with a willing buyer. An internet study of one thousand cactus sales revealed that 90 per cent were illegal. Collectors of rare cacti require only two things: a ridiculous amount of money and a very low level of intelligence. That's only my opinion, though, as some may not be rich.

There are about fifteen hundred species of cacti, and all but one can be found in the Americas. About a third of those are considered endangered. Cacti are very slow-growing plants and can live to be over one hundred years old. One of the more sought-after species of cacti is something that can only be described as butt ugly (not that all butts are ugly). The living rock cactus is a drab-coloured glob less than ten centimetres high. If you can picture a fresh, steaming cow-pie with small rocks inserted into it, you're close.

Large prickly poaching rings run by organized criminal groups operate in places such as Mexico, the United States, South America and more. Similar to most poaching operations, the bottom of the crime chains are normally poor locals who can't afford to resist the temptation of quick cash.

Some sophisticated operations start by sending criminals posing as tourists to locate the rare plants. They will take a camera and pose as a botanist or photographer interested in seeing the rarest (and most valuable) plants and discreetly record the location through GPS. A local person will then be sent in to collect the plants, getting paid pennies on the dollar for their work.

In one case goatherds were asked to collect some rare cacti while herding their goats over a vast area where a particular species was known to exist. The goatherds collected over ten thousand plants, likely making the rare plants nearly extinct in that location. The plants made their way to China and Korea and sold for a tidy $200,000.

In another case a local game warden in a park in Africa was asked to show visitors some rare cacti they wanted to photograph. He obliged but unknowingly had led some criminals to the location of the plants, and the next time he returned there, the plants were gone. In this case a poaching ring was broken on future trips, with Japanese "tourists" caught and convicted. They were forbidden to ever return to the country. Perhaps one form of punishment would be to strap a few cacti to the poachers' butts or lower anatomy and send them home! Maybe we should call them prick collectors.

These collectors should not be confused with the many dedicated botanists and education facilities that legally own and care for endangered species. Sul Ross State University in Alpine, Texas, is one such facility, containing about thirty-five hundred succulents. Many have been seized from poachers and can't be returned to the protected locations in case they are not from that area. Genetic diversity must be maintained, and placing plants in a park where they may not be native to the area is of concern. Plants can be transferred to private property where genetic concerns are not as great.

In 2015 five people flew from Europe to Los Angeles for a three-week "vacation" to ostensibly photograph plants. "Igor," the Russian leader of the group, had been to the US before for a similar purpose.

In this 2015 evidence photo, "Igor" is hiding rare cactus seeds in rice to be smuggled from Texas to Europe and Russia. *Photo: Undercover officer, US National Parks Service.*

This time, authorities were onto him and, using tracking devices and undercover officers, discreetly followed his meandering trip through remote deserts all the way to western Texas.

Mr. Igor had a personal collection of over two thousand live cactus plants at home. He estimated he'd owned over ten thousand plants over the years. His group was not just collecting the plants, they were returning to rare locales he'd meticulously recorded on previous trips to collect seeds or pods from mature plants. They were caught at the airport with over seventy plants plus seeds from endangered, protected plants hidden in a bag with jalapenos, in a box of rice and among electronics.

Many poachers can't help but brag about their conquests. Igor was no exception, posting pictures of himself on Facebook collecting the protected plants and cradling his prized cacti like a newborn baby. Igor's types are collectively known as "cactophiles," putting them in a group of "dirty old men in potting sheds." He received a fine of $535 and was allowed to go home. A lot of work is needed to educate judges about the severity and profitability of this crime.

A more recently discovered cacti-poaching ring was busted through a lengthy and complex investigation in Texas. The investigation involved the US Fish and Wildlife Service (USFWS), Homeland Security Investigations (HSI), the US Department of Justice, the US Postal Service and the National Parks Service (NPS).

Most previous cases had involved European smugglers picking their own plants. This case focused on locals in the Big Bend region in southwest Texas and the living rock cactus previously mentioned.

The case began with an investigation into illegal immigrant workers in which a warrant was served on a local farmer employing them. The officer noticed a bunch of cactus plants during his search and reported the findings to other agencies. Officers determined that the farmer was supplying a local seller with markets in Asia. One single violator in this case made over $300,000 in six to seven months of operation.

In Asia the cactus plants are gifted to newborn children to nurture the plant throughout their life. Ancient customs are difficult to change. Efforts to lessen the demand would be the best tool to save many of these plants from extinction. China is inundated with illegal importations of animal parts such as those of rhinos and other threatened species. Its officials are therefore reluctant to be concerned with mere cactus plants.

Some might think these customs are wrong and have to change. But North Americans can't be too critical given some of our past dealings with species now extinct or threatened. For example, in 1886 the Smithsonian Institute was concerned it didn't have any good buffalo specimen mounts for the museum. Buffalo were near extinction. What did they do? A Smithsonian crew went to eastern Montana and "collected" twenty-five of the few remaining buffalo. They were carefully skinned for taxidermy mounts. Six were mounted and displayed for over seventy years before finding their way home to a small museum in Montana. They thought they were doing the right thing. I'm certain we are doing things today that will be ridiculed a hundred years from now, maybe even five years from now.

Living rock cacti investigations are complicated by the fact these cacti can be harvested from private land and sold within the US. Seeds can be sold outside the US. This is allowed because the living rock cactus is not yet listed as endangered. Buyers will pay even more for plants collected from within Big Bend National Park. Trails within the park that once had hundreds of plants in certain locations are now devoid of all but a few remaining plants.

In the Big Bend case, four cactus traffickers were fined nearly US$120,000, a total of nine years' supervised probation, one year of unsupervised probation and forfeiture of seventeen firearms. I didn't know cacti were that dangerous! I expect that, as with any poaching ring, these people would be involved in other crimes. The value of the cacti would also make theft a serious possibility.

These convictions have helped reduce the internet trade and likely driven the crime further underground. Education of the public, judges, investigators, land owners, developers and anyone else who may negatively impact these plants must be an ongoing effort in order to lessen the decline of these rare species that are seldom recognized as a poaching threat. Until then, game wardens will have to tackle cactus poachers one prick at a time.

HUNTING FOR DUMMIES

Facebook can be a wonderful thing. An individual—an adult male—on Facebook was pictured with dead wild turkeys, and someone saw the photo and reported it to New York's environmental conservation officers. A youth season was open at the time, but the officer tracked down the man and went to his home to check it out anyway. The man confessed to shooting three turkeys. When the officer asked where the meat from the birds was, the poacher hung his head and turned to the kitchen, where a cooked turkey was being served. Further questions revealed that the man had been barred from possessing firearms. The officer charged him and seized all the uncooked meat, and dinner was allowed to proceed. I'll bet the poacher really enjoyed choking the bird down as he thought about what it was going to cost him.

NARWHAL TUSK
SMUGGLING

NARWHALS ARE TRULY A UNIQUE SPECIES ON OUR PLANET WITH their fairy-tale, unicorn-like spiralled tooth or tusk extending up to three metres on larger animals. They are mainly found in the Arctic waters of Canada and Greenland. Arctic inhabitants have hunted narwhals for centuries to provide valuable meat and fat to their northern diet. The spiral tusk is also ideal for carving. Many countries including the US have banned the import of narwhal parts because of their concerns about encouraging poaching. Canadians can legally purchase and own tusks in Canada but require special permits for them.

The world population of narwhals is estimated at around 123,000 animals (2017). Their harvest rate is estimated at less than 1 per cent, or about one thousand animals per year. They were listed as near threatened in 2008 even though there has been no sign of a population decline. Some non-governmental organizations (NGOs) attempt to create an artificial concern simply because they don't agree with activities such as hunting. There are always people willing to be called experts who use selective data to "prove" their point. Conservation concerns could develop as Arctic ice melts, but no one knows for certain whether or how the narwhal's food sources might be affected. The narwhal could be exposed to more hunting pressure, or populations could disperse and be less available for hunting. Increased ship and boat traffic could also impact these unusual creatures. However, the best evidence available does not indicate any conservation concerns through current traditional Inuit hunting practices in the Arctic.

The value of tusks varies dramatically depending on the length. A fully intact tusk can be worth $3,000 to $12,000, while a rare double tusk can bring up to $50,000 or more. These crazy values caught the greedy eyes of RCMP constable "Jimmy Lowlife" while he was stationed in the Arctic, in Iqaluit and other northern communities. Lowlife's interest would turn him into one of the most sought-after wildlife smugglers in North America. Greed can strike anywhere.

Mr. Lowlife started buying tusks from the locals in Nunavut while working as an RCMP officer in 1999. He sold them in Canada, where it was legal, provided that documents were included. At the same time, a United States Fish and Wildlife Service officer in Ohio located an ad on eBay that led him to discover Mr. Lowlife was the seller. The officer contacted Lowlife, who used his police status to successfully claim his innocence. He even used RCMP letterhead to fax information back and forth! It makes me wonder what role he would have played in a "good cop, bad cop" scenario. In his correspondence he asked, "Why would an RCMP officer with twenty-five years' experience even try such a thing?" That was cheeky. The buyer in the US was convicted and Lowlife was given the benefit of the doubt and issued a warning.

Lowlife's parents lived in New Brunswick. As Lowlife's fortunes rolled in, he decided to buy both a summer home in New Brunswick and a home where he lived in Alberta. Lowlife also built a third house in Texas. The builder was very pleased because Lowlife always paid cash for his work.

In 2002, retirement gave Lowlife loads of time to develop a scheme of illegal smuggling of narwhal parts into the US. Like most poachers' schemes, Lowlife's was sophisticated but not intelligent. He increased his purchases of narwhal tusks and, flashing his RCMP badge (even though he was retired), smuggled them into the US through a small border crossing in Maine. The tusks were often stored in a hidden compartment under the box of a utility trailer he pulled behind his truck. The compartment was painted the same colour as the bottom of the trailer to avoid detection. Lowlife sometimes strapped tusks to the underside of his pickup, wrapped in hand-sewn bags coloured the same as the underside of the pickup. He'd modified the underside of the truck to accommodate the long tusks.

Meanwhile in the US, an eBay ad had prompted investigations into narwhal tusk buyers that all seemed to point to Mr. Lowlife. An international team of investigators was assembled to work on Operation Longtooth. A more appropriate title would have been Operation Bonehead. They tracked tusks flown from legal Arctic sellers to Winnipeg, from where they were trucked to New Brunswick. Lowlife had a US postal address and two US bank accounts, complete with "legitimate" businesses in the US, to launder money. Lowlife always used his friendly Canadian cop routine when dealing with authorities. Sorry! You can't always trust a Canadian, eh?

In 2009, Lowlife and his wife made one of their many trips to the US with two large tusks tied up and hidden under his pickup. He approached the border as he'd done dozens of times before. When asked whether he had anything to declare, he pulled out his tarnished RCMP badge and declared himself legal. He crossed the border and, to avoid detection, backed into a secluded old logging road well out of sight of the main road.

Little did he know that an USFWS officer was watching from the bushes as Lowlife crawled under his truck to untie the tusks and place them in the wooden crate in the box of his pickup truck. He drove to the courier and sent them off to his buyer. All was good, except that an American buyer had been caught a short time before and ratted him out to avoid jail time. Lowlife's purchaser on this day was an undercover USFWS agent.

Months later, seven search warrants were executed at locations in Alberta, Texas, California, Hawaii, Alaska and New Jersey to gather evidence for numerous violations. Les Sampson was the lead Canadian investigating officer with the Canadian Wildlife Service. He later ended up in Beverly Hills, California, interviewing one of Lowlife's customers, an innocent elderly man who carved ivory and had purchased tusks he believed were legal. He had legal documents for all the ivory in his ivory tower overlooking Beverly Hills, purchased over decades through his antique business and estate sales. He was unaware that some of Lowlife's documents were forged and charges were not laid in this case.

Two of Lowlife's customers in the US received hefty sentences for their illicit purchases of narwhal tusks. Dealers from New Jersey and Boston each received thirty-three months in prison plus fines and forfeitures of cash and tusks. A Ukrainian co-conspirator living in the US was given a nine-month sentence for lesser offences. He served his time and was immediately deported.

At his New Brunswick trial in 2013, the full scope of Lowlife's enterprise was revealed: between 2003 and 2009, he smuggled at least $2 million worth of tusks in forty-six different transactions to a network of US collectors and criminals. This time period was used because it contained the most complete evidence gathered, even though it was known Lowlife made many purchases prior to 2003. He also smuggled illegal walrus ivory tusks but was not charged for those. He forged documents in the US to claim that some of the tusks were from earlier than 1972, making them appear to be legal and worth far more than tusks without papers.

During Lowlife's trial, the courts also heard that he had sold his house in Texas and transferred sizable amounts of cash to an account in Mexico just as the case was unfolding. What defence could he possibly have? He claimed post-traumatic stress disorder from his time on the police force. It's possible he did have PTSD, so I'd never want to say what I really think about his defence in this case. He was sentenced to a fine of $385,000. That may sound good, except that he had likely profited millions. He paid the courts $280,000 on that day alone.

His battle did not end there. Thanks to a successful extradition to the US, he faced charges of conspiracy, smuggling, tax evasion and money laundering. He probably had to do his own laundry after he faced his sentence in a US district court. The judge gave Mr. Lowlife a tongue lashing like few had ever seen. Lowlife's arrogance vanished as he was sentenced to serious prison time in Pennsylvania, five years and two months. His enforcement background made it necessary to isolate him from other prisoners. Some might say he should be let into the general prison population for a day. I wouldn't agree with that, but perhaps a longer sentence would be suitable. Lowlife still owes the remaining $105,000 of his fine in Canada. He will probably be arrested upon returning to Canada and could spend more time in an orange jumpsuit if the fine isn't paid.

HUNTING FOR DUMMIES

Deer decoys provide some of the best entertainment a wildlife officer can have. Wisconsin officer John W. Buss had a couple of good ones. When his fellow officers in Wisconsin decide to operate a deer decoy, their policy dictates they must make the public aware of the setup. That may sound counterproductive, but really, not many poachers watch the news. They are more likely to be in the news. To follow agency policy, John contacted the local television station and requested that the operation be mentioned on the 6:00 p.m. and 10:00 p.m. news the night before they set up the decoy.

With the decoy in place, it wasn't long before a black Bronco came along, slowed and stopped. The driver got out and fired at the decoy. When John apprehended the poacher, he said, "My wife is gonna kill me! The worst part about this is that I watched this last night on the news." Yes, there were two dummies in the story, the shot-up decoy and the shooter.

POACHING FIREFIGHTER

PRIOR TO 2013, COLORADO PARKS AND WILDLIFE (CPW) OFFICERS had fielded complaints for several years that elk and deer were being spotted with arrows in them in one particular neighbourhood. The officers got a great break when a concerned citizen called in and reported having seen a dead elk covered by a blue tarp near their property. Three deputies near the area responded to the call. They arrived and greeted a man dressed in camo with blood on his hands. The man took off running, leaving the elk and some gear behind. The deputies also called CPW officer Murdoch to attend the scene. The officers' body cams had recorded the whole incident, including the poacher running away. The poacher was now the quarry.

Officer Murdoch and the deputies approached the headless elk and began a thorough search of the area. They found a backpack, knives, water bottles and a bunch of small items. They also found a hat down a slope where they believed the poacher had escaped. They obtained a search warrant for the backpack, which contained the poacher's wallet and identification, along with a cellphone. The phone held pictures and locations with major pieces of evidence. One picture of an elk taken a couple of years before led an officer to the photo's exact location, where he found some elk bones that were later analyzed and matched with the mounted heads of one of the poacher's elk.

Officers were able to locate where the poacher was likely hiding by searching online for his name and finding it in his father's obituary that listed a sister with an address close to where the elk had been shot. Officer Murdoch returned to the kill site with another officer and searched the area again. Nearby, they found a bull elk head stashed in the bushes, identical to the elk in the pictures on the phone they had seized. They also found another backpack matching one in one of the pictures on the phone. A compound bow and bicycle were hidden with the bull elk head.

Several months later, after gathering and analyzing all the evidence, three CPW officers travelled to Texas and were joined by three Texas officers to visit the home of Mr. "Loser." It turned out he was a firefighter, one of the noblest of professional callings. Boastfully, he toured them through his impressive home, showing off deer and elk mounts in many of the rooms, but he went quiet when they started asking about the bull elk. The officers meticulously gathered evidence and testimony from other family members and associates before returning to Colorado.

Meanwhile, officers in Colorado searched the poacher's sister's house. Her living room featured a large trophy elk above the fireplace that belonged to Mr. Loser. Lo and behold, this was the elk they had been looking for! At the same time, officers in Texas interviewed other people related to the case.

It turned out Loser had held an elk licence only once, in 2013. In that year, he took an elk in an area he didn't have a licence for. After that, he didn't bother getting a licence. He shot all the animals with a bow. He often hunted in a residential area near his sister's place in Colorado. He also hunted on his sister's property. He'd ride around on his bicycle with his bow, looking for elk. He'd get off the bike, hide it, then go after whatever trophy animal he wanted. It's amazing what people can get away with in residential areas!

In 2019, Loser was charged and convicted of a felony and eleven other minor offences. His fines and restitution totalled nearly $60,000. Loser was charged with violations for five elk and one deer seized in the investigation. As a condition of his probation, he was given two years to provide two elk racks and a deer rack that the officers had never been able to locate during the investigation. He is also eligible for a lifetime ban on hunting.

This investigation required an incredible amount of work to piece together. Officer Murdoch and all those who assisted did an amazing, thorough job that all started with a concerned citizen seeing someone with a dead elk. The evidence at the scene was not enough to prove anything. It took many hours of work and "thinking outside the box" to bring about a successful conclusion. The investigation even included undercover officers attending church, not to ask for divine assistance but to locate a possible suspect they were looking for.

Loser apparently likes beef as well. On July 21, 2018, he was indicted on three counts of cattle theft in Texas for crimes dating back to 2013. Riding a bicycle must require a lot of protein calories.

HUNTING FOR DUMMIES

A property owner in Maryland had been watching a large non-typical deer for years. Then a jealous neighbour snuck onto his property, shot the deer and dragged it home. Local game wardens came knocking after word of the big buck spread faster than a cold through a daycare centre. The poacher claimed to have shot the buck on his own property; however, wardens were able to track the blood trail back to his neighbour's field. The poacher's own friend, who'd helped drag the deer to his home, sang like the proverbial bird. Besides losing a friend, the poacher kissed the big buck bye-bye and had some explaining to do to the judge.

THE BUMBLE BUCK

A twenty-four-year-old wildlife officer from Oklahoma, Cannon Harrison, thought he'd try his luck on a dating site called Bumble. Bumble requires the woman to make the first move. Harrison received a message from a local lady late one night. He asked "Sweetheart" how she was doing. Sweetheart replied, "Just shot a big ol' buck! Pretty happy about it."

Harrison suspected a prank from someone he knew. He's from a county of twenty thousand people where he'd worked for a couple of years, so many people knew him. Rifle season had closed but bow season was still open. The officer played along, expecting the joker to reveal herself. He asked whether she'd shot it with a bow. Her response: "Well, we don't need to talk about that." Through a series of late-night messages, she admitted she had shot it on their ranch with a rifle and a spotlight.

Harrison used his investigative skills to track the woman down through social media and gained knowledge of the approximate location of the ranch she lived on. Early the next morning he and another game warden showed up at her door. She didn't have a clue how she'd been caught until Harrison told her. After the citation was issued, Sweetheart showed Harrison a picture of the deer. It turned out her rack wasn't that big. She told him it was her first deer. She got her date through Bumble all right—a court date!

Sweetheart and her poaching partner co-operated fully and avoided jail time by paying the $2,400 in fines. The deer head was confiscated as well. The deer became known as the Bumble Buck. You might expect some hard feelings from Sweetheart after this incident, but apparently Oklahoma ladies don't carry a grudge. Sweetheart agreed to date Officer Harrison after the incident. She'd bagged her second Bumble date! They even went to her parents' place for Christmas dinner (I wonder if they ate venison). Not all poachers are bad people. Some can change their ways.

HUNTING FOR DUMMIES

South Carolina officer Jeff Day took some poaching violation paperwork before a local judge one day. The judge said, "I want you to write lots more of those tickets." The officer wasn't quite sure how to respond, but he quipped, "That will make a lot more work for you too." The judge said, "I get thieves, drug dealers and drunks all the time. I know when a game warden walks into the courtroom I'm going to hear a good story."

On another occasion Officer Day presented a trespassing case in which a woman was fishing inside a closed area with signs clearly posted everywhere. Before he approached her, Day had snapped a photo that showed seven NO TRESPASSING signs with the woman right in the middle. The judge asked her whether she had anything to say for herself. Wisely, she didn't respond. How could she explain casting her line among the seven NO TRESPASSING signs visible in the picture with her? Day had no need to present any verbal evidence—it was a good story, all told in just one picture.

WEIRD ONE IN WYOMING

THIS CASE STARTED LIKE MANY, WITH A CALL FROM A CONCERNED citizen who'd witnessed what he thought to be a violation of wildlife laws on property west of Sheridan, Wyoming. The complaint first went to a retired Wyoming game warden who was the father of a current warden, Dustin Shorma. Shorma would be the lead investigator in this horrific poaching case.

Shorma and fellow warden Bruce Scigliano began a lengthy surveillance on the property, and eventually they observed Mr. "Lam" kill a deer. While on watch, they also noted several other dead deer visible on the property. Records were checked and showed the man did not possess a hunting licence. Lam had taken a hunter safety course and purchased a deer licence once before, but did not have one at the time. The indiscriminate slaughter became worse. Witnesses told the officers they had seen Lam beating a deer to death over the head with the metal hook on a towrope. It had been shot but had stood up when he started to tow it away.

Officers continued to monitor the property and gather more evidence for a search warrant. Local sheriffs joined a team of game wardens to serve the warrant on November 27, 2018. Two officers searched the house and located two rifles, empty brass and other evidence. Lam refused to talk to the officers that day. Two other officers searching the property located 113 dead white-tailed deer and one antelope. Eighty-one deer were on his property and another thirty-two had wandered onto adjacent property before they died. All appeared to have been shot and no meat had been taken. Witnesses also reported seeing the man (I'm being generous) towing dead deer around the property with his lawn tractor. Officers performed necropsies on all the deer, painstakingly going through the

29

bodies that were in various stages of decomposition. The bullets they recovered matched the rifles later seized from Lam. He shot most of the deer with a .22-calibre rifle.

Eventually, Lam owned up to killing the deer and spoke to the officers. He felt the deer were infringing on his solitude on the property. He'd moved from New York to build his dream home on the private property and the deer were constantly getting too close. He didn't care whether they were bucks, does or fawns. The .22-calibre rifle resulted in many deer making it to adjacent property before dying. When deer got too close to his house, he shot them and dragged them away. He pled guilty to multiple charges and a plea bargain was agreed to on August 1, 2019. The plea bargain helped him avoid a maximum of twenty years in prison.

The judge heard the statement prepared by Lam for the courts. He expressed remorse and apologized to the community. His defence was that he still struggled to deal with the sexual, emotional and physical abuse he had received as a child. But he didn't claim this as a plausible excuse for his actions and agreed to seek counselling upon release from prison. Let's hope so. He made this timely decision after the case became public. Psychological trauma shows up in lots of criminal behaviour. Certainly, much of it is legitimate. Some people, however, are just liars, and it's very easy to become cynical when this defence is raised at sentencing. Let's just hope it was true in this case and, for the sake of everyone and the wildlife, he gets proper treatment.

Lam was given nine months in jail and $254,000 in fines and restitution. He brought a certified cheque to the courtroom, paid the fine and went directly to jail, just like in the game of Monopoly.

TURTLE TRAFFICKING

WHO WOULD POACH A TURTLE? OF COURSE, I REFER TO THE TYPE OF poaching dealing with the indiscriminate harvest and selling of turtles. It's a huge problem in any area where they grow in both the US and Canada. The international pet trade, especially in China, will snap up turtles as fast as poachers can deliver them for ridiculous prices in the thousands of dollars per turtle for the right rare species.

There have been several major turtle-poaching rings taken down recently in Florida, South Carolina and Oklahoma. The Oklahoma case is a great example of a concerned citizen taking the time to report the crime, keen investigating officers, interagency co-operation and smart prosecutors all combining for a successfully prosecuted case. The poacher wins if any link in the chain is weak.

The following case involved the collection and sale of ornate box turtles and three-toed box turtles. Box turtles can live up to one hundred years. They are an important part of any ecosystem where they live. Some eat carrion, fish, snakes and worms. They often consume fruit and pass the undigested seeds as they move to new areas, sort of a slow-moving seed spreader.

This case started in a motel in Mannford, Oklahoma, where a group from Arkansas had been staying for a few days. The cleaning woman became suspicious when the occupants kept declining to have the room cleaned. On the third day, she peeked through the open door and noticed a number of large clear plastic tubs with live turtles inside them. She reported her findings to the local police station. They in turn called Oklahoma Department of Wildlife Conservation officer Karlin Bailey. Karlin called a senior officer in Tulsa, Carlos Gomez, and his supervisor. Unbeknownst to the officers, the USFWS had been working on a major turtle-poaching case. They

31

had identified a key player of an international ring in New Jersey but had been unable to get a solid lead to pursue the investigation further—until this case.

The three devised a plan to surreptitiously watch the motel to gather more information on the five guests in the two rooms of interest. Things moved rather slowly (as one might expect in a turtle investigation), but eventually they were able to approach the two rooms simultaneously and start their investigation.

The turtle poachers were relatively co-operative. It turned out the key player had been charged for trafficking wildlife in his home state, and he expected a similar small-ticket offence for these turtles. He rolled over and told the whole story, describing their operation.

The group would slowly drive through the countryside early in the morning when turtles are most active, pick them off the road and bring them back to the motel. He was paying others in the group $5 a turtle, boxing the reptiles up and shipping them by air courier to a Mr. "Gamey" in New Jersey. Gamey paid $25 each for the turtles, then sold them to his buyer for $100 each. The buyer would sell the turtles to at least one more middleman. They would eventually be sold for $500 to $1,000 each when they reached the overseas market. (These turtles are considered a symbol of wealth in China and are highly desirable as pets.)

The head poacher had shipped two hundred turtles the day before this arrest and had two hundred more ready to go the next day. He had recently shipped about a thousand of them. The officers seized the turtles, containers, cellphone and vehicle. The poachers would have a very slow trip back to Arkansas without their vehicle.

Officer Gomez had nowhere to take the two hundred live turtles, so he took them home. His wife and daughter did as many warden families do—they took care of whatever animal the warden dragged home. In this case, the Gomez family put the turtles in their secure backyard and cared for them. These turtles hadn't been near water and food in who knows how long. A quick internet search led the turtle-sitters to a local grocery store, where they described their predicament to the produce manager. The store was delighted to help out and gave them all kinds of expired produce. The turtles were especially fond of strawberries. The Gomez family took care of the turtles for several days.

Officers contacted the USFWS, who were elated to hear the connection to Mr. Gamey, the key target of their poaching investigation. They devised a plan to approach Gamey, offering turtles for sale. They used the two hundred turtles from the Gomezes' backyard to arrange a shipment. I'm not sure whether they deputized the two hundred turtles or promised them some strawberries, but they did keep their mouths shut until the sting was over.

The investigators were fortunate to have a district attorney who took the time to learn the details and educate the judge so an appropriate sentence could be delivered. Gamey was convicted and ordered to pay $250,000 to the Oklahoma Department of Wildlife and $100,000 to the USFWS. That may sound high to some, but Mr. Gamey had been operating for many years. He opted for the large fine rather than spend time in jail. He was also given two years' probation.

Who knows how many such operations exist or what overall impact poachers are having on turtle populations? As with most wildlife populations, the real problem is often identified too late, and animals are constantly under pressure from habitat loss as well as poaching.

Another important factor in maintaining wild populations is avoiding the introduction of non-native species into the wild. For example, in North America the red-eared slider turtle was and sadly still is a popular pet with kids because they are easy to care for and don't take much space. But many carry salmonella. Once people tire of them, many are released into the wild and become an invasive species. Red-eared turtles are in the top one hundred invasive species in the world and are not worth poaching. And please, do not ever release them into the wild.

HARD TO SWALLOW

A NEBRASKA STATE TROOPER ON PATROL WAS LOOKING FOR A reported stolen vehicle. He happened upon a vehicle parked on a bridge with no one in it and got out to look around. He heard some noises coming from beneath the bridge so he went under to have a look.

Three Burmese foreigners were shooting barn swallows. They were shooting the adult birds with pellet guns then gathering up the baby birds and putting them all in a sack. The sack contained 210 birds, some alive and some dead.

The trooper found more surprises when he returned to the apartment where the three lived. The apartment reeked from the smell of birds cooking. Some cooked birds were in the fridge and others were in pots on the stove. All three men were arrested.

I know it's important to be tolerant and understanding of those less fortunate who make their way to North America in hopes of something better from life. Many only practise what they know and that is survival. If something moves and has a pulse, it is viewed as food. Wildlife officers are exposed to scenes such as this one far too often. Perhaps there should be some training included for all immigrants when they become citizens in a new country to bring more awareness to our wildlife resources and the laws that protect them.

OKLAHOMA DEER POACHER

AN OKLAHOMA LANDOWNER REPORTED POACHERS SHOOTING DEER at night on his property. The landowner was a deer hunter himself and had food plots to attract deer set out as part of his legal hunting operation later in the fall. Needless to say, he was quite perturbed to find lowly night hunters on his property.

The landowner purchased a game/trail camera that sent pictures to his cellphone. He captured images of a poacher heading into his property at night with a flashlight and rifle and leaving the property carrying a deer. Wildlife officers subsequently made several attempts to capture the poacher through frequent discreet patrols and checks in the area, to no avail. The poacher was next seen on camera poaching six white-tailed deer before the season opened.

Wildlife officer C. Gomez received a panicked phone call late one evening that the poacher was in the field—right now! Officer Gomez contacted three other officers to assist in the patrol. Two of them agreed to make their way to the poaching field, one by patrol vehicle and one in his personal vehicle. The third man Gomez contacted, a junior officer, also drove to the field in his personal unmarked vehicle. The junior officer lived closest to the site and was told to locate the poacher's vehicle but not to approach the poacher or go into the field.

Officer Gomez made the half-hour drive to the site as fast and safely as he could. Meanwhile, the junior officer located a vehicle and reported it to the officers on their way to the location. Officer Gomez called a deputy sheriff, who agreed to send another officer. Tulsa police were contacted and sent support. Having so much support for one violator is not a normal occurrence in fish and wildlife enforcement. Eight vehicles were responding: Officer Gomez, another wildlife officer in his personal vehicle, a wildlife officer in a patrol vehicle, the junior officer in his vehicle, a sheriff and several Tulsa policemen were all making their way to the poaching location.

The junior officer in his personal vehicle arrived first and was watching the poacher's vehicle from a distance when he saw the headlights of the police cars approaching the area. All the lights and traffic must have caused the poacher to panic. He quickly loaded his deer in his truck, made a U-turn and headed off in the opposite direction.

The wildlife officer jumped into his car and commenced the chase. The police and sheriff turned their lights on and joined in. Everyone loves a parade. The officer was relieved to know he had backup. The only problem? The police and sheriff thought the officer's unmarked vehicle was the poacher and stopped *him!* The officer quickly jumped out and produced his badge. Precious seconds had passed and the poacher was disappearing fast. The police resumed pursuit but had to follow at a legal speed due to high-speed chase policies. The four "chase" cars could see the poacher about a kilometre ahead and they were losing him.

Meanwhile, Officer Gomez was approaching the turnoff when a vehicle flew by him in the opposite direction. Gomez saw the police lights off in the distance and realized he had just met the poacher. He turned around and began the chase. Several kilometres later the poacher blew a front tire on his vehicle and came to a stop. His vehicle was a fancy pickup with a lift kit and giant off-road tires not suitable for high speeds.

The four-car cavalry—and a helicopter that happened to be on night patrol—arrived just as Officer Gomez began dealing with the poacher. It must have looked like a scene from a movie. Of course, the media had heard about the chase through their scanners and arrived on the scene of this "major" takedown.

The truck, deer, rifle and clothes (with deer blood) were seized later. The Hispanic poacher saw Officer Gomez's nametag and immediately began speaking in Spanish, claiming they were family and asking for a warning only. Not flippin' likely, señor.

The poacher turned out to be an illegal immigrant from Honduras. He was living and working in the area with his family. His poaching charges were added to the multiple charges related to endangering others in the high-speed chase. He was later convicted and received a fine of $10,000 and forfeited his truck, rifle and deer. He was held in jail for about six months before being deported back to Honduras. *Adios!* It's not uncommon for illegal immigrants to poach wildlife. As mentioned in the swallows story, many come from countries where anything edible is fair game. Fortunately in this case, things ended safely for the public and all officers involved.

HUNTING FOR DUMMIES

Here's another great decoy story from Wisconsin officer John W. Buss. A decoy was set out and waiting when a vehicle came along and the driver got out. The man staggered along the road toward the decoy, obviously drunk. He fired a shot at the decoy. An officer yelled, "State warden! Unload your gun!" The drunk turned to the officer and slurred, "Thasss smy deer!" He then turned and fired three more rounds into the decoy, blowing its head off. Yep. The decoy dummy was headless and the real dummy was clueless.

UTAH ELK REWARD

IN JANUARY OF 2020, UTAH DIVISION OF WILDLIFE RESOURCES (DWR) officer Jonathan Moser was patrolling a local area where a herd of elk had been spotted frequently. Everyone in the neighbourhood enjoyed watching the animals; it was as if they were part of the community. During his patrol, Moser spotted part of the herd moving off in the distance. He noted something unusual just over a small ridge. He jogged over and found a large, dead six-point bull elk. Twenty metres past it, he found another dead bull. Both appeared to have been recently shot with a large-calibre rifle and left to die. Moser dug through the carcasses, scanning them for evidence. Soon after that, a resident in the area reported a third elk that had also been shot. Moser found a .22-calibre bullet in its carcass. Over the next two weeks, three more dead bull elk were reported in the same general area. Two had definitely been shot with a rifle and one appeared to have died naturally.

The community was in an uproar, with many offering advice on how to conduct the investigation. It seemed that *csi* and *Forensic Files* had made everyone an expert. Moser had completed all the forensic work he could do and had to rely on a witness or evidence to go any further. Community members started a GoFundMe page to try to catch the poacher. In two and a half months, the reward was over $21,000. Several leads were followed up on, but to date the culprit has not been located. Sadly, it's not uncommon for poaching stories to have an ending like this one. Officers can only hope the reward will entice someone to come forward.

MYSTERY MEAT

ERNIE COOPER WORKED FOR THE CANADIAN WILDLIFE SERVICE for many years before retiring. He currently runs an environmental consulting business and is considered one of the top Canadian experts in identification of wildlife from anywhere in the world.

Cooper was called to assist the BC Conservation Officer Service in a wildlife search warrant they were executing. The officers had found some frozen animal carcasses they couldn't identify, so Cooper headed over right away to assist. He arrived at the residence while the search and investigation were still in progress. When he walked into the house, the wife and children of the suspect were seated quietly on the couch. Cooper made his way to the deep freeze to help the officers identify the animals. Inside the freezer was a variety of meats including frozen raccoons, a crocodile penis and a house cat. I'll bet they didn't have to feed that cat much.

The undercover officers learned that the suspect, Mr. "Meathead," would buy any meat he could get his hands on. He even had a live owl in the house. He would buy roadkill animals from anyone willing to pick them up. Why was he such a meat lover? It turned out Meathead was actually selling the meat to a local ethnic restaurant. That is a fact! It may make you nauseated, but it's true.

During his interview, Meathead was asked whether he was married and he said yes. His wife heard the question and yelled out, "Not for long." I wonder what she served Meathead for dinner.

THE CLOWN CAR

OFFICER RICH BERGGREN OF NEBRASKA STOPPED A SMALL SUV with tinted windows in a remote area where people had been known to catch fish. He described what he saw as a "clown car," with seven people squeezed into the small vehicle. He cautiously approached the car, then asked the occupants a few questions before realizing they were foreigners and did not speak English. At the same time, he smelled something horrible coming from inside the SUV.

Suspicious now, he went to the rear of the vehicle to look in the hatch. Under the hatch was an eighth occupant, a young boy (twelve years old, it would later be determined) sleeping beside a backpack and a bloodied machete.

The boy awoke and became the English interpreter for the group. They had been fishing, he said, but upon further questioning he admitted that no one had a licence. The officer looked in the backpack and found one carp with its eyes removed. He looked deeper into the bag and pulled out what he described as a large bratwurst ready to pop, with a tail attached. A closer look revealed its identity and the source of the stench, an opossum (commonly called possum in North America). It turned out the group had been sitting around a fire the previous evening when the possum had innocently wandered through the camp. Its tracks were stopped with a shot from a well-aimed slingshot. They had hung the whole possum over the fire until all its hair was burned off.

Officer Berggren asked what they planned on doing with the hairless, partially cooked critter. One in the group rubbed his belly and said, "Yum, yum, spices!" Since the group had only one fish and the hairless possum, Berggren decided the best penalty he could issue would be to let them go free to eat their stinking possum.

CAT TALE

IF YOU ARE A CAT LOVER YOU MAY WANT TO SKIP THIS STORY. IT'S not a poaching story. It's a cat story from a game warden in the US. I won't disclose the location of this feline fatality because I'm certain the warden has suffered more than his share of catcalls.

Officer "Lucky" was on duty in his marked patrol vehicle, driving through a rural area he frequently passed through. It had been a rather uneventful day to that point, when suddenly a cat ran across the road directly in front of him. He pounded the brakes just as he heard a thud. It's an awful feeling to hit any animal, but this surely must have been someone's pet. Lucky came to a stop and glanced in his mirror. There wasn't any traffic coming, but he noticed the cat lying in the ditch and still moving a bit.

Killing injured animals is never a fun part of the job, but sometimes it has to be done. He backed up his patrol vehicle, got out and finished the poor cat off with his sidearm, then drove away, feeling bad about the events that had just happened.

He was heading home for the end of his patrol when he received a call from his supervisor. A woman had called in to complain that a uniformed game warden had shot her cat. Officer Lucky explained the whole story to his boss. His boss said the woman was adamant that he had not run over her cat, but shot it dead.

Lucky pulled his vehicle over, got out and walked around to look at the front. The cat he had hit was attached to the front of his vehicle and was stone dead. Oh no! He had shot a second, healthy cat that had just happened to be lying in the ditch. If there were ever a prize for the most embarrassing warden story, this would be a winner.

CREATIVE LOBSTER POACHING

HISTORICALLY, LOBSTERS WERE SO PLENTIFUL THAT NATIVE North Americans used them to fertilize their fields and bait their hooks to catch fish. When Europeans first settled in Nova Scotia, storms would wash tonnes of lobsters onto the beach. They were gathered up to be used as food for the poorest people or to fertilize the fields and gardens. Servants in the state of Maine rebelled against their employers by writing a clause into their contracts that limited them to having to eat lobsters no more than three times a week. Do you think that would fly today?

I don't know how it happened without social media, but some wealthier folks decided lobsters were good to eat, and thus was born an entire industry that remains strong today. I'll take a guess at how the change took place somewhere in a wealthy home in Boston:

"Honey dear, we're out of Russian caviar. Can you zip out and pick some up?"

"But that would take three months, dear. Can't we order in from Skip the Voyage? Besides, my ship is in the shop getting barnacles removed. I'll try to find something right after I finish my beer."

Later, the husband returned with a sack of lobsters. Mother was not happy. She threw them out the window. They landed in the hot springs just before the husband did.

The poor famished husband bobbed around in the hot springs with the now-cooked lobsters. He'd heard that peasants actually ate these things, so he cracked one open and tried it.

"Honey! You gotta try this!"

And that's how lobsters became a coveted food for the wealthy ... maybe. While that may not be precisely accurate, it's certain that once lobsters became valuable, poachers entered the scene.

Clawed lobsters are found only on the east coast of North America, not the west coast. (California has spiny lobsters, but they are quite different). That is, except for the case of a Vancouver animal rights activist who purchased a live lobster and released it into the Pacific to save the poor thing from a boiling pot of water. Someone else found it on the shore and thought they'd witnessed a new lobster migration phenomenon. It turned out it was just a free dinner. No one should do such things, because invasive species (species transported by humans to non-native areas) are a problem all over the world. Just eat the tasty crustaceans already or stick to your greens.

In Canada, many World War II veterans were hired as fishery officers to control the ever-expanding fisheries on the east coast. One Royal Canadian Air Force pilot turned fishery officer, Ron McKinnon, worked in Alberton, Prince Edward Island, and quickly became known as the lobster poacher's enemy. Before the 1948 lobster season, McKinnon was catching poachers, but they were also catching on to him and getting wiser. He noticed that the piles of traps in town were beginning to get smaller, but he wasn't catching anyone with lobsters during the day or night.

McKinnon devised a plan. He arranged for a couple of patrol boats to go into the harbour while he took a plane in the air. From his aerial vantage point he quickly located numerous sunken traps and directed the patrol boats to their locations. The day before lobster season opened, his team was able to pull up over one hundred traps containing over twenty thousand live lobsters. They were all released alive and the traps were smashed. The despairing, angry faces attached to the poachers on shore could only look on helplessly. After that, poachers began painting their sunken traps green and tying seaweed to them to avoid detection.

Any game of poacher/warden hide-and-seek is always evolving. McKinnon uncovered a myriad of other techniques poachers used to hide lobsters. He noticed a few milk cans on porches of people who had no cows. They contained illegal lobsters. One poacher used a large gasoline truck to hide lobsters. One of the most ingenious methods he discovered was that of a woman he suspected of poaching pushing her baby carriage down the street. He greeted her cordially and asked to see the dear child. Before she could respond, he pulled the covers back to reveal fifty pairs of sad lobster eyes staring up at him. "No resemblance to you, ma'am," he said before busting her. And now you know why game wardens can be very suspicious of most anyone.

The California spiny lobster is less well known than the east coast lobster. These clawless crustaceans are highly sought-after, with prices reaching over $30 per pound. The state has a tightly controlled commercial fishery along with a recreational fishery with seasons and size limits. The lobsters are caught with round hoops that are baited and lowered to the ocean bottom. When the lobster walks onto the hoop, he's hooped. Then it's a quick trip up the elevator of death as the fisher pulls the rope to the surface before the lobster has time to jump off. They can also be grabbed by hand, but their spiny tails can inflict serious injury. The hand method is mostly used by those further down the evolution chain. The most effective illegal method is to snag the lobster with rod and reel using baited treble hooks.

The spiny lobsters prefer to hang out at the Santa Monica pier. Experts aren't really sure why. It just may be that Disneyland is too busy. Poachers like to fish right off the pier with rod and reel. They stash their illegal catch in whatever container they can to avoid detection. Poachers will often hide their catch in garbage cans, just in case the game warden comes along. Game wardens have found that the best method of catching poachers is to have a couple of plain-clothes officers hanging out while others are stationed strategically to observe the activities. Uniformed officers wait in the parking lot until information is relayed to them about incoming lobster poachers from the pier.

California game warden Bob Farrell was assigned the observation point from the men's washroom in the harbour master's office. Farrell had to stand on a ladder to see out the window. The things a warden has to do. At least he wouldn't have to stray far from his post to relieve himself.

The night was moving along with about a dozen poachers bagged and tagged at a $1,000 fine each. Around midnight, a very large couple wandered down to the pier. He was about three hundred pounds and six-foot-four, she just slightly smaller and pushing a baby carriage. Surprisingly, he pulled out a fishing rod, bullied his way to the rail, dispersing people with his bulk and his unpleasant personality, and began snagging lobsters. He looked like a pit bull walking into a group of poodles. After catching a lobster, he hollered for his sweetie in profanity-laced outbursts. She scurried over with the stroller and the lobster disappeared under its hood. The poacher was cussing the entire time, apparently the victim of a small vocabulary. He caught a couple more crustaceans, placed them in the stroller and prepared to leave.

The officers were shutting the operation down for the night, so they let Farrell out of the washroom to deal with the couple with the baby carriage. He approached them, asking the large man what he'd caught. The man replied, "I ain't caught shit." When Farrell inquired about the stroller, the big guy gestured to the woman and said, "No, not mine—hers." Farrell asked a few more questions, trying to elicit a two-syllable word from the man, but he was evidently fed up and turned to walk a short distance away.

Then the officer with Farrell went over to the stroller and stuck his hand in. He squealed like a little boy and jumped back. "There's a real baby in there!"

Regaining his courage, he lifted the pad beneath the baby and peered into the stroller bottom, where he located the three lobsters they had recently observed going into the stroller. The ticket was issued and the man hauled away to jail. Momma had to drive home with the real baby, but without the lobster padding. Maybe the baby carriage as a lobster smokescreen isn't so original after all.

One beautiful summer day, fishery officer Jeff Irwin of New Brunswick was on his day off. He decided to go diving for scallops in the St. Croix River with the local judge's son. Jeff knew the area well and took the younger man out in a small boat to dive and collect their limit of scallops. Afterward, they climbed back into their boat to head in to shore.

On their way back, they noticed another diver in the area who appeared to be solo and without a boat. The current was a bit strong, so they decided to help the diver out and offer him a ride in. The man gladly accepted and threw his bag into their boat first. The bag contained four live lobsters. As the diver crawled into the boat, Jeff advised him it was against the law to dive for lobsters.

"They were biting me and they crawled into my bag," the man said lamely. Jeff told him he would be fined and charged for the illegal lobsters. Without hesitating, the man stood, dived back into the water and swam away.

"I know where you live!" Jeff yelled. He had recognized the lobster poacher when he climbed aboard—the man was a direct descendant of world-renowned chocolatier Whidden Ganong. (Ganong is sort of like Hershey in the United States, except better chocolate.)

Jeff released the live lobsters, then went to shore with his star witness, the local judge's son. They loaded their boat and gear along with the poacher's gear into their vehicle and headed to his residence. They arrived just as "Choco-man" was getting out of the water after swimming for forty-five minutes. Apparently, being raised on chocolates can affect your ability to think clearly. Choco-man refused to co-operate and ended up being hauled away to jail. He later paid his fine and had his gear forfeited.

The moral of the story is, if you are out poaching, don't climb into a boat with a fishery officer and the local judge's son.

There wasn't a fresh or frozen market in the 1940s; canneries were the destined market. This made it easy to check on catches and size limits of lobsters. Poachers solved this problem by starting their own secret canneries hidden in the bushes. After officers located them from the air, they moved into some caves to further avoid detection.

Poaching often resembles a war more than a game. A sad story from 1926 emerged when fishery officer A. LeBlanc failed to return from a lobster patrol in New Brunswick. Three days later his body floated ashore with a fractured skull. The murder was never solved. Fishery officers have been shot at, spit on, assaulted, threatened, had their children assaulted, their patrol boats burned, their offices and homes vandalized and burned all by lobster poachers.

There is no honour among poaching thieves either. Some so-called legal harvesters would sabotage poachers' boats by wrecking their outboards or setting the boats on fire. Some poachers worked together to alert others of incoming fishery officers. One accomplice was paid to sit in a truck by the bay and simply honk the horn if the fishery officer was coming. A more ingenious method was that of a woman near the bay entrance who would hang clothes on the line if an officer was arriving. That worked until the officer saw her hanging clothes in the rain and figured the trick out.

Today's techniques are more advanced, but the lobster-poaching game is still played by far too many. A complication is the First Nations fishery's constitutional right to fish for food, social and ceremonial purposes. Fishery officers find that although those lobsters are supposed to go to feed people and support ceremonial activities within the band and community, they are often sold in large quantities. There really isn't an effective way to prevent them from getting to the market illegally.

Tensions have ebbed and flowed over the years. However, the constant threat of poaching along with reduced catches and high prices can boil over at any time. In June of 2013, three Cape Breton fishermen were charged with second-degree murder after they caught Phillip Boudreau stealing lobsters from their traps. Mr. Boudreau's overturned boat was found full of bullet holes and smashed by having been run over with a larger boat. Mr. Boudreau's body was never found. Of course, some blamed the government, which is a common reaction. Desperate people doing desperate things have no one to blame but themselves. What are lobsters really worth?

Today, fishers use modern technology to hide their gear, making it very difficult to find and check. Officers, however, also use technology to combat poaching by placing tiny electronic tags in the lobster when they find illegal traps set. They then scan the catch when it reaches the lobster buyers and locate the illegal catch. Officers can also use waterproof markers containing ink that shines brightly under a special light to mark lobsters caught in illegal gear. And satellite tracking devices are placed on suspected vessels, under warrant, to follow the course of the vessels at night and in bad weather to identify where their illegal fishing gear has been set.

More recently, legal Canadian lobster fishers have protested what they view as poaching. The First Nations fishery is allowed to take place before the commercial opening, and commercial fishers allege that some of this catch is finding its way into illegal sales markets. Fishery officers are caught in the middle of the political games being played. It's a dangerous place to be. Both sides have legitimate arguments, except for those who are truly poaching or selling illegally. Catching someone selling illegal lobsters requires resources that few locations can afford. It's a battle that has raged for over one hundred years. Until everyone, including commercial fishers, First Nations, resource managers, fishery officers, politicians, the public and the courts, are willing to work together, the problem will continue. Officers having connections with the lobster fishing community is still a key factor to properly monitor this multi-million-dollar industry. Legitimate lobster fishers know the detrimental impact poaching has on their livelihood and the future of their fishery. Poachers don't care.

HUNTING FOR DUMMIES

Some hunters do make honest mistakes in animal identification. It's especially difficult with some migratory birds. Other hunters simply shouldn't put down the television remote. In 2016, one proud Michigan hunter went to the wildlife check-in station to show off his beautiful six-point white-tailed deer. The officer listened patiently to the hunter's story as they walked around to the back of the truck to find a very large six-by-six bull elk! The guy left the elk behind but took his story home—along with $11,000 in fines.

TURKEY THUGS

IT'S AMAZING HOW QUICKLY A VIOLATION CAN GROW INTO A MON-ster. Mississippi Department of Wildlife, Fisheries and Parks officers had a recent example when they nabbed a whole flock of turkey poachers. The investigation began with four suspects who were served warrants on Easter weekend, just before turkey season opened.

These guys had already shot a bunch of turkeys before the season. Officers seized guns, phones, USB drives and other electronics loaded with additional evidence. There's no honour among turkey thugs either, I guess, because more and more information came from those four guys that implicated more and more poachers.

Officer Calvin Fulton said he and other officers diligently went through all the data and laid charges only in cases where they had two sources of evidence to tie a poacher to one violation. The searches spread to other counties and states until the total violation count was 282, with over one hundred turkeys taken by fourteen different poachers. This was the state's largest turkey-poaching bust in history. One of the poachers was charged with shooting twenty-six turkeys, yet he had never held a turkey licence. The case continues to expand into Kansas and Oklahoma with the assistance of other state agencies and the USFWS investigating cross-state violations. Let's hope some of these turkeys get put away.

THE EIGHT-POINT DUMMY

A YOUNG MAN DECIDED TO SHOOT A DEER WITH HIS COMPOUND bow in "Somewhere," Utah. That would have been okay, except he did it right in town and in January (that's two dummy points for hunting in town and out of season). He and a few friends dragged the deer into his residence and put it in the bathtub (that's two more dummy points). The party started, and one thing led to another until someone decided to Snapchat a photo of the deer in the bathtub (dummy point #5). An online observer called the Utah DWR and reported the suspicious photo.

Officers attended the location and found the deer kill site near the residence. They also saw blood on the steps leading into the house. They obtained a search warrant and knocked on the door, but there was no answer. The house was quiet, so they made it clear, with loud conversation, that they were leaving the area. Then they watched and waited for eight hours before they knocked again and were greeted at the door. They presented the warrant to the resident and started the search.

The strong smell of bleach throughout the house was overpowering. It turned out that the occupants of the house had been trying to cut up some of the evidence and flush it down the toilet (dummy point #6). The officers found deer meat packed in boxes hidden in a closet (#7). The bloodied head and cape were finally located in the closet of the poacher's two-year-old daughter, hidden under her pink clothes (dummy point #8).

The poacher and his buddy who helped drag the deer into the house ended up paying $8,000 in fines and restitution. If bad decisions were brains, this guy would be a genius.

LOUISIANA ALLIGATOR

IN 2018, LOUISIANA DEPARTMENT OF WILDLIFE AND FISHERIES (LDWF) game warden Jake Darden responded to a call about a unique alligator-poaching case that turned out to be very easy to solve. The call reported that an aggressive alligator had bitten someone.

The story he heard was that two men had been walking along a seawall pathway that people often used for fishing or recreational walks. The area had a lot of alligators living in it. Darden learned that two would-be alligator poachers, "Dumb" from Louisiana and "Dumber" of Pensacola, Florida, had tried to deal with a 1.4-metre alligator with their bare hands. They seemed unaware that smaller alligators like the one they encountered are very aggressive and quick.

Dumber was the senior of the two, and I expect he was showing Dumb how a Floridian could manhandle an alligator. He planned to grab the alligator and throw it into the water. The alligator bit Dumber several times before he got away. Dumb grabbed a large piece of limestone from the shoreline and beat the alligator to death. But there was no open season at the time, and that's against the law. I'm not sure whether there's a law against catching alligators by hand, and I'm not sure why there would be. I would think natural selection should work in humans too. I would have paid money to watch that. In fact, I get in stitches just thinking about it.

Warden Darden located the dead alligator and was able to connect the two poachers in the crime to the hospital visit. (I don't think they needed to do a bite-mark match.) The warden interviewed Dumb, who tried to convince him the alligator had been aggressive toward them and that was why he'd killed it. Dumber said he'd just wanted to grab it and throw it into the water. The two had been drinking at the time, so any level of intelligence they did possess was impaired even further. Dumb said he had no regrets for killing the alligator and stuck to his poor excuse.

Dumb and Dumber were charged for killing an alligator out of season. They were fined $840 each, ordered to perform forty hours of community work and take an online course given by the LDWF. The state could also have imposed a restitution order for the value of the alligator, $375.80 at the time.

HUNTING FOR DUMMIES

Saskatchewan conservation officer Kevin Fitzsimmons was splitting wood outside his cabin by a campground when a lady surprised him from behind.

"Excuse me," she said. "I found a Lady's Slipper."

He tried some humour, responding, "I don't know of anyone missing one." Then he turned and continued the conversation.

"What are you going to do about it?" she said.

"What do you want me to do?"

"You should have someone stand guard over it."

Kevin explained that he was the only one working and, in any case, they were common to find in the area. But she wouldn't stop. Before she left, her final words were "Well, at least you can build a fence around it."

Kevin never built the fence, and thirty-nine years later, these orchids are still found in the campground.

CALIFORNIA SHOCKER

THIS IS THE TYPE OF CASE THAT WILL SICKEN EVEN THE MOST experienced wildlife officer. It started with an anonymous phone call to the California Department of Fish and Wildlife (CDFW) in March of 2018. The caller had witnessed a resident—I'll call him "Psycho"—shoot a hawk with a rifle. Officers attended the property near Standish, California, located in the Cascade-Sierra mountain range of Northern California, but no one was home. From the public road, they could clearly see a number of dead raptors lying on the thirty-two-hectare property. The area is rich in wildlife and especially in migratory birds. The open grasslands are an ideal habitat for raptors of all kinds.

A plan was put together to gather evidence. Wildlife officers, in plain clothes and equipped with spotting scopes, set up surveillance of the property. It didn't take long before they had seen enough to leave and return with a search warrant. Officers attended the house first and dealt with Mr. Psycho.

After that, seven officers, some with dogs, set out a grid pattern to begin the long, gruesome search of Psycho's property. The officers found a total of 159 birds, all apparently shot with a rifle. The count included seventy-five red-tailed hawks, Cooper's hawks, northern harriers, a prairie falcon, flickers, woodpeckers, magpies and a great horned owl. Some had recently been shot and others were badly decomposed, with only the skull remaining.

Each bird was carefully collected and labelled for evidence. A search of the house located an embalmed mountain lion. A recently killed bobcat lay in the front yard. What kind of person was Mr. Psycho? He was an insurance agent and former member of the local chamber of commerce with a university degree in psychology and criminal law!

In 2018, 159 dead birds, mostly raptors, were shot and left by a California property owner. He didn't want the raptors killing the game birds he liked to hunt.
Photo: Patrick Foy.

The birds were sent away to the USFWS forensics lab for analysis. The world-renowned wildlife lab methodically analyzed each animal—at least, those that still had flesh or bones intact—and determined they had all been shot with the two rifles owned by Mr. Psycho. The detailed forty-page report was vital to seal the case. Mr. Psycho pled guilty to ten counts and received ninety days in jail and a $75,000 fine, and his two rifles were ordered destroyed. He was also given a five-year prohibition from hunting or owning a firearm.

This baffling display of human behaviour is disturbing to most people. No one knows how many other animals he'd killed before a responsible, concerned citizen called in. This wasn't a one-time shooting spree. This man must have shot at anything that moved whenever he saw it. A reasonable explanation for the carnage was never given, and alarmingly, this guy will be allowed to hunt and own firearms in the future.

HUNTING FOR DUMMIES

Tennessee Wildlife Resources Agency officers had a pair of doe and buck decoys set up in a field. The decoys were working so well that a group of white-tailed does were feeding around them. "Dim Don" came driving along and couldn't resist the sight of the big buck. Dim Don knew all about decoys and should probably have recognized the decoy as the exact same one he'd been caught shooting at about eighteen months earlier. Of course, the live deer scattered, leaving the two defenceless decoys facing Dim Don. He bailed out and shot the decoy buck. Officers arrested him and gave him a court date. Dim Don had a defence, though—he claimed the officers had trained pet deer around the decoy and he felt that was a form of entrapment. The judge didn't take the bait and convicted Dim Don.

I have to ask, who ties this guy's shoes in the morning?

CONCHES AND COCAINE

WHAT COULD A BEAUTIFUL SLOW-MOVING QUEEN CONCH SHELL have to do with cocaine? You might be surprised, but nothing surprises a fish and wildlife officer.

The conch has always been a source of meat for Caribbean residents. The large-shelled animal has a meaty texture like that of scallops. It has long been exported in an estimated $60 million industry, with about 80 per cent of the harvest going to the United States. A conch can live thirty years, and they normally live in large, clustered communities, sometimes hundreds in a single location. This makes them vulnerable to overfishing and poaching. Florida once had a stable population of conches but overfishing forced a commercial closure in 1986. The next year, a total closure was imposed.

One might expect a recovery after a closure, but the opposite often happens. The demand increases, prices rise and poachers move in to clean up what's left while it's worthwhile. In 2003, international pressure was put on countries such as Haiti, Honduras and the Dominican Republic to stop exporting conches before their stocks were depleted too. The countries obliged and implemented a ban on exports. This caused prices for conch meat to rise by five times to $4.50 per kilogram, turning it into a logical criminal currency. The global trade in conch meat in 2020 was over $200 million—another sad example of implementing closures and restrictions without adequate resources to enforce them.

A conch investigation started in 2006 during a routine food safety inspection of a truck at an Ontario–New York border crossing. The Food and Drug Administration inspector located nine hundred kilograms of frozen product labelled Frozen Whelk (a type of shellfish) Meat, Product of Canada, with a Florida destination label attached. The inspector opened the cardboard boxes to find internal packages labelled Fresh-Frozen Peeled Conch Meat. The mislabelled boxes were seized and DNA samples sent that confirmed it was conch meat. There weren't any food-safety issues, so the US Food and Drug Administration referred the file to the USFWS.

How and why would conch meat—only sold in the Caribbean—be shipped from Canada all the way back to Florida? How would it have gotten to Canada in the first place? The officer knew he was onto something and suspected the product had come from Haiti. Import records in Canada confirmed this. Investigators kept digging and determined that the end buyer was a major seafood dealer in Florida. Still more digging revealed a connection to an importer based in Vancouver, BC, who had arranged for the product to be shipped to eastern Canada. The conches were being shipped by container from the Caribbean right past their eventual, final destination in Florida, up the east coast to Canada, shipped by land to central Canada, then back down the east coast of the US by truck to Florida. These conches were travelling the world! Were they getting air miles for their travels?

Canadian authorities, alerted by the seizure, were on the lookout for more frozen product from the Caribbean. Several months later, an eighteen-thousand-kilogram shipment (twenty US tons) of conch meat with a wholesale value of $200,000 was discovered in Montreal, having arrived from Colombia. Some of the shipment had been sold locally, but the remainder was seized.

Officers then received information that another similar-sized shipment was coming to Halifax, Nova Scotia, on a container ship. The sender had gotten word of the previous seizure and had tried to have the container redirected to Honduras, but Environment Canada officers had already detained it. Someone would be getting cranky by now, having lost over $300,000 worth of product. The complex investigation tapped into the resources of both USFWS and EC officers. About 25 per cent of both agencies' officers were working on the case, which was called Operation Shell Game.

The big break came from a Colombian-born man, "Chocho," who owned a seafood company in a region of Colombia with waters rich in conches. Someone had given him an offer he couldn't refuse, and he became a cocaine smuggler for the Colombian cartel while still operating his conch exporting business. One of his conch shipments to Florida was seized because of improper permits. To avoid having authorities look for conches in Florida, he devised a plan to ship the conches through Canada, then have them trucked through the United States to Florida.

Meanwhile, Chocho's cocaine shipments were getting more lucrative than the conches. In November of 2000 he agreed to transport a whopping twenty thousand kilograms of cocaine. The cocaine was smuggled in small shipments on fast-moving boats travelling at night. A multi-agency police operation intercepted a big chunk of the cocaine shipment, and Chocho ended up in the safest place you could be after losing a shipment of cocaine belonging to a big cartel—jail. He was in jail in Colombia before being extradited to the United States, another move that likely made his life safer. USFWS agents interviewed Chocho. He spilled the beans on the conch business. He admitted to occasionally trading cocaine. In Chocho's confession in Florida he stated, "Cocaine is used as a currency down there [Colombia] and it's common in the seafood business to pay for seafood with cocaine." This is nothing new to the poaching world. I know of several examples where poachers were paid in drugs to supply wildlife to illegal markets.

With the new information, agents were able to obtain warrants in Florida, Toronto and Vancouver to search for electronic documents related to the conches. Following the warrants being served and armed with new information, USFWS and EC officers met in Florida. They interviewed the unco-operative owner of the seafood importer identified through documents and confirmed by Chocho. Eventually, the evidence toppled the lies and the importer sang like a bird. The twelve-plus tonnes of seized product in Canada was only the beginning. Records revealed that this single company had imported sixty tonnes of conch meat between 2003 and 2006. This was more than the entire export quota for Colombia. It was estimated that this amount could be over a million animals. It was later revealed the conches were also coming from Haiti and other places outside Colombia.

The two main players were charged in Nova Scotia and Florida for a host of violations including conspiracy. They received a meager $10,000 fine in Florida and a $20,000 fine in Nova Scotia. This would just be the cost of doing business. Another Vancouver criminal, "Ling," was fined $78,000. He claimed poverty and shut his Vancouver business down before flying to Los Angeles. I guess total poverty hadn't struck yet.

Within days, Ling travelled from Los Angeles to Mexico to start his next seafood business. He hired a Mexican driver to accompany him and bring two large totes of live ling cod from the west coast across Mexico to a more remote crossing, north into the US and on to Los Angeles, where the live ling cod would be illegally sold to Korean buyers. While Ling was in Mexico, Florida authorities had laid more charges from the conch business against him. He was arrested for both violations and flown to Miami to answer the additional charges.

This complex investigation and the time it consumed to complete are a great example of the lengths to which poachers will go to avoid detection. Money is no object for poachers. If their costs go up, the product price will rise. The same is not true for the fish and wildlife officers trying to suppress the illegal trade. Their resources are usually minimal and unlikely to keep up with the poachers in many cases. The best hope for threatened wildlife is an informed public willing to report violations and not purchase product they suspect is illegal or threatened. Undercover operations must continue to be part of the plan. There seems to be no limit to the number of people willing to poach.

POLAR BEAR POACHING— MYTH INTERPRETED

ON EASTER SUNDAY 2013, ENVIRONMENT CANADA WILDLIFE OFFI-cer Richard Labossiere of Winnipeg received a phone call with information originating from a confidential informant in the Arctic (no, it wasn't a cold call). The tipster indicated that a private jet from Mexico had just taken off from Iqaluit, Nunavut, with a group of Mexican hunters who intended to illegally export their polar bear hunting trophies. They'd be landing soon in Winnipeg to refuel before heading home to Mexico. Labossiere and two other federal wildlife officers, Blair Lacroix and Marc Boiteau, all abruptly left their respective Easter Sunday feasts (and Easter egg hunts) and arrived at the airport at exactly the same time as the private jet landed to refuel. If they'd been any later, the plane would have left the country. Perfect timing does not always happen.

The officers remained out of sight until the four passengers and two pilots were in the terminal waiting for their plane to fuel up. The officers then entered the waiting area and identified themselves to the father, his two sons, a godson and two pilots.

The search of the plane and luggage revealed three polar bear hides stuffed in duffle bags, three narwhal tusks and two polar bear skulls. The group did not have permits and couldn't have obtained one for any of the contraband because of an import ban of marine mammal parts into Mexico. All wildlife parts were seized and the men from the plane were arrested and interviewed.

They had to remain in Canada for a week. Two of them spent a few days in jail until their $20,000 bail money arrived from Mexico. The bail was to help prevent them from skipping the country. If they

61

A live polar bear near Churchill, Manitoba, waits for the ice to form before heading out to hunt seals in November 2018. *Photo: Lorraine Nelson.*

did leave the country, they'd lose their bail money and have a warrant issued. Who'd have thought the US might need a *northern* wall to stop Mexicans from entering their country?

"Juan Deportez" was a wealthy rancher and father of the boys. His past included convictions for trying to smuggle a lion, three tigers, a bobcat, a leopard, two jaguars and three black bears into Mexico. In this case, the group was charged for the polar bears and narwhal tusks. They paid their $80,000 fine in cash. I didn't know ranching was so profitable! They must have supported their ranching with some other revenue streams. My parents raised cattle and could only afford a Chevy pickup. The Mexicans were allowed to fly home minus the bears and tusks.

Polar bear–poaching cases like this are rather rare these days. The white bears were overhunted worldwide in years past. The

United States banned the import of polar bear hides or parts in 2008 and has tried to extend the ban worldwide since. Canada, home to over half of the world's twenty to thirty thousand polar bears, does not see hunting by northern residents and limited sport hunting as a problem as long as it's properly regulated.

Because of the sustainable population of polar bears in Canada, northern communities are allocated a quota of bears to harvest. They can take the bears themselves or sell them, through a hunt, to wealthy hunters (but not Americans or citizens of other countries with an import ban). The communities that sell the trips are paid well for these unique hunts. This practice results in fewer bears being harvested than in areas that don't allow non-resident hunting. That may surprise you. The reason is that a legal foreign hunter wants to shoot only a large bear and has a limited time to harvest one. But not all these hunters are successful, leaving the bear alive while generating over $20,000 for the sale of the hunt to the local community. On the other hand, if a local resident shoots the bear themselves they can sell the hide. A bear hide can be worth $5,000 to $25,000 depending on size and quality.

Poaching polar bears is extremely difficult without being detected. Poachers would have to fly into a remote Arctic community and completely rely on locals for guidance. Everyone in the community knows what's happening, and anyone assisting poachers would be reported by others who prefer to follow the law, as in the case described above. The bears are worth more to those in the community than they are to a poacher.

To help track harvested polar bears, Canada has implemented a passive integrated transponder (PIT) microchip tagging program. Inuit communities strongly support the program. Any bear harvested is reported to a conservation officer, who will gather information about the bear kill and inject microchips in a variety of locations in the bear hide. DNA samples are also collected from the harvested bear and input into a national database to also assist in the tracking of the bear hide. If the bear hide ever finds its way outside the community, it can be tested and identified. Informing the public of this program helps spread the word and shows poachers they will likely get caught if they purchase or transport a bear hide illegally.

There are numerous debates over the existing polar bear population. What is certain is that bear populations have increased since being globally protected in 1973. That might surprise many people who saw the picture of the starving polar bear in a major global magazine a few years ago. The photographer tied the starving bear to climate change even though there was no evidence to support that statement. The bear likely was dying of natural causes and no other bears like it were photographed. The photographer eventually admitted that she could not connect the photo to climate change. The lesson should be to always stick to facts when hitting alarm bells. Far too many "influencers" make outlandish claims on topics they have little knowledge of.

Bans and strict controls on the liberal hunting practices of the past have likely been the biggest reasons for bear population recovery. There are nineteen subpopulations (non species) of polar bears in the world. Several are in decline, but most, including Canada's populations, are healthy and expanding. Local Inuit hunters and residents provide the best indicators of population status. They live in the same habitat as the bears and feel that their numbers are increasing. Yet some southern-based environmental groups with deep pockets and strong lobbyists want you to believe otherwise. Some environmental groups will use furry animals to gain public support (and funding) even though they may not be in danger. The east coast seal hunt in Canada is another great example of this. The seal population was one of the best-managed resources around. Populations were increasing and harvests were closely monitored and controlled. But because seals have cute, big eyes, lobbyists appealed to the public's emotions, and eventually the seal hunt was stopped. Now the seal population is growing unchecked and they continue to make cod stocks difficult to rebuild.

Current bear populations are five times what they were in the 1950s and four times what they were in the 1970s, when protection measures were implemented. The population has been stable in Canada for the past three decades.

My wife Lorraine and I travelled to Churchill, Manitoba, in 2018 to witness these magnificent animals ourselves. The bears congregate in the Churchill area, lazing around while waiting for the ice to form before heading out to hunt seals. They will wait up to four months after eating their last meal! Climate change could reduce their hunting season on the ice; however, polar bears have survived through previous climate changes. No one can positively say how the bears will fare in the future. As an example, a study of this population from 1984 to 2004 showed a decline from 1,200 to 935 and speculated that by 2011 it would be 676. Today, there are 1,013. Even experts can get it wrong

I believe that climate change can often be a game of political football played with big dollars to "prove" their beliefs. I would tend to believe the voice of Inuit residents and scientific population estimates over highly funded voices from some "conservation" groups. I can positively say that strongly funded enforcement programs have to be part of any plan to protect our wildlife. But rarely are those with expertise in enforcement asked for input or opinion in population estimates or management decisions of wildlife. This seems odd given they are the ones most closely associated with the wildlife. The same could be said by most anyone who has donned a uniform. I'll leave that for another discussion.

PERSEVERANCE
BEATS POACHING

SO MANY CASES ARE BUILT FROM TINY SCRAPS OF EVIDENCE GATH-
ered over time. South Dakota Wildlife Conservation officers (WCOs)
had such a case that began in the fall of 2017. Officers kept receiving
reports of headless deer found throughout several counties. They
checked the kill sites and discovered whole deer carcasses without
any meat taken. The heads were missing but there were no obvious
bullet holes or signs of being hit by vehicles. Officers gathered DNA
evidence from the deer carcasses. They also picked up a few items
from some of the locations, including blue paper towels, plastic
Holiday brand water bottles and empty orange packs of Pall Mall
100s cigarettes.

The evidence was meaningless without more information; however, its collection would become crucial down the road. Officers
worked numerous night patrols for about six weeks in the late fall
in the areas where deer had been killed. Attempting to get any
lead whatsoever, they stopped and talked to landowners, hunters
and other law enforcement officers. It was frustrating to know that
ten more dead deer were found during that time span without any
further clues.

Finally, a break came when a Flandreau police officer provided
some information that led WCOs to the main suspect, "Woody." WCO
Chad Williams made an early-morning visit to Woody's house and
found his vehicle parked on a public street. Chad approached it and
looked through the window to see orange packs of Pall Mall cigarettes, a roll of blue paper towels, plastic water bottles and a large
white-tailed deer rack. Bingo! Officers took all their evidence,

obtained a tracking warrant for Woody's vehicle and monitored his residence with electronics. Little did Woody know that two weeks later his poaching crimes would come to an abrupt halt.

wcos and the Sioux Falls police served Woody with a warrant twelve days before Christmas Eve. (Hmm, this might make a new Christmas song.) They seized fifty-three deer racks, many stored in the rafters of his garage (Rudolph would be horrified). Even more were found in the backyard, in a shed and in the basement. They also found two freshly killed deer heads severed from the neck. They seized several firearms, a bloody utility knife, a bloody hatchet, a bloody meat saw and bloody clothing before taking blood samples from the garage floor and from the pickup box.

You'd think someone with fifty-three deer heads would give up right away, but not Lyin' Woody. He initially claimed they were all roadkill or crippled so badly that he shot them to put them out of their misery. What a thoughtful person! But his lies caught up to him and eventually he admitted that some of the deer were not injured until he shot them with a .22 rifle. This explained why there weren't any obvious bullet holes in the deer. He would drive around between 4:00 and 6:00 a.m. with a spotlight, on his way out to hunt water-fowl, and shoot the deer with the .22. Certainly, many deer would run away, wounded and suffering, and die later because he was using such a small bullet. Poachers just don't care. The small-calibre hole would often avoid detection unless the carcass was closely checked. Woody's cellphone revealed more evidence about where deer were shot and when.

Officers interviewed a number of Woody's family members, friends and acquaintances, who all knew he had many deer heads, yet no one had questioned him about it. This is another sad example of how a poacher can be extremely brazen, yet many still don't care enough to report them.

ALABAMA OUTRAGE

EVERYONE HAS HEARD THE TERM "EASY AS SHOOTING FISH IN A barrel." The question I have is "Why would you do that?" I'd just tip the barrel over, dump the water out, bonk the fish and eat them. It would be a lot easier than getting your gun and wasting a bunch of bullets trying to hit a fish. Plus, there wouldn't be a bullet hole in the fish. You wouldn't have to be as careful. You wouldn't make unnecessary holes in a perfectly good barrel. Some things just don't make sense. Something easy to do, though, would be to go hunting in a zoo. Yep. Someone did just that.

The Birmingham Zoo in Alabama had a pen of white-tailed deer, including a majestic ten-year-old mature buck nicknamed Bucky. Zoo workers walked into the deer exhibit on November 19, 1983, to find a pool of blood and drag marks leading to a large hole cut through the enclosure fence. The deer's headless carcass was found three days later in a nearby ditch. Public outrage ensued, rewards were offered and taxidermists were called, but the case went cold.

Four years later, in 1987, a proud Mr. "Weasel" entered his massive buck in the Alabama Deer Hunter's Exhibit. He was proud of the buck he'd shot with a bow in a nearby county. A small crowd gathered around as the massive buck was scored. But the scorer recognized the head of the dearly departed Bucky, and Weasel was busted. Bucky was seized but charges could not be laid, as the statute of limitations had passed. The citizens of Birmingham were scandalized!

The public ridicule and outcry that followed Weasel around were a huge penalty. A song was even written about him that played relentlessly on the radio. He was fired from his job. Time passed and so did Mr. Weasel, eighteen years later.

Over thirty years later, at 10:00 a.m. on December 31, 2018, conservation officer Kerry Bradford of Alabama received a panicked call from a property owner located right next to a busy interstate highway. Everyone loves to see deer as long as they stay off the road, and travellers on that interstate saw them almost daily. The caller himself saw them often; in fact, he had put out game cameras in an attempt to nab poachers hunting illegally on his property, which was open only to bow hunters with access permission. On that day, he'd heard a long volley of shots and immediately called the conservation officer. Shortly after, Bradford arrived on the scene with Hoover police assisting him.

The officers found four brazen poachers covered in deer blood and hair. Only one of the four men could speak English. They had just one deer with them but admitted to shooting several more. They had two rifles and two shotguns and claimed to be just hunting. A search of the area led the officers to believe there were more men who had gotten away with some of the deer. None of the four had a hunting licence or any form of identification. A call was made to US Customs and Immigration. Those officers arrived and determined that all four men were from Guatemala and were in the country illegally. One had been deported once before. Their problems just got worse. They had no legal right to have guns and were charged for federal felony offences.

The public outrage and media frenzy were reminiscent of Bucky thirty years earlier. Some vehicles passing by had seen the deer and were livid. The four were held in custody until federal weapons charges were laid. They all pled guilty and were held to await extradition hearings. No doubt the ghost of Bucky would be pleased.

RESTORATIVE JUSTICE

THE BATTLE AGAINST POACHERS CAN SEEM FUTILE AT TIMES. THE length of time, cost of the courts and low court penalties offer little deterrence in many cases. Educating the prosecutors and the courts is helping, but there is another way. Restorative justice (RJ) is a dramatic shift in how to deal with violators.

Restorative justice is a set of guiding principles to resolve a dispute. The process focuses on a positive outcome for the victims, the accused and the community without assigning specific blame. Trained facilitators (fish/wildlife officers or local boards) lead the process with the goals of offender accountability and repairing the harm caused by the offence. With RJ, the recidivism (repeat offender) rate is much lower than with the court system. RJ is usually done in a matter of weeks versus months or years with the courts.

But many agencies and officers are reluctant to try something new. Common responses are "It's not tough enough" or "That's not for me." I was one of those people until a fellow officer, Jim Michie, persuaded me to attend and observe a healing circle near Williams Lake, BC. Prior to this, Jim had already worked in his community to develop an enforcement protocol between the RCMP, the Conservation Officer Service and the Department of Fisheries and Oceans.

I travelled to the small reserve where the RJ matter was being held. The first thing I noticed was that no lawyers were involved. I liked it already! The case was about a woman who'd been physically abused by her husband. He sat in a circle with his wife, his sixteen-year-old son, some elders from his community and a few officers from the agencies. The emotions came pouring out as the wife and son spoke. My palms were sweating as I heard the gripping stories. I watched in amazement at how the process quickly dealt with the offence. Everyone had a chance to speak, unlike a traditional court. There was no yelling or court theatrics. Did I mention no costly lawyers? The victim felt better, the son felt better, the community felt better and the accused felt remorse in front of them all. He later said he'd rather have gone to court because it would have been easier than this.

I came away with a clearer understanding of the process and supported Jim in developing a provincial approach to RJ. Jim developed and led the first RJ program for fish and wildlife offences anywhere in the world. Officers throughout BC received facilitator training. The conservation officers, led by Andy Mackay, followed a similar path. Yet few officers were willing to accept or try the process. We didn't push it but instead focused on letting those who wanted to try it first. Not every community is ready for this either. Ultimately, it can only work if the accused is serious about trying it. If it fails, the court option can be used.

Despite these obstacles, the DFO persevered and began using RJ for other offences. Many people think the process is for First Nations cases only, but it has been used successfully for commercial fishers, sport fishers and environmental crime. Relationships with First Nations also improved. The outcome is limited only by the creativity of those involved in the process. The DFO made concerted efforts to improve relationships through other processes as well. There has not been a single serious confrontation with fishery officers in many years in the Pacific region (BC and the Yukon). RJ and building relationships have been the two biggest reasons.

A major environmental crime occurred in Trail, BC, involving Teck Resources, a large mining company that directly or indirectly employed most of the community. Their operations had spilled leachates and mercury into the river running through town. Conservation officer Andy Mackay decided to try RJ to address the violations. The town mayor, local businesses, officers and company executives attended the RJ process and heard from anyone who chose to speak. The company lawyer sat in the back as an observer.

In the end, it was agreed that the company would pay $325,000 to be held in trust for the community for projects. The community used some of the money for purchasing bear-proof garbage containers. They built some nature trails with interpretive signs. Other money was matched by the local fish and game club and put into an endowment fund. The company agreed to review its piping configuration and establish procedures to prevent discharges into the sewer system. The company also launched phase II of its effluent spill reduction program budgeted at $5.5 million to reduce the risk of spills. And it agreed to a long list of other measures to improve its operations. I doubt the normal court system would have resulted in such measures and timely improvements to the mining operation.

The company executives who attended the RJ session should be applauded for their willingness to try something outside of the accepted way of dealing with a violation. There is a short video on YouTube, "Restorative Justice Encourages Collaborative Solutions," that interviews those who participated in this process. Everyone was a winner, especially the fish. If any agency is willing to try RJ, it should be approached slowly and only started in situations where everyone wants to be part of it. Successes will result if others are willing to give it a try. It won't always work but it's worth an attempt, and if successful will reduce recidivism.

ALASKA POACHER REBORN

LEGENDS ABOUND IN ALASKA. PEOPLE WHO LIVE THERE ARE PART of the wilderness that surrounds them. They share a unique nonconformist "leave me alone" attitude distant from the rest of the United States. Sixty percent of Alaskan residents moved there from the lower forty-eight for adventure and solitude in the outdoors. One in sixty residents have a pilot's licence.

Most Alaskans hunt big game and many southerners flock to Alaska for a chance to hunt a monster moose, bear or sheep. About 450 outfitters provide some of the best hunting experiences in North America. "Chuck" was probably the most notorious big-game outfitter in Alaskan history. He was known for finding the biggest animals around—he just wasn't known for following the rules. Chuck used aircraft in many of his hunts and catching him was a challenge that required a long-term undercover operation.

Undercover officers were assigned to the case in the 1980s. A Spanish-speaking officer was chosen for the operation because two main Mexican "targets" were going hunting with Chuck. Through a complex, sometimes hair-raising operation the officer infiltrated Chuck's hunting camp when the Mexicans were there as guests. The Mexicans were initially suspicious of the officer because his Spanish accent wasn't quite right; they thought he might be a wildlife officer. Chuck threatened to kill him if he was an officer. The Mexicans did some background checks through their Mexican connections (which checked out okay) and the officer was welcomed. The threats associated with working as an undercover officer are tremendous. They have to act cool and calm no matter what happens around them. They might even have to lie like a poacher. Undercover officers operating in the Alaskan wilderness have no readily available support.

Chuck took the now trusted "guest" on a bear hunt. He did as he had done dozens of times before: he flew around and found a decent bear, dropped his client off on the ground, then chased the bear toward the poacher with his plane. It was not legal or sporting, but it was very effective. The undercover officer gathered enough evidence from that hunt to charge and convict Chuck and the Mexicans. Chuck's hunting outfitting business was shut down and his licence removed.

But the allure of fortune was too great, and Chuck would not be kept down. He had made hundreds of thousands of dollars guiding poachers, and most poachers can't resist the lure of a big catch. Chuck started up a fishing lodge in Alaska and attracted the same wealthy customers and politicians he'd had for the hunting operation. The fishing lodge became a front for Chuck's continued illegal bear guiding. He didn't have a licence to guide hunters, but you really don't need a licence if you're poaching in any case. Chuck used the same diehard old habits as before. He'd take poachers out for a flight, find a large bear, drop them off and chase the bear toward them. It would take another undercover officer several years to crack into his organization again. The officer developed a close relationship with Chuck, eventually becoming the man's favourite customer and being given priority for the best hunts.

One day, Chuck took the officer on a plane trip to hunt brown bear. Where do you take a very special customer bear hunting? Chuck spent five days flying over Katmai National Park and Preserve before finding a huge, 2.8-metre bear for his customer. Yes, the officer shot the bear that Chuck herded directly to him. I don't know whether the officer had a choice—that was really the only way to catch this poacher enabler. Evidence was gathered on a number of poachers, customers and staff.

Chuck and many of his workers, pilots and customers were charged. One of Chuck's pilots, who was willing to testify against him, fell off a cliff and died before the trial. The wife of another of his guides committed suicide. Chuck was fined $100,000, spent a year in jail and had several airplanes forfeited. Fishing lodge records revealed dozens of other clients, resulting in many more seizures and charges.

A uniformed USFWS officer visited Chuck in prison. The officer persuaded Chuck to be part of a poaching video his agency was making. The show would feature former poachers talking about the errors of their past and hopefully persuade others to either stop poaching or help catch those who might try following in their "foolsteps." It was a great idea and may have convinced some; however, you don't have to look far to find another poacher.

A final example: in 2011, another famous Alaskan hunter operator was charged. Mr. "Chase" operated Fair Chase Hunts (funny in a sick sort of way) as one of his outfitting efforts. He guided for nearly forty years in Alaska. He estimated his clients took over one hundred brown bears and over three hundred sheep. He didn't use aircraft and was outspoken against those who did. He was a self-proclaimed conservationist. He did break the law, though, and was fined $125,000 for a long list of violations including poaching in the Arctic National Wildlife Refuge. I wonder whether he thought hunting in a zoo was okay too. The seventy-eight-year-old plea-bargained the fines to avoid jail time as he was dying of cancer. In his failing health, Chase admitted to many of his violations and tried to vindicate himself of being a felon. But I'm afraid it was too little, too late for ol' Chase. It's too bad he didn't come clean decades earlier.

BIRD HUNTING IN HAWAII

BIRD HUNTING IN HAWAII IS LIKELY THE LAST THING MOST PEOPLE think of when talking about these precious islands in the Pacific. But the Big Island has a diverse, bountiful population of pheasant, quail, chukar partridge, francolin (ground-dwelling flightless birds) and turkey. All of these birds were introduced but have a thriving presence offering great bird hunting.

Bob Farrell was a game warden with the Department of Land and Natural Resources. He was patrolling the Big Island with two experienced fellow wardens when they stopped a few bird hunters to check their licences and bag limits without incident. After that, they were driving along a country road when Farrell noticed a motorcycle parked down a side road, partially hidden in the bushes. The bike had an empty rifle scabbard on the side and a hunting dog kennel mounted on the rear. It was parked in an area closed to the use of motorbikes for hunting.

Farrell stopped his truck and walked over to the bike, but he found no sign of the operator. He climbed a ridge and kept low to scan the countryside with his binoculars. Still not spotting a hunter, he returned to join the other two officers. One of them was standing by a concrete guzzler (a water catchment station designed to hold rainwater for wildlife in the dry seasons). He had found a camouflage jacket covering a couple of plastic bags about twelve metres from the motorcycle.

One bag contained a small, dead pig (pig season was closed) and the other contained three francolin (the daily limit) and a chukar. The officers covered the find, backed up and drove down the road a ways to wait for the poacher. He would have to pass by, as it was the only road out of the area. They had waited only thirty minutes before the bike came bouncing down the road with the hunter and his trusty springer spaniel poking its head out of the kennel. The bike continued past the officers before turning down a side road.

Farrell followed in his truck and the bike stopped. When questioned, the hunter claimed he had just wanted to stop for some shade. He was polite and friendly, producing his licence and proudly showing the officers three francolin and a pheasant. Farrell recalled noticing that one of the francolin birds under the jacket had had a double spur on the legs. None of these birds showed that, and what had happened to the chukar? The pheasant was a hen and thus not legal to shoot.

Now the story began. The hunter claimed his dog was such a good dog that he'd caught the hen pheasant himself, and the hunter felt obligated to finish it off. He didn't want to waste it (maybe he was taking it to Grandma's?). Farrell continued to question the poacher, but the man stuck to his story. He claimed he was an honest guy with no reason to lie to an officer. Aren't they all?

Farrell pointed out that the jacket he'd found covering the stashed birds was the one Mr. Honesty was wearing. At that, the poacher folded like a cheap tent and admitted there were some francolin in the bottom of his scabbard. "Oh yeah, and there's a chukar too. My dog killed that one too and I had to finish it off." By this point, I'm sure the dog was not impressed with his new job as fall guy for his owner. More questions and more complete honesty: "I've shown you everything—nothing more to show, I swear."

Farrell finally said, "You know what? Just show me the damn pig." The dejected hunter hung his head and said, "It's under the dog." The dog looked as sad as his owner as the officer pulled the hidden pig from under the pad inside the kennel. The poor dog knew what was coming next. The owner said, "The dog killed that too."

The poacher left without his shotgun and all the animals he'd shot, but with one very sad, embarrassed dog.

ALLIGATOR POACHERS
IN FLORIDA

IN 2015, THE "TOOTHLESS" ALLIGATOR FARM WAS ESTABLISHED IN southwest Florida in the heart of alligator country. Four young men decided that selling alligators to the farm would be a great way to make some extra cash. They pulled in to the farm one day with their pickup filled with sixteen live alligators they had poached over the previous two nights. The alligators had their limbs and mouths taped to avoid injury or escape during the hour-long trip. They ranged in length from thirty centimetres to 2.5 metres. The buyer, Mr. "Goodguy," looked the pile over and issued a cheque for $1,600. The beaming young driver looked at the cheque and said, "Not a bad paycheque for two nights' work. Better than selling dope!" (Unless you are one.)

What the young criminals didn't know was that they were selling their catch to Goodguy, an undercover agent hired by the Florida Fish and Wildlife Conservation Commission during a two-year operation targeting alligator poachers.

There are about ninety licensed alligator farms in Florida, generating about $8.5 million for the lucrative hide and meat markets. This doesn't include contraband products outside the legal market. Hides, both legal and poached, can be worth $40 a foot, and alligator eggs go for up to $60 each. After Hurricane Katrina wiped out many Louisiana alligator farms, the search for eggs to replenish their operations caused egg prices to skyrocket.

Alligators have survived for millions of years. A popular food and hide source in the 1800s, they were hunted to near extinction. Millions were hunted over the years, until their numbers dropped to

Alligator eggs can fetch up to $60 each. In 2015, Florida officers completed a large undercover operation resulting in over $80,000 in fines. *Photo: Florida Fish and Wildlife Conservation.*

fewer than a hundred thousand US-wide in the 1950s. Florida banned hunting them in 1962. The federal government extended the ban across all states in 1967. A remarkable recovery resulted. In 1987 they were removed from the endangered list, and a controlled, licensed harvest commenced. Alligator meat and hides found a renewed market over the ensuing years.

Many feel the popularity of a couple of television shows, *Swamp People* and *Gator Boys*, contributed to a renewed surge in hunting alligators and the quest for alligator meat. From 2013 to 2015, prices for the reptile's meat doubled, and more people wanted to hunt them. The profits from farming alligators also increased along with the temptation to poach.

The price of alligator eggs was driven up to the aforementioned $60 each. Permits can be issued to harvest eggs from nests on private land. The permit holder will pay an amount per egg directly to the landowner. Inevitably, the temptation became too high to declare the number actually taken. The only way to enforce such a law is with an undercover operation.

A permit has a number of conditions attached. One important conservation condition was that the permit holder could only remove eggs from half of the number of full nests they discovered. This law is just plain goofy. It is absolutely impossible to enforce. If you found twenty empty nests before finding one with eggs, I would think you have a conservation problem. With this licence condition the permit holder could still take those eggs but not the next full nest. At a value of $60 per egg, this condition is probably ignored most of the time. This is a common problem in fish and wildlife management: seemingly logical decisions are made with the best intentions, but enforceability is difficult if not impossible.

Enforcement of alligator hunting laws is further complicated by the fact that First Nations are permitted to harvest alligators on their reserves. They are not allowed to sell them. Again, the temptation arises for non-Indigenous people to team up with First Nations, creating a good cover for poaching alligators. This undercover operation was located in a very poor region of Florida where 30 per cent of residents lived below the poverty line. The temptation to poach and make money would be high.

Goodguy worked the operation for two years. He befriended many long-time targets of the agency. He accompanied poachers taking alligators from the local reserve, assisted with unlawful egg collections and purchased hundreds of poached alligators. Violations included but were not limited to selling eggs, hides and meat, selling alligators taken from a reserve, killing a protected bird, theft and racketeering, and a host of charges were laid. Racketeering charges are generally used for criminal enterprises or organizations, and poachers are increasingly being placed in this category. Some of the people charged certainly fit that description. One egg collector had illegally poached over ten thousand eggs worth over half a million dollars. Over sixty officers conducted raids on residences, resulting in nine people being charged.

One of those charged owned an alligator farm. Of course, he blamed the government for his predicament after he was charged. He had worked as a corrections officer for sixteen years in a state prison. He blamed a change in politics for closing down a bunch of prisons, leading to his layoff. He knew a lot about alligators and quickly learned the value of the industry by starting his own alligator business. Maybe they'll have to reopen those prisons to accommodate his new occupation.

One of the illegal egg harvesters sold eggs to a millionaire buyer in Louisiana for the latter's alligator operation. The buyer was less than a model citizen, with criminal convictions including illegal political campaign contributions, a fatal hit-and-run and aggravated child rape (he settled with the family by paying them $2 million). Others were almost normal people without serious criminal records. And naturally, some of the accused claimed innocence, that they'd been set up, that the undercover officer was drunk—anything to try to deflect their own stupidity and responsibility.

The poacher proven to have profited the most received a three-year jail sentence, forfeiture of two boats and four trailers, plus ten years' probation. Others received up to ten years of probation, and the entire group of them must pay over $82,000 in restitution.

SURPRISE! SURPRISE!

CONSERVATION OFFICER JIM CORBETT WAS AT THE HOSPITAL IN Quesnel, BC, checking on his wife. She had been in labour for twenty-eight hours before delivering their first child. He hadn't been in to work for a few days, so on his way home he decided to stop by his office and check for messages. He listened to the voice messages, including one from that morning. It was from a man reporting a dead doe that had been gutted and hidden in some bushes. The caller had left his name and number, so Corbett returned his call.

He met the man at the poaching location. They walked into the site, being careful not to leave visible footprints on the road in the snow. Corbett determined that the deer had been recently shot and thought the poachers would return, since the carcass had been gutted and hidden. After thanking the fellow who had reported the incident, Corbett decided to hide in the bushes and wait for the poachers to return. He donned his long raincoat, found a comfortable stump out of sight near the deer and prepared for a long wait.

Sure enough, late in the afternoon a truck stopped and five people spilled out. One guy said, "Go get the deer!" They heard a vehicle coming, so pretended to be sharpening a chainsaw until it went by. After the vehicle had passed, Corbett watched two guys run to get the deer and drag it to the pickup. The five of them then stood contemplating the deer lying on the ground.

That was the moment Corbett walked out wearing his raincoat over his uniform and approached the group without saying a word. No one seemed to notice the extra guy standing there. Of course, poachers don't notice a lot of things. They were all looking down at the deer and talking about it. As Corbett wiggled into the group, the smartest one looked up and said, "Hey, it's the game warden!" One on

82

the lower end of the intelligence scale responded with "Don't scare me like that." Reality finally connected and they all stood staring in shocked amazement.

"Who shot this deer?" Corbett said. In their surprised state, one of them readily admitted to the crime. Corbett took the keys out of their pickup and walked the guy back to his own truck, asking, "What made you think you could ever get away with something like that?" The poacher said, "We knew your wife was in the hospital having a baby, so we thought you'd be off."

The incident would become legend in the community. None of the poachers ever learned how Jim Corbett could possibly have known about their deer, or how he could have appeared out of nowhere and stood among them before they noticed him. Never underestimate the stupidity of a poacher.

HUNTING FOR DUMMIES

You have to love a judge who really thinks before passing a sentence. A judge in Grayson County, Texas, convicted "Robin Dudd" of using a rifle in bow season to hunt deer on private property without permission. The offence means automatic prison time in Texas. Dudd was fined $18,000, prohibited from purchasing a hunting licence for five years and sentenced to spending every weekend of hunting season in jail for the next five years.

WHOOPING CRANES

WHOOPING CRANES HAVE BEEN A REMARKABLE RECOVERY STORY of a bird near the brink of extinction. In the early 1940s, there were only about twenty birds left. Today, they number about eight hundred, including three small populations of introduced birds in the southern US. Not everyone is cheering about this success story, though. Yes, there are even whooping crane poachers.

Whooping cranes are sometimes shot intentionally by farmers and landowners in the southern United States. It would seem the cranes like to feed on crawfish raised in ponds, and the pond owners feel they have the right to shoot these rare birds. Where are all the environmental groups who try to save other animals? They usually focus more on fuzzy, huggable-looking animals with big, sad eyes. It's great that they try to save those, but there is so much work they could do on our own continent to save some of the more endangered, less cute animals here.

The practice of draining swampy land for agriculture only magnifies the problem. The former wildlife habitat is turned into farmland, and the loss of habitat leaves less natural space for the wild birds. Birds then eat the crops that are planted. Sandhill cranes are a larger problem with crop predation due to their sheer numbers. And as whooping cranes increase in number, they will also be subject to more poaching.

It's been estimated to cost $110,000 to raise a whooping crane in captivity for release into the wild. You'd think that restitution laws would mean large fines for those inclined to shoot them. Yet few poachers are ever caught, and if they are, penalties are all over the map. In 2016 a young man killed two whooping cranes and was given a $25,810 fine, two hundred hours of community service and a five-year hunting ban. In South Dakota a poacher paid $85,000 and lost all hunting privileges for two years. A Texas man served six months in jail and was barred from hunting for life. On the other end of the scale was an Indiana man who killed a whooper and paid a $1 fine and $550 in court costs.

A whooping crane shot in Louisiana in July of 2018 was the twenty-ninth one shot in that state since they were listed as endangered in 1969. It would take over $3 million to raise and replace those twenty-nine birds through captive methods. Very few of the twenty-nine poachers were caught. Most were just chronic poachers and a few were accidental shootings through identification error. Extinction is only a few dodos away.

HUNTING FOR DUMMIES

A New York environmental conservation officer responded to a call about a young wild fox entangled in a soccer net at a local daycare centre. The job can be entertaining on many days, and others are sheer sport. The young fox was removed uninjured and released into some nearby trees. Can you imagine the puzzled parents when their preschoolers came home and told them about the fox in the soccer net? The story would have been even better if there'd been a grapevine nearby.

ORCHID SMUGGLERS

IF POLAR BEARS ARE THE APEX PREDATOR IN THE WILD, THE DELI-cate orchid has to be near the other end of the scale. Most orchid owners are legal operations, but smuggling rare exotic plants is a thriving part of the illegal trade in nature's creations.

The same officer who dealt with the polar bear poacher was the lead investigator in this unique file. Richard Labossiere was a twenty-year veteran wildlife enforcement officer with Environment Canada in Winnipeg when he received a call about a shipment of Lady's Slipper orchids imported into Winnipeg from Taiwan. It might surprise you that orchids grow in Manitoba. In fact, there is a whole world of Manitoba botanists, collectors and government-owned botanical facilities looking for unique legal plants to share.

Unfortunately, some orchid owners are drawn into the alluring world of poaching. Can you imagine an orchid poacher's story? "There I was, deep in the remote jungle of Brazil. I was on the last day of my ten-day safari when I spied this beauty through my Swarovski 10x50s from fifty metres away. I silently stalked it, then pulled out my twenty-gauge stainless steel shovel and bagged it. It's the rarest orchid in the world. I get goosebumps every time I look at it on the mantel."

When Labossiere received the call from Canada Customs, he immediately said he would conduct the inspection. There was a slight problem, however—he knew next to nothing about endangered orchids and needed to brush up on the subject, and fast. Labossiere quickly headed to the airport with his plant identification book, a local orchid expert and a customs officer. The shipment contained over two thousand orchids! As they carefully unpacked the fragile plants (none were in bloom), they discovered that, oddly, between pairs of larger orchids plants were smaller, bare-rooted orchids, meaning they had dormant roots without foliage. These orchids caused the local expert to reel with excitement. He believed they were a rare Paphiopedilum (Paph) species. The shipment contained a total of 211 of these smaller, protected plants.

The accompanying paperwork listed 211 orchids of a different species that was not as rare. This would have been legal in the shipment. The local orchid expert was not 100 per cent sure of the identification; however, the fact that an attempt had been made to conceal them made it all look very suspicious. Just then, the owner of the shipment arrived at the airport to claim the orchids. He was the manager of an orchid nursery. He said the orchids were not the Paph variety but rather a "hybrid" greenhouse-bought species. Officer Labossiere doubted the story and seized the 211 plants, plus 538 other orchids that had been used to conceal them. Great idea, except what do you do with nearly 750 orchids?

The Assiniboine Park Conservancy offered to care for the plants. A special tag and serial number was attached to each one of the plants for evidentiary purposes. All was good except no one could positively identify these as Paph orchids because they had no blossoms. The plant normally flowers every two years. The officer called every orchid expert he could find. Many thought they were indeed the rare orchids, but without flowers for positive identification, they were not willing to testify in court. DNA wasn't an option either because DNA labs didn't have Paph orchid DNA to compare these plants with.

The only option was to wait for the plants to bloom. Miraculously, three months later the first flower arrived. Officer Labossiere must have felt like handing out cigars. A few months later a second one bloomed. An orchid expert was located in Ottawa who would be willing to testify in court. The flowering Paphs were carefully packaged and shipped first-class on Air Canada to the expert for identification, then returned to Winnipeg. One was identified as a rare wild natural hybrid from China and the other was a pure wild species; both were listed and highly protected.

Good news travels fast in the orchid underground. Perhaps too fast, as someone stole one of the flowers right out of the conservatory greenhouse. Labossiere sheepishly attended the police station to report the stolen orchid. The police officer did a double take when Labossiere made the report. "Now I think I've heard everything," he said. The orchid community was abuzz, and everyone was out to get the dirty thief. Then the plant mysteriously reappeared at the conservatory—without its flower. In order to prevent any further thefts, the wildlife officer placed all the seized orchids in locked dog kennel cages—without the dogs, of course.

Over the following months most of the orchids bloomed. Each was carefully sent to the expert in Ottawa for identification. Labossiere conducted interviews and executed search warrants of the buyer's business, residence and vehicle used to transport the plants. Computer records revealed three prior shipments of Paph imports from Taiwan dating back to 1997. After two and a half long, laborious years on the case, the business and its three board members were charged with multiple violations under the appropriate legislation.

It became important to absolutely prove that some of the orchids were wild collected plants versus others that were hybridized in a greenhouse. Both were illegal; however, the ones taken from the wild were rarer, and presumably the courts would deal with that offence more severely. But there wasn't a Canadian expert who could testify that the seized Paph orchids had indeed been collected from the wild.

In past years, Labossiere had tried to get approval to attend the Convention on International Trade of Endangered Species (CITES) conference. He was finally allowed to attend the 2002 conference in Chile. There, he located two world-renowned orchid experts, one from Switzerland and the other from England. Both would positively say the plants had been collected from the wild, based on the photos of the seized orchids that Labossiere showed them. The experts eventually analyzed photos of all 211 plants and provided an expert report for the pending trial. They pointed to old leaf damage and discolouration and root damage that clearly proved to them the plants had been removed from the wild and then grown in a greenhouse for one or two years before being sold.

The expert reports and amount of tireless investigative work resulted in a guilty plea from the orchid nursery in July of 2003. They were fined $15,000 for the illegal importation, plus forfeiture of all the orchids. Of that amount, $5,000 was earmarked for a permanent display of the orchids in the Winnipeg conservatory facility. The business was also ordered to display CITES information pamphlets in their storefront location for three years. Finally, they were ordered to advise Environment Canada before any future imports arrived.

It's not uncommon to see this type of dedication and patience from a fish and wildlife officer. It's not as common to show such endurance on what many would consider a boring case. Officers show remarkable investigative skills and creativity. I've been told by a number of prosecutors that a file from a fish and wildlife officer is usually more thorough and complete than most police agencies'. Experts' assistance in any case is also extremely important. Their passion needs to be shared by everyone to control poaching and smuggling of all plants and animals. Labossiere's dogged determination over the thirty-month-long case earned him the handle of "Officer Orchid."

NORTH DAKOTA'S BIGGEST

MR. "DITZ" AND HIS SON "HOMER" OWNED AND OPERATED THE "Bonanza Valley Lodge," a business with two lodges in a scenic valley in North Dakota. The area teemed with migratory birds, upland game, deer and other wildlife. North Dakota is the top duck-producing state in the US. It's not uncommon for areas to have 100 to 150 wetlands per square mile. The state is a duck factory. The lodge is located in the middle of this region rich with wetlands.

The lodge attracted many law-abiding customers. However, it also developed a reputation of doing whatever the customer wanted because the owners and their guides encouraged lawbreakers. Fishing and hunting lodges will attract the type of client the owners allow. A law-abiding owner will generally attract law-abiding customers. Guests who like to work outside the law will find each other and find a lodge better suited to them. This operation attracted many clients, with unimaginably horrific consequences for the wildlife.

A typical day at the lodge involved three hunts—a morning waterfowl hunt, an afternoon upland bird hunt and an evening waterfowl hunt. If the limit was taken in the morning, it didn't seem to matter. The lodge dump contained hundreds of wasted birds.

In 2005, North Dakota Game and Fish (NDGF) developed and implemented an undercover operation that would eventually blow the lid off the lodge's resource-pilfering attitude. The officers at NDGF were fairly new to undercover operations (which began in the late 1990s), but they'd had success in the few they had run before this one at Bonanza Valley Lodge. A lot of background work is required before launching into an expensive undercover project like this one.

The undercover officers were shocked by the type and number of violations they witnessed. A decision was made to shut the lodge down immediately after only one season of the undercover operation. In October of 2005, a group of thirty uniformed officers from NDGF and the USFWS descended on both the north and south lodges and the homes of Ditz and Homer. An NDGF officer invited the prosecuting attorney along to witness the search operation. This provided the prosecutor with some valuable insight and exposed him to details that couldn't be matched by a description. He saw a shelterbelt of trees with rotting carcasses of geese, ducks and swans strewn about. He saw a freezer stuffed full of goose and duck breasts with no markings of who they belonged to. Presumably, these were for those guests who might want to take a few birds home with them. Many guests didn't take any and just kept shooting.

The resulting charges included unlawful transport of wildlife, unlawful sale of wildlife, unlawful hunting of deer, swans, ducks, geese, raptors and upland birds. A number of guides were swept up in the mess too. Accurate record keeping was frowned upon and discouraged by the owners. Over-limits were frequent. Guides would be compelled to claim some over-limit birds if they were checked, thus many birds were simply thrown in the dump to rot so guests could shoot some more.

Investigators painstakingly analyzed the hunting ledgers for the lodge. They commonly found false and missing information for guests and limits. The investigation led officers to charge ninety-four guests for a host of violations. Those guests paid over $20,000 in fines. The seven guides convicted paid $10,000 in fines and probation. The lodge owners, Ditz and Homer, paid $90,000 in fines, served eighteen months of probation, had their hunting privileges in all of North America revoked, paid $10,000 in restitution, forfeited two shotguns and were given a lifetime ban on guiding and outfitting anywhere in the United States. Who knows how many animals were killed before the brief undercover operation went down? The Ditzes shut the lodges down and sold them. Ditz did apologize to the judge for his mistakes. But an apology hardly seems enough for such calculated crimes.

Most private lodge owners and their guests are law-abiding people. However, if the opportunity for greed goes unchecked, crazy things like this will and do happen. At 103 violators, the tally was the largest number of people charged in one investigation in North Dakota history. It's a record no one wants to see broken.

HUNTING FOR DUMMIES

A Delaware poacher saw a recent photo of a huge flock of geese in a local magazine. He headed out to the location named in the photo and started harvesting a few fat geese. His goose was cooked when officers showed up with him hunting inside a federal bird refuge.

CRACKING A BLACK WALNUT CASE

WOODWORKERS WILL CRINGE WHEN THEY HEAR THAT OUR FORE-fathers used black walnut for things like fence posts, shingles and poles due to its resistance to rot. The slow-growing black walnut tree can live to be over one hundred years old and is found through-out eastern Canada and the United States. Today, the black walnut is highly desirable for high-end furniture and woodworking. The largest old-growth trees are often on private land or in parks in the middle and southern United States. They generally favour riparian zones along watercourses. Their removal can impact fish as well as other wildlife. Our historic misuse of this resource has followed the path of many other species. Of course, demand drives the price up and a new poacher is born—the black walnut tree poacher.

Poaching of this species has become a problem in a number of states, especially Iowa and Missouri and more recently Nebraska. Some officers feel the increase has occurred due to low scrap-metal prices. The previous collectors and thieves of metal and wire have turned to a more lucrative commodity, black walnut. Obviously, it's not nearly as difficult to sneak up on a black walnut tree as a white-tailed deer, and the reward is more valuable. A large piece of black walnut can bring hundreds or even thousands of dollars to the poach-ers. As long as there are buyers for the wood, there will be poaching.

Two men in Iowa were charged for taking black walnut trees from a state park. Another person went to jail after being caught with thirty-two trees taken from federal land—one of those trees was valued at $10,000. Poachers sometimes use electric chainsaws (to save the environment—not!) to reduce the noise and chance of getting caught.

In February 2019, Nebraska conservation officer Rich Berggren received information about a call from a concerned citizen who had seen a vehicle in his neighbour's field and thought it might be illegal hunters. Officer Berggren arrived at the property and came across some truck tracks through the snow in a soybean field. There didn't appear to be any tracks coming out of the field. He followed the tracks into a grove of black walnut trees and found a partially hidden truck surrounded by some toppled walnut trees. The black Suburban with deeply tinted windows (the vehicle of choice for criminals) was pulling a trailer with a bunch of trees piled on it. The lack of chain-saw noise led Berggren to the truck. He could barely see through the heavily tinted windows and was cautious in his approach. You never know whom you might be dealing with. He heard some noise inside only to find the driver sound asleep. Poaching trees is hard work and he was having a nap.

The officer looked around the area and found eight fresh stumps. Deputies and police from Waterloo, Nebraska, showed up to assist. The poacher's defence? Someone had told him the area was going to be cleared for development and he could have all the trees. Of course, he didn't know the guy's name or where he was from. At first, the landowner wanted the poacher charged for theft. He later declined to press charges, likely for fear of retaliation. The only charge was for criminal trespassing. The judge gave the man a $25 fine, less than a parking ticket. This is yet another example of the courts needing to be educated about the impact and extent of this type of crime.

EEL-ICIT CRIME

THE POOR, DEFENCELESS EEL MIGHT BE THE RODNEY DANGERFIELD of the wild—they "just don't get no respect." There is a massive, lucrative global trade of baby eels (elvers) and frozen eel meat. Eel poaching is a worldwide problem, particularly in Europe, eastern Canada and the eastern United States.

Eels have an amazingly complex life cycle. The European eel hatches somewhere in the Sargasso Sea (between North and South America, near Bermuda). The larvae develop into a form shaped like a willow leaf and drift in the Gulf Stream for a year before they turn into elvers, sometimes called glass eels because their bodies are clear at this life stage.

As elvers drift in close to Europe, they begin migrating up rivers, where they spend most of their four to twelve years of adult life. The American eel follows a similar life cycle, starting in the Sargasso Sea and migrating north before moving into freshwater streams. The mature adults eventually migrate all the way south again to spawn. Little is known about this stage of their life. I guess they're kind of shy.

If eels are kept in fresh water and not allowed to migrate to spawn in the Sargasso Sea, they can live to be one hundred years old. If I were an eel I think I'd rather head south for some sun and fun rather than abstain and get old.

Eels have been a desirable meal in Europe, Japan and more recently in China. I shouldn't knock those who eat things that give me nausea, but I will. Eels have been eaten since medieval times in Europe. The popular French "reverse eel" recipe involves deboning the eel, turning it inside out, stuffing it with something that tastes good, sewing it up and cooking it in red wine. Yum, yum! I think I'd just drink the wine.

Live elvers (baby eels) can fetch $2,000 per pound in Asian markets. They are often shipped in watertight suitcases fitted with oxygen bottles.
Photo: Florian Büttner.

Japan consumes a major amount of the world's eel catch. Eels became especially popular in a dish called kobayashi. To supply this increased market, the Japanese have turned to aquaculture, mainly to control the size and flavour of the eel. This industry has turned to foreign overfished stocks for elvers. Eels are especially difficult to breed in captivity—they may be more private than rabbits.

The small, licensed eel fisheries in Europe are constantly threatened by poaching. Legal fishers, using boats and nets, are assigned to fish in certain areas while the poachers scoop up the elvers in closed waters, causing prices in the legal fishery to drop and threatening the stocks. Europe's eel populations have dropped about 5 per cent per year over the last fifty years. They are now at about 10 per cent of historic averages and continue to decline, yet the seizures of illegal eels continue to climb. They are simply worth too much money in the Asian market.

An enforcement group in England called Border Force caught sixty-seven-year-old "Scooby Goo" smuggling elvers from Europe to Asia. His main supply of eels came from Spain, Portugal and France. The European eel is protected and nearing extinction. During his smuggling operation from 2015 to 2017, Mr. Goo is known to have smuggled about $62 million worth of elvers! How did the courts deal with Mr. Goo? Apparently, $62 million can land you a good lawyer. His lawyer argued that because of Mr. Goo's age and other health issues he should not go to prison, because of the threat of contracting the coronavirus. Goo's two years of jail time were suspended. If you're starting to feel warm right now, it's not likely a fever.

Elvers have to be transported live from Europe to Asia for aquaculture. One method poachers employed was to place the live elvers in containers supplied with oxygen underneath larger shipments of frozen fish. Mortality rates can be high, but that just means you catch some more. The Sustainable Eel Group's 2019 annual report states that the value of live eels can go from $115 per kilogram in Europe to $2,300 per kilogram in Asia. At that value, private jets have been used within Europe to fly live elvers to their aquaculture buyer in nearby countries. Hong Kong customs records have shown illegal shipments of elvers from France, Spain, Bulgaria, Italy, the UK, Greece and Australia. In 2012, law enforcement agencies arrested fourteen people from four countries and seized 1.5 tonnes of elvers and a private jet. One Spanish shipment was found in a warehouse inside 364 suitcases, each equipped with oxygen. There are no limits to smuggling when the commodity is valuable enough.

The threatened European fishery means higher prices for North American elvers. Maine has a fishery for elvers with a state limit of 450 licences, each assigned a maximum of two kilograms of catch (licences were capped based on historic catches of those who'd caught at least two kilograms annually). In 2019 the fishery brought in $20 million, with fishers getting up to $1,300 per kilogram. Nine licences came up for grabs through a lottery system that brought 3,600 applicants. The real lottery might be easier.

Canada's eel poachers and fisheries are mostly located in New Brunswick and Nova Scotia. They used to be fairly modest fisheries until Europe banned exports and protected their species. That conservation measure simply increased the pressure on any other wild stocks in the world. Prices went from $6 a kilogram in the 1980s to over $900 a kilogram in 2015, and even higher in recent years. This crazy value is putting pressure on North America to declare its eel a threatened species as well.

In 2015, a Canadian poacher with over three hundred kilograms of live elvers arranged for a sale to a buyer at a bargain price of $350 a kilogram, a third of the value. Mr. "Keel" took a sample in a bucket in his car to show the buyer in a prearranged parking lot. The deal was struck and the buyer—an undercover fishery officer—took the whole shipment in exchange for a court appearance. Mr. Keel had stolen the elvers and the car he delivered them in. He was sentenced to five months in jail and fined $17,500. He had been convicted of a similar crime before and will likely continue to poach in the future. There is just too much money to be made and so little risk of getting caught. Canadian officials recently seized eighteen tonnes of frozen eels in the port of Vancouver, destined for Asia. It was the largest single seizure of illegal wild animal product in Canadian history. It was but one small part of a ninety-two-country worldwide wildlife sting operation trading in any plant, animal or fish with a value.

Eel smuggling is a graphic example of wildlife smuggling that exposes the extent of the inflated values driving the poaching industry. Based on 2017 figures, poaching criminals have only a 1.3 per cent chance of getting checked by wildlife authorities compared with the chances of other types of criminals getting checked by police. That's why many thugs switch to this type of crime. The courts, too, will usually be more lenient against wildlife crime. I could go on and bore you with a continued long list of countries and violations. It's safe to say that eels are slipping through our borders in extraordinary numbers as stocks continue to spiral downward. Eels are slippery and slimy and decidedly not cuddly. You don't hear any conservation group crying, "Save the eels." But the eel is as important to wildlife diversity as any other plant or animal.*

* Special thanks to German eel specialist Florian Stein (who says their group does cry, "Save the eels") for educating me and providing so much information about eels.

DESERT SHEEP POACHER

MY SEARCH FOR POACHING STORIES LED ME TO MEET MANY remarkable fish and wildlife officers from all over North America. I was overwhelmed with responses for stories. Ninety-two-year-old Nando Mauldin was one of the most amazing people I met during the hundreds of phone calls I made. After many years as an officer with New Mexico Game & Fish, he retired and later served with the USFWS.

During the 1960s, Mauldin was working undercover for Montana and Washington state, where for one operation he posed as a feather and ivory buyer. One day, he visited a taxidermist shop looking for feathers, and he was distracted by a beautiful desert sheep the taxidermist had on his table. Knowing the sheep were found only in New Mexico, Nando pretended to be a jewellery salesman from that state and expressed interest in the sheep. When he told the taxidermist that he knew the sheep had been available only in a once-in-a-lifetime draw, the man said it was from Mexico. He also claimed that he sent many hunters to an American guide who took them across the border to hunt sheep in Mexico. He'd sent the guide enough hunters to earn his very own sheep trip, and he intended to go soon. Nando said he'd be interested in talking to the guide. Over the course of the conversation, Nando talked his way into accompanying the taxidermist on his hunt for a $5,000 fee. The taxidermist would call when the trip was arranged.

Through past intelligence gathering, Nando knew of an American poacher named "Carlos" who arranged such trips, and suspected he could be the same guy. Carlos was near the top of Mexican authorities' most-wanted list of poachers. Nando called his boss to arrange funds for the hunting trip, and a few days later the taxidermist called with the flight dates. They would meet in San Diego and be driven to Mexico by the guide Carlos. But a few days later the taxidermist called Nando to say he'd had a disagreement with Carlos and would not be able to take Nando as a second hunter after all—the taxidermist would be going alone.

Nando quickly made a series of calls to determine the taxidermist's flight number, which he then passed on to his undercover agent colleagues in San Diego. The next day, Nando received a call from the San Diego agents advising that they'd observed Carlos picking up the taxidermist at the airport, and they'd followed the pair to the Mexican border, where the federales were waiting to pick up the pursuit. Later in the day, another call came in that Carlos and the taxidermist had both been arrested in Mexico. They'd also searched Carlos's residence and found a printing press under the bed. The press had evidently been used to make Mexican sheep-hunting licences.

Two months later, Nando returned to the taxidermist's shop in Washington. When he asked about the desert sheep trip, the taxidermist was visibly upset. He explained they'd driven about three hundred kilometres into Mexico in Carlos's small pickup when three federales stopped them. They had only one set of handcuffs, so they cuffed Carlos to a limb on a tree and tied the taxidermist up with ropes. They searched the pickup and seized the guns and the vehicle.

During the search, Carlos was suddenly seen hanging limp from the tree limb. One federale was a medic and realized Carlos was a diabetic. They poured some soda into him and he came to life. The taxidermist was put in the back of the federales' pickup while Carlos rode in the cab and one of the federales drove Carlos's pickup.

It was a three- or four-hour drive to the Mexican prison, during which the taxidermist succumbed to the sweltering heat. His nose started bleeding and bled so much it poured out the back of the pickup. He was placed in a four-by-four-metre prison cell with a bunch of other prisoners. The cell was so disgusting that he couldn't bring himself to wash his hands in the filthy sink for a week. A large, boisterous guard occasionally brought them food. The taxidermist said he'd considered lunging for the guard's gun to try escaping. Finally, his family managed to raise the $36,000 bribe to have him released. He said, "I wish they'd use poison gas to terminate every living thing in Mexico." It sounded like a week in Mexico should have been the sentence for more poachers.

Nando struggled not to smile. He said, "It could not have been me that set you up, as I intended to go hunting with you, and except for your disagreement with the Mexican guide, I would have been in jail with you." He parted on good terms.

Several years later it would seem Carlos managed to get released from Mexican prison. A vehicle registered to him was found in Mexico, totally burned. Carlos was never seen again.

UNDERCOVER IN
THE 1950S

THIS IS ANOTHER FASCINATING STORY FROM NANDO MAULDIN. HE was originally hired as a wildlife officer with New Mexico Game & Fish in 1950, at the young age of twenty-two. He was a keen young officer with new ideas and didn't always see eye to eye with his supervisor. (I'm glad that never happens today, right?) He got fed up with how things were being handled and walked out. A few years later, a senior warden remembered the good things he'd seen in Nando, so he contacted him and rehired him.

New Mexico shares borders with more states than any other. The state borders Texas, Oklahoma, Utah, Colorado, Arizona and the two Mexican states of Chihuahua and Sonora. Although often mistaken for a mostly desert ecology, New Mexico has vast mountainous regions rich in wildlife resources. A lot of New Mexico contains large areas of land formerly owned by the Spanish. Wealthy ranchers have purchased tracts of land for modern-day ranching. All this open country and wildlife makes for plenty of national forests to protect.

Nando's boss provided him with a horse, a small tent and a sleeping bag before sending him off into the mountains of New Mexico to keep an eye on the wildlife. He was on his own without any means of communication or support. He absolutely loved the job. It may have been a test of his abilities: if he came back, he was worth keeping. If he didn't come back, at least the horse might. Nando passed the test with flying colours. The boss figured he was ready for another task.

New Mexico was being inundated with logging camps. Camps with crews of ten to fifteen guys moved into the mountains with heavy equipment for road construction and logging. The wildlife resources were plentiful and offered fresh meat for the hard-working crews, even though taking it was against the law. There was little chance of ever being checked by a game warden. Nando was sent into the camps as a prospective labourer. I'm not sure whether he got paid as a game warden *and* as a logger, but if he did, he earned it. Nando's job was to become part of each camp until he had gathered enough wildlife violations to call in the authorities. The wardens would roll in and literally haul everyone in camp off to jail, sometimes in an open cattle truck. If they couldn't pay their fine, they stayed in jail or worked the fine off at $5 per day.

The plan worked extremely well until Nando showed up at the fourth camp. One day, he was travelling along in his old pickup, which was equipped with tire chains for slogging through the muddy roads. He came upon three loggers stuck in the mud. The three of them approached Nando's truck, and one guy said, "We got it figured out. Three camps have been shut down and you've been at all of them. You're the problem. We'll take care of you." Nando pulled out his six-shooter, pointed it at them, told them to get out of the way and drove off. That was Nando's last undercover operation in that area.

A DIFFERENT TIME

IN THE SPRING OF 1957, AN ANONYMOUS CALL CAME INTO THE Albuquerque, New Mexico, office where Nando and his supervisor Bill Humphries worked. The caller claimed two people were selling deer meat to the local zoo. (The irony of local deer being poached to feed non-native species in a zoo!) Bill knew the manager of the zoo to be a recent immigrant who didn't know much about state wildlife laws. Bill and Nando frequented the zoo to help the manager rope and treat sick animals, and during these visits they gathered information about the suppliers of the deer meat. The manager had nothing to hide because he didn't know it was wrong.

Rather than just catch the delivery crew, the officers wanted to trace the source of the deer meat. They determined that the sellers were from a tightly knit Mexican community about 160 kilometres northwest of Albuquerque. They decided to solicit the services of a New Mexico brand inspector. The Spanish-speaking inspector they contacted quickly agreed to the task and easily infiltrated the community where the sellers lived. Several days later, he returned to report his findings.

The inspector advised the officers that the person killing the deer was an older Mexican man. One of the two people delivering the deer was the man's daughter. The inspector had an exact description of the property, including the inside of the house. He described a small "shrine" attached to the side of the house capable of holding several people, inside of which a large podium covered with a white cloth concealed a hollow space below. That space held a large glass bowl filled with smoked deer jerky (perhaps a way to increase church attendance?). The Mexican's daughter and the man delivering the meat were employees of the zoo, and the money for the deer meat was being split evenly between the three of them. There was a loaded .30-30 behind the front door that the old guy intended to use on anyone interfering with his business.

The brand inspector and Humphries, his boss, were asked to assist the game wardens with the property search, and they willingly agreed. The plan was for Nando and one of the inspectors to search the Mexican's house, while the other two would arrest the sellers at the zoo. The officers arrived at the remote home early the next morning but the old guy wasn't around. They served the warrant on his wife and began their search. Nando located and unloaded the rifle behind the door first and put the bullets in his pocket. They seized the jerky hidden in the shrine. They found deer hides, hooves and hair from twenty-seven recently killed mule deer. Meanwhile, the two at the zoo were arrested and held by Humphries and the other inspector.

Nando and the brand inspector returned to the house early the next morning. The old guy was in the yard and ran for the house. Nando caught him at the steps and a struggle ensued. As he struggled, the man yelled obscenities in both Spanish and English. With the inspector's help, Nando arrested him and put him in the car without serious injury to anyone. They hauled him to a jail cell with the other two from the zoo.

All three received a fine, extensive jail time and several years of probation. The poaching world of 1957 has a lot of similarities when compared with today. Every generation has its share of people willing and able to exploit wildlife resources if they can make a buck.

BELUGA WHALE IN SASKATCHEWAN

THIS IS ONE OF THOSE "ONCE IN YOUR CAREER" MOMENTS. Saskatchewan conservation officers Chris Maier and Cal Schommer visited a location after a caller said he wanted them to look at the old taxidermy collection his uncle and great uncle had amassed over sixty years. The collection had been in a museum years ago, but limitations of time and space meant the collection was no longer needed. The uncles had purchased two old buses to store the pieces in, and they'd sat inside for decades. The family wanted to keep some of the mounts and give the rest away.

The officers explained that some items could be sold and others required permits. They were willing to issue permits for those the uncles could legally possess. As the owner led Maier and Schommer to the buses, he said he would rather give the collection to the agency to make the best use of it. They were astounded to find three or four hundred animal mounts of all kinds. It was as if a modern-day Noah had filled the buses before heading for the ark. There were species that no one would be allowed to own, ungulates of all kinds, raptors, song birds, ducks, bears, wolves, coyotes, grayling walleye, shore birds, badgers, and many more. In the middle of the bus was the biggest surprise—a 4.5-metre beluga whale!

Two weeks later, the officers returned with a large trailer and began sorting through the pile. They loaded anything that looked good enough to keep. Many of the mounts were faded and had been destroyed by mice. The owner even had nicknames for some of the mounts. The taxidermy archaeological site was carefully sorted.

It took several trips back and forth to the office before the buses were empty.

Over the next few months, the officers cleaned and distributed the mounts to local fish and game organizations, ministry offices and Environment Canada. One eagle went to a wildlife rehab centre to be used as a companion bird for orphaned eagles. This was recycling, Saskatchewan style. The beluga whale was kept. If you're ever out beluga whale poaching in Saskatchewan, be careful—it could be a decoy.

POACHING FOR
PROFIT IN OHIO

FEW PEOPLE KNOW THE AMOUNT OF MANPOWER IT TAKES TO DEAL with the worst of poachers. The Ohio Department of Natural Resources (DNR) dubbed their biggest poaching case in history Operation North Coast. The case involved a ring of operators in the Lake Erie area who illegally caught fish and shot deer, then sold them through a complicated network of processors and buyers.

Over a period of two and a half years, officers conducted about two hundred interviews, examined hundreds of digital records, executed search warrants, gathered physical evidence, attended approximately one hundred court hearings, and seized ninety-six deer and turkey mounts, thirty-five sets of antlers, ninety kilograms of sport-caught fillets and 180 kilograms of processed deer meat.

Mr. "Worthless" was the main player in part of the operation. The Ohio DNR had fielded twenty-seven complaints against Worthless leading up to the operation. He was tracked for eighteen months and was caught spotlighting, selling deer sausage, using other people's licensed tags and much more. They would misreport deer through the electronic reporting system. This resulted in more serious charges similar to other corrupt activities for profit. Worthless also was in the drug business. He'd shoot deer, have sausage made, sell the sausage, then buy drugs. The group would have spouses and friends buy tags and falsify records to the ODNR so as not to draw attention to one person. Many deer were never tagged.

Other undercover officers were working simultaneously on an unrelated fish-poaching operation. They had been ready to end the fishy guy's business but he died before they could arrest him. Rather

Over one hundred deer mounts were seized in 2016 when Ohio officers ended a thirty-month-long undercover operation. *Photo: Ohio Department of Natural Resources.*

than shut the entire undercover operation down and go home, the officers turned the focus of their limited manpower on another commercial deer-poaching operation run by Mr. "Zany." Zany turned out to be an even bigger find. He boasted of the size and number of deer he'd shot. He kept meticulous details about his hunts in a personal diary. His phone contained hundreds of pictures and information that would lead investigators to a bunch of other violators. He worked with a couple of key partners. The trio focused on bucks—the large antlers for their poaching egos and the meat for sausage sales.

A large amount of the meat made its way to "Smokin' B," a meat-processing business that turned the venison into sausage and other meat products they sold or traded illegally. The processed sausage was put in packages that were labelled Not for Sale, but that didn't seem to deter anyone from buying the stuff. Officers proved that the processor had profited off the criminal actions too. He had processed forty-four deer (from others besides Zany), nineteen of which were illegal. He'd processed over 1,360 kilograms of meat and made about $8,500 for the processing alone. Buyers were charged in the operation as well. Prosecutors did a good job of treating the business seriously and proceeded just as they would have with any other corrupt activity. They used organized criminal laws that resulted in many felony convictions.

The investigation went back only two years for violations. At first, Zany and his two partners were known to have taken forty deer, only three of them legally. They were convicted of laundering and numerous other charges. But when the massive, co-ordinated search warrants were executed, the officers searching Mr. Zany's house had some surprises. One trophy room contained forty-eight deer head mounts. They took over sixty deer from him alone. They returned a few of the mounts later, when proper documents were produced. The best find, however, was his daily hunting diary. It was discovered tucked above some ductwork in the basement. It contained a treasure trove of information that officers were able to link to numerous illegal animals taken and to implicate numerous other individuals. One poacher was even purchasing tags in his ex-wife's name without her knowledge. I wonder whether he was paying alimony with sausage.

Others involved committed a range of serious crimes with deer and fish as well. Money laundering and racketeering charges formed a part of the dozens of charges eventually laid. These included the illegal harvest of deer, falsifying records, shooting from a vehicle, involvement in corrupt activity, sale of wildlife, improper use of firearms and tampering with records. Zany was convicted and paid $40,000 in restitution, forfeited his truck, forfeited forty-four deer mounts, lost seven years of hunting privileges and was given thirty months in prison.

The third portion of the operation started with an ad on Craigslist with fish for sale. People online told the seller what he was doing was illegal, but he continued to sell fish. An undercover officer purchased sixty-two kilograms of fillets in one single transaction. This fellow was also nailed with felony charges for his commercial operation. He was also in the moonshine business, a sort of Crimes-R-Us department store.

In total, forty-six people were charged with ninety-one felonies and seventy-three misdemeanours. Eight were given prison time, and a total of $225,000 in fines and restitution orders was levied. It was a shining victory for all the officers involved.

Two of the accused were convicted of theft by deception for using a walleye caught in Lake Erie to enter a fishing tournament on the Maumee River. They won $375 for their entry and paid over $13,000 for their crime. (That sounds like the return I get if I try the stock market.) Another criminal in the group baited deer off his back porch. A motion sensor would activate a light on the deer bait and he'd shoot deer right from the window of his house—perhaps while watching a hunting show.

This massive investigation shut down the largest known poaching ring in Ohio's history. Two of the one hundred officers working on the case spent over one thousand hours poring over information and tying the pieces together. Who knows how many others were operating or how much poaching went on while these officers were occupied with this massive file?

Enforcement was much easier years ago with less legislation, fewer challenges of charges and less technology working against officers. Most criminals know how to use technology too. A few may not walk upright, but those types are usually found at the bottom of poaching rings such as this one. It was an amazing result from an even more amazing example of fine work by the Ohio DNR, the prosecutors and the judges who heard the cases.

KANSAS—
HIGH-PRICED BUCK

DEER-HUNTING SEASON WAS APPROACHING IN KANSAS IN 2011. A young hunter had been tracking a large white-tailed deer with a game camera on a piece of property on which he intended to hunt when the season opened. He showed up on opening morning to find the body of a large white-tailed deer with the head missing—"his" deer. Thinking the big deer might have been poached, he called a Kansas wildlife officer, Jesse Gehrt, who showed up to gather evidence from the large deer in case other evidence materialized in the future.

The young hunter was dismayed at the loss of a chance at the big buck. Rather than just leave things up to the officers to resolve, he decided to try a bit of investigating himself. He attended the local monster buck classic several months later in hopes of finding the deer entered in the contest. He took his game-camera pictures with him. Sure enough, he located the large buck's antlers in the show— they had scored B&C 198 and 7/8ths inches.*

The young man reported his findings to wildlife officers at a different table in the trade show. The officers initially seized the deer but changed their minds and returned it until after the show. The deer's antlers were measured up and it won the biggest buck of the year, coming within inches of the Kansas state record for a deer taken by a bow.

---

* The Boone and Crockett scoring system is the most widely recognized and popular method of measuring the size and other characteristics of white-tailed deer trophy antlers.

But the winner's victory was short-lived when the officers came along to again seize his deer, this time permanently, and have a long chat. The man confessed to shooting the deer with a handgun at night by the road. The tag he'd used was marked for a different county. His crimes were dealt with and the deer was forfeited to the state.

The story would end there, except a landowner's son near where the deer had been shot claimed that *he* should own the deer. He was a deer outfitter who had seen the deer on his mother's property (which he insisted was *his* property so he could claim the deer) and the loss of hunting trips amounted to two paid hunts. Surprisingly, the judge agreed with him and awarded him $8,000 restitution for the deer that had been ostensibly poached from his mother's property. He didn't stop there, though. He insisted that the wildlife division should award him the deer antlers.

Meanwhile, a local taxidermist donated his time to mount the deer for the wildlife division. The deer would become part of a display for public education. That would be a great ending, right? Wrong. It seemed the outfitter had some major pull with local politicians and legislators. He was successful in having legislation passed that gave the landowner the right to own an animal that had been taken illegally, as long as they weren't involved in the crime. However, the legislation was not retroactive, and he continued his fight. He had T-shirts printed with the slogan KANSAS WILDLIFE AND PARKS STOLE MY DEER. He attended public meetings and made a scene with verbal outbursts and disruptions. The deer head was removed from the public display and stored away, and the legislation was changed again to include all wildlife taken illegally, no matter when. The saga finally ended with a political decision to auction off the deer head at a closed auction. Bass Pro Shops and the outfitter attended the auction. Bass Pro started at $10,000. The auction ended with the outfitter's bid of $16,001.

Today, the outfitter/poacher is the proud owner of a deer that someone else poached—shot at night with a handgun—of which he got possession under bad legislation by falsely claiming he owned his mother's property and thereby deserved the deer. He vows to sue the wildlife agency now. Sometimes it's best to not try to understand actions such as this. Common sense is not always that common.

I expect that this political decision to appease a voter has resulted in major challenges to wildlife officers. The new legislation gives property rights for animals to an individual, when they really belong to everyone until they are legally harvested. This legislation should employ a few lawyers for years to come. What kind of sportsman would even want to display an animal with such a crazy story? But there's more.

This poacher had been involved in a far more serious crime five years earlier while out poaching with his brother. He was driving his truck and his brother was the gunner. He stopped the truck while his brother shot a rifle out the window at a flock of geese in a field. The geese were decoys put out by an eighteen-year-old hunter who was hidden in a blind nearby. The bullet from the rifle killed the boy instantly. The poacher's brother went to prison for thirty-two months for involuntary manslaughter. He claimed he was shooting at a coyote.

Click your heels, Dorothy! It's all just a bad dream.

WARDEN FRIENDS ARE POACHERS' ENEMIES

IT WAS HUNTING SEASON IN OHIO AND THE DEER-POACHING COMplaints were coming in to Division of Wildlife officer Nick Turner. Deciding which complaint to address first is a combination of experience, gut feeling and good luck.

Officer Turner decided to respond to the most recent complaint regarding a headless buck found on a field on some private property. The owner was fairly certain the headless deer carcass was that of a huge non-typical buck he had seen recently. He showed Turner game-camera pictures of the buck so he would recognize the antlers if he encountered them. Turner also looked over the deer carcass, noting a small-calibre rifle hole in the animal. No meat had been taken.

The officer decided to utilize a decoy set up on the owner's field at a later date. He called another officer—Craig Porter 11—to join him for a Veterans Day evening patrol. The two made a number of hunter checks before pulling into the field where the huge buck had been poached and set up their decoy.

A church near the field would be their convenient cover, allowing a good vantage point from which to wait for possible spotlighters and perhaps some divine assistance. As Turner and Porter wandered around the church, they couldn't help but notice all the military headstones in the graveyard. They paid a fitting tribute before their long night of waiting began. They had just settled back into their truck when they saw the light. Not the light you normally sing about seeing at church, but a vehicle scanning the fields and bushes with three separate spotlights. It was a gift from above!

Officer Turner discreetly backed their vehicle out and followed the poacher's vehicle. As they approached, it stopped in the middle of the road right by the decoy. The element of surprise was on the officers' side, and they jumped out and cautiously approached the vehicle. A young engaged couple and the fiancé's father were in the vehicle. Maybe they were on their way to church? The officers searched the vehicle, finding a rifle, several live rounds of ammunition, three spotlights and a bloody knife. Turner interviewed the son while Porter interviewed his fiancée. Pop had to wait, giving him a bit more time to dream up a story. The young couple claimed to simply be on their way home; however, the route they had taken to their destination—apparently Greenbrier, West Virginia—meant they were either extremely lost or were out poaching.

Officer Turner called an officer in West Virginia, Todd Petrunger, who was very familiar with the two poachers. Pop had been convicted eleven times in the past ten years and his son had been charged nine times in the past seven years. It looked like the son was a quick learner; he'd just had a bad teacher. The fiancée must have felt guilty being so close to the church because she confessed first and admitted they'd shot a deer a week earlier and another the week before that. Meanwhile, Officer Petrunger had started his drive to the poachers' residence in West Virginia.

The girl waited outside while Turner interviewed Pop. Suddenly, Pop's dashboard cellphone lit up. Officer Turner read the message—it was from the fiancée. The intended recipient was Pop's wife, but the fiancée had mistakenly sent a group text, including one to Pop. The message read, "Get rid of everything and don't text back." Just when you were starting to have faith in the young lady, she did that! Turner called Petrunger with this new information to alert him that some evidence might be hidden or gone by the time he arrived.

Petrunger and a crew of officers arrived at Pop's residence, greeted by a very nervous wife along with a sister and brother. The officers soon had their hands on seventeen fresh deer heads from several outbuildings and in garbage bags thrown over the bank near the house. One large deer head was recognizable as the buck on the property owner's game camera. A bullet recovered from the deer carcass was later analyzed as an exact match with the rifle in the truck. DNA from the kill site was an exact match with the same large buck in Pop's freezer. All of this work took months to complete. It was a great example of keen officers gathering all the evidence they could, even though they didn't know whether they'd ever find another clue to match.

Pop was fined over $11,000, forfeited his rifle and deer heads, had to serve five days in jail and was given a five-year loss of hunting privileges. It was a strange sequence of events in which the sitting judge was the son's attorney (how convenient). He declined to hear the case because of a conflict of interest. Ya think? The son's case took too long to address (likely deliberate procrastination until the statute of limitations had passed) and his charges were dropped. Did they learn? Nope. The son was caught again in Pennsylvania the next year. These guys belong in a group of those who have zero regard for wildlife and who will poach without a conscience as long as there are deer to shoot.

Officers Turner and Petrunger worked tirelessly on the investigation, even though they barely knew each other at the time and worked for different agencies. They became friends and have hunted together a number of times since. I suppose they can thank this group of low-lifes for a friendship that might not have happened without this incident. These two young officers certainly dispel the myth that younger officers don't like to work as hard as the old guys used to. I talked to both of them and they share a passion that should lead to many, many unhappy poachers.

DOVE'S BLIND

IN LATE AUGUST OF 2015, OHIO WILDLIFE OFFICERS RECEIVED A TIP from someone who'd seen three guys in a field hunting doves using a blind and decoys. Hunting from a blind with decoys is legal, but the season had not yet opened. They were set up within sight of a major highway and using "mojo" moving decoys. The two officers surreptitiously made their way to the reported field and approached the hunters undetected. Officer Cottrill came up behind them.

Poachers are normally more alert than these three. As the officers approached the blind, they could see some wheat nearby being used as bait. That is illegal as well. Hunting out of season and using bait—this would be a good bust. But wait—like a cheap infomercial, there's more! Look again and you'll get another charge for free!

The blind was built out of marijuana plants. Very tall marijuana plants. This, of course, was not legal in Ohio. I wonder, were they wearing tie-dyed camo and flashing peace signs at the officers? The three were in possession of forty-five doves, much "higher" than the limit, even if the season had been open. When they were searched, the officers found a marijuana pipe and some freshly picked marijuana buds. Asked why they'd started hunting before the season opened, one of the poachers replied, "We gotta work this week and decided to hunt on the weekend." It was an honest answer; it just didn't help in this situation.

The officers issued a few coupons for a variety of violations. One of the violators had no identification, so Officer Cottrill walked with him to the residence on the same property, where the officer found more drug paraphernalia, fresh marijuana leaves, a hawk-tail fan and talons. There was a reason the guy didn't carry his identification. He had an outstanding warrant and was hauled away to jail. This case would have made a great Cheech and Chong movie.

THE BEAR TRUTH

THIS IS NOT A POACHING STORY, BUT IT SHOWS WHAT CRAZY SITU-ations wildlife officers can find themselves in. In the early 1980s, John Edwards was a conservation officer stationed in the Battlefords Provincial Park in Saskatchewan. One hot summer day in a year of drought, he received a call from a rancher that a bear was killing his cattle. It made sense: in a dry year without vegetation, bears will look for other food sources. He hopped into his patrol vehicle (a highly inappropriate 1979 Chev Bel Air station wagon) and drove the 120 kilometres to investigate.

The distraught rancher related how he had lost three head of cattle to bear predation in the last month. Edwards asked to see the kill sites, so off they went in his vehicle to investigate. The first kill site was an area of trampled vegetation, about sixty-five metres in diameter. Only bare bones were left, as this kill was about three weeks old.

He took Edwards to the second kill site. This too was just bones—it had occurred about a week before. The trampled area of the skirmish was half the diameter of the first. Edwards determined that the cause of death was crushed neck vertebrae. Then he was taken to the site of the most recent kill, still only a day old with lots of meat left. This time, there was only a small area of vegetation disturbance. This bear was getting very proficient at cattle killing and had to be destroyed.

Edwards called his boss, who came out to assist. They set up a blind for the ambush, and sure enough, the bear returned near sunset—a sow with three cubs in her wake. Now things got complicated. There was no hope for the sow—she had become too efficient at killing cattle and would not change. They shot the sow and scurried around trying to catch the three bears. Where was Goldilocks when she was needed? They captured two but one escaped.

The cubs were transferred to the Moose Jaw Wild Animal Park. Fast-forward to mid-October and Edwards received a call from the very same rancher, reporting that he had captured the escaped bear cub. Evidently, his wife had felt sorry for the missing cub that had returned frequently to the farmyard and she'd been feeding it. But it was growing pretty big and now threatening her dog and poultry. The rancher, in typical "can do" Saskatchewan farmer fashion, had constructed a bear trap out of two by fours, chicken wire and plywood.

Edwards showed up and gave the lecture about not feeding the bears before walking over to the makeshift trap. Now the question was, what to do with this critter? Moose Jaw had enough bears already, which left only two options: remove the bear out of sight and destroy it, or transport it north to the provincial forest and release it, a trip of at least a hundred kilometres. The bear seemed quite calm in the makeshift trap and looked healthy (no doubt because of the rancher's wife's daily menu), so Edwards decided to take the time to transport it to the forest and give it a second chance.

He and the rancher loaded the flimsy trap and bear into his station wagon and he headed north. The bear remained fairly calm, if not exactly happy. John stopped briefly at home to show the bear to his wife, then left to complete the remaining fifty kilometres. Just like an impatient kid in the back seat moaning, "Are we there yet?" the bear was becoming increasingly unhappy, gnawing at its prison cell in its frustration.

Pop! A quick glance in the rear-view mirror revealed that the bear had gnawed through the wire on the top of its makeshift cage, enough to get a couple of centimetres of its muzzle out. With about twenty minutes to go, Edwards decided to step on the gas, increasing his speed to about 120 kilometres an hour.

Another glance back and the bear's head was now completely out of the cage. The solution was still more speed. Edwards turned on his emergency lights and kept going as the bear continued to tear through chicken wire until it was fully out and wedged between the car roof and the cage. Travelling at 140 kilometres now, Edwards eased onto the road's shoulder and began to apply the brakes. *Thud!* The sudden reduction in speed had launched the bear clear over the back seat and onto his lap. The bear chewed and clawed as Edwards fought back with a fist, steering with the other hand and still travelling way too fast. There were no distracted-driving laws back then.

He slowed right down, turned the car into the ditch and reached for his handgun in the glovebox. That plan was overtaken by the thought of trying to explain a bullet hole inside his car. The bear was now down by Edwards's feet, in control of the gas and brakes. He whacked the bear a few times with his bloodied fist before it clambered over to the passenger's seat. The bear had just been beaten by a conservation officer and would have a great story for its lawyer. It crawled into the back seat as Edwards's car came to a stop in the ditch. He lowered the electric rear window and his bear buddy jumped out.

Edwards was furious. His adrenaline was pumping with a justifiable mix of rage and fear. He got out of the vehicle, fully intending to shoot the damn bear. The bear stopped and looked back, clacking its teeth. Like the loser in a valiant mixed martial arts battle, Edwards tipped his bloodied hand and let the bear go before turning to see that three cars had stopped to witness the event. If he had shot the bear, it would have been three days of explaining to the media. The next day, Edwards noticed bear feces all over the dashboard and front seat—at least, he thought it was the bear's. The sweet smell of bear crap in the hot sun lingered for days despite his best cleaning efforts.

IT'S A FALCON CRIME

FALCONRY HAS BEEN AROUND FOR THOUSANDS OF YEARS. IT WAS popular in medieval times, especially for royalty and wealthy folks. Using falcons (and hawks, eagles and owls) to catch game birds or small mammals was not only sporting, it provided fresh meat for the table. The sport of falconry, although still popular, waned somewhat in Europe with the invention of the shotgun.

Still, in the United States there was a solid base of aficionados, and the first organized falconry club was started in the 1930s. Its members obtained many of their birds from the wild. Their use of falcons was legal and populations were steady until the use of DDT in agriculture. DDT was banned in the early 1970s because it caused soft eggshells and reduced chick survival. The birds have made a remarkable comeback since then, to the point where many have been removed from the endangered lists. Today, there are about two thousand licensed falconers in North America, according to the North American Falconers Association (one falconer suggested the number is over twice that). Some licensed falconers in the past have helped replenish areas where falcons once ranged but had become endangered. Breeding falcons in captivity requires exacting conditions and care only knowledgeable falconers can provide.

The Middle East, with the wealth of its sheiks and oil barons, has huge aviaries of raptors to support their traditional passion for falconry. I was offered a glimpse of what North Americans would view as a surreal world of Middle Eastern falconry by a former Environment Canada wildlife officer who attended a couple of conferences in Abu Dhabi years ago. Traditionally, wild raptors were captured during their migration in the spring and used for hunting during the summer before being released back into the wild in the fall. Some Middle

Easterners feel these traditions should still be followed, but many have switched to owning their own birds.

The wildlife officer explained that many royal family members, sheiks and other falcon owners take the summer off in the United Arab Emirates (UAE). The more traditional falconers take their camels, hunting dogs and falcons into the desert for the entire summer to hunt. Others take their private jets to neighbouring countries where wildlife is more plentiful and hunt there for the summer. They take falconry as seriously as Canadians take hockey and Americans take football. There's nothing wrong with that, providing it's legal.

The visiting officer went on to explain how he was shown a large, hangar-like building that was air-conditioned for the falcons housed inside. It contained about three hundred birds, each on its own personal stand. They are cared for like royalty.

The officer also visited the falcon veterinary hospital. He was shown a huge bank of cabinets (like map filing cabinets) in the specialized clinic. Each drawer contained falcon feathers collected either from natural shedding or from dead birds. If a hunting bird breaks a feather through hunting or handling, a new feather is found to match and is carefully sewn or glued in place rather than waiting for the feather to grow back naturally. The process is called *imping* and involves joining the broken feather to its replacement by inserting a thin piece of wire or bamboo inside the feather at the joint. It's held together by adhesive glue. The UAE spends millions of dollars on its falcon hospitals, clinics and breeding facilities. Before anyone thinks that's a huge waste of money, I'd ask, what do we pay football and hockey players? How much is spent operating and stitching them back together for sport? All these falcons get paid is a bit of meat and a lot of care. It's all about traditions.

More recently, the Middle East has started a newer sport called falcon racing. Birds are released and fly over a 366-metre distance, lured by a handler swinging a decoy to attract the bird. Huge money is bet on this sport and its popularity is growing. Its big advantage is that it can be done at one location and without searching for the dwindling prey populations in the desert. And birds aren't exposed to lengthy flights in extreme heat. There will be traditionalists for a long time yet, but this sport does seem to be a little less harmful to the birds.

Now back to North America and falcon poaching there. In the early 1980s, Canadian and American agencies combined in an undercover sting operation to address what they believed was a raptor-poaching problem. Called Operation Falcon, it was primarily led by the USFWS, but when targets in Canada emerged, Canadian agencies joined in. Many owners in the falcon community felt their members were being "baited" into violations. A few of the key poaching targets managed to avoid arrest by leaving the country or returning to their homeland (e.g., Germany and the Middle East). Falconers were upset to learn that the undercover operator in Operation Falcon, hired by the USFWS, had previously been convicted of a falcon violation. They also didn't approve of using wild eggs and birds as "bait" to catch would-be smugglers.

Tactics and methods used in undercover operations are not always supported by the general population, but sometimes these covert methods are the only way to catch the real bad guys. I spent days uncovering the truth, discovering facts that many falconers never really wanted to know. I read dozens of articles and talked to a number of falcon experts, including the undercover operator and the lead investigator of Operation Falcon. They provided court documents and first-hand information. Their version of supported facts was very clear and very different from what falconers had told me. A falconer had suggested that I read a book written about Operation Falcon. When I did, I was dumbfounded to find it had been written without input from the USFWS or the undercover operator. Facts from a courtroom are much more credible than those from others with ulterior motives. It may be more prudent of the falcon community to applaud Operation Falcon rather than attack it, and instead try work with officers to keep their sport free of criminal activities.

Over one hundred birds were seized in Operation Falcon. Some falconers were upset with the handling and care of their birds, yet the seized birds were all housed in newly built facilities. It was true that some birds were in rough shape, but that was because the birds had not been properly cared for by their previous owners/poachers before they arrived. The project certainly shed light on falcons and how an undercover operation can often expose entrenched problems. Those with political connections and deep pockets can sometimes wrangle support and avoid prosecution. Democracy isn't perfect.

Poachers are making huge profits in many fields of wildlife. Falcon poachers may not be great in number but they are difficult to catch unless operations like this one are launched. Poaching falcons is one of the most lucrative of all crimes.

The operation led to sixty-eight convictions, most for misdemeanour charges. Community service and a total of $501,071 in fines were levied. Seven outstanding indictments are being held for people who escaped the country. One falconer charged ended up as a personal handler of falcons in the Middle East. During the operation, a Saudi crown prince came to the US to buy a white gyrfalcon for $50,000 and flew home with it. When Operation Falcon was completed, the US request for extradition of the prince was denied. Instead, the Royal Embassy of Saudi Arabia paid $150,000 to the US Department of Justice.

I also discovered an old case from the late 1970s, just before the undercover operation began. Two California Hawking Association members were caught on the Queen Charlotte Islands (now Haida Gwaii) with a wild peregrine falcon in their motel room. Officers knocked on the door and a physical confrontation ensued. One of the culprits took off with the falcon and an officer gave chase. Community members recognized the officer and headed the poacher off, but not before he had gotten rid of the falcon. This "upstanding" member of an American hawking association had killed the falcon and thrown it under a house to hide the evidence. The officers found it. The two poachers were fined $2,500 each and released. I doubt these two disclosed this story to their club. That would have resulted in their removal—or at least the club claims so.

Although the government often tries to do the right thing, it certainly isn't always right. As an example, the Canadian government ran a falcon breeding program that operated in the 1970s and '80s. The facility had breeding pairs of gyrfalcons that successfully produced fertile eggs, but the government directed its staff to make the eggs infertile because of the value of the eyas (chicks). There was concern they'd make their way into illegal markets. Falconers were outraged and persuaded the government to hatch the eggs, and one of the resulting chicks was given to a reputable falconer who raised the bird in his licensed facility. Then one day he was called and asked to give the adult bird back to the government! I guess it was sort of like an election promise.

That falcon was to be a gift from Prime Minister Pierre Trudeau to King Khalid of Saudi Arabia. I don't think that would fly today. A special escort was assigned for the bird to accompany the prime minister to Saudi Arabia. The bird was taken to King Khalid's personal live collection of raptors in a large room with about one hundred falcons, each with its own handler. The Canadian falcon would not be lonely. This is another glaring example of how times can change what was once considered acceptable.

There are few falcon poachers in the world, but those who do poach make a pile of money. The world's main falcon poacher, Mr. "Moron," has also focused on removing eggs from nests and selling them. Eggs are easier to gather and smuggle. Mortality is high but that doesn't matter to a poacher. You just have to take more if you break a few. Moron is likely the biggest falcon poacher of the past thirty-five years. He was born in Africa but moved to Ireland to continue what his father had taught him—how to gather and sell falcon eggs.

Moron was first caught and charged in the remote northern Quebec town of Kuujjuaq in May of 2002. Moron and an associate travelled to the community under the guise of being photographers for *National Geographic*. They hired a local helicopter and pilot to fly them out to some remote, untouched cliffs where falcons nested. Suspended from the chopper, Moron rappelled down a rope, plucking the rare eggs from nests while the pilot carefully manoeuvred around the cliffs. If the pilot had not been so skilled, this story might have ended there, and falcons would be happier.

Moron paid $5,000 cash for his flight and took the eggs to his hotel room, where he had set up an incubator. The residents of the small community were suspicious, and someone reported them. Local resident officers Saunders and Watt arrived with the police. The two had been recruited only a couple of years prior through a new program focused on hiring local Inuit for enforcement work. Joined by the Quebec provincial police, they visited Mr. Moron. He tried to claim the eggs weren't falcon eggs. The locals knew better. He tried to say they were for an egg collection. That didn't fly either, as the eggs were in an incubator.

The officers consulted with legal experts, who agreed to charge the poachers with illegal possession, and issued the maximum fine at that time of $7,250. Moron paid his fine in US cash and left the next day without the eggs or his incubator. The eggs were flown to a birds of prey recovery facility.

Moron's activities would not stop, though. He has been arrested five times on three different continents for smuggling eggs and birds. In 2010, a janitor in the British Midlands airport noticed an empty egg carton with a red eggshell in it after Moron had been in a particular washroom for a long time. He alerted authorities, and Moron was arrested with ribbons of surgical tape holding woollen socks filled with fourteen eggs taped to his abdomen. His excuse was that his physiotherapist had told him to do this to hold his abdomen muscles tight, thereby strengthening his lower back. Maybe that helicopter pilot did slam him against the cliffs a few too many times?

In 2016, Moron was sentenced to four and a half years in jail in Brazil for smuggling eggs. He managed to skip the country before he was arrested. In 2019, he was sentenced to three years in prison after being caught with nineteen eggs strapped to his paunch worth an estimated $130,000 at an airport in the United Kingdom. The judge declined an extradition request from Brazil for fear its deplorable jails might violate his human rights. I doubt this will be the last of this falcon criminal. To falconers who say there isn't a problem, wake up and work with the authorities rather than against them.

CORAL SMUGGLING

IN JUNE OF 2007, OFFICERS WITH THE CANADIAN BORDER SERVICES Agency inspected a six-metre shipping container from Indonesia with ninety-five hundred kilograms of what they believed was live coral. The coral was in small, waxed cardboard boxes with plastic bags filled with seawater inside. The shipment was headed for an aquarium business in Winnipeg, Manitoba. They placed a call to Environment Canada for assistance.

There are numerous species of coral. Some species are okay to import without permits, others can be imported with permits and the rarest protected kinds are not allowed to be imported at all. This shipment was analyzed by experts and found to be Scleractinian rock coral. Aha! you say. You're right. They're protected and importing them is illegal.

An Environment Canada officer in Winnipeg, Trevor Wyatt, called the business owner, "Dick," and asked about the shipment. Dick explained that the shipment was entirely of "conditioned stone." Dick said the Indonesia exporter mixed cement and stone together before placing them in the ocean for a while until some coral began to form on the outside. The product would then be designated as sourced from aquaculture and not require any permits. He had all the papers to support his claim. Pinocchio would have been proud! He went on to say he was importing the rock to build a fence at his home in Winnipeg just like the ones he'd seen in Indonesia. But I think even Pinocchio would doubt that one, given that the rocks were stored in seawater.

The officers let the shipment leave Vancouver but had it redirected to their Environment Canada warehouse in Winnipeg, where Wyatt and others carefully unpacked every box and determined the shipment was 100 per cent illegal wild coral. Dick arrived to claim the shipment and insisted they were wrong. Over his protests, he was served with a search warrant for his business, including all electronic devices and computers. The forensic analysis revealed a detailed two-records system. He kept one set of documents for inspectors and one set for customers and shippers. He had also traded in illegal live clams and seahorses. Dick kept to his fabricated story right to the end. Consistency is usually a good trait, except if you're consistently lying.

The coral was unpacked and stored in a locked semi-trailer. This allowed it to dry out and the rotting smell to dissipate (there was no means or time to ship the coral back to Indonesia). The dried coral was stored in another container and held for five years before the trial was held. The span of time was needed because Dick was still insisting they were wrong despite the mountain of evidence against him.

Dick tried his tale one more time in the courtroom. The judge called his evidence "evasive, contradictory and argumentative." He also indicated that Dick had doctored records to hide what he was doing. His defence lawyer tried to claim that Dick's business would be ruined if a large fine were levied. The judge handed down one of the largest penalties ever for such a case, with a $135,822 fine including over $10,000 to store the coral for five years before trial. That's a lot of clams! The fine was based on an approximate retail value of the shipment (the cost of picking, packaging, shipping and delivering the coral was about $20,000).

"LIKE A HERD OF PELICANS"

ZEBRA MUSSELS ARE AN INVASIVE SPECIES THAT CONTINUES TO infest North American waterways. The tiny shellfish is believed to have arrived via foreign freighters in the Great Lakes. From there, recreation boats have transported them to many regions throughout North America. (Boaters are constantly reminded to wash their boats off before entering another body of water.) The massive, fast-growing mussel colonies take over natural habitat and food sources for native plants and animals. They also block off water intakes and sewer outlets, causing tremendous damage and costs.

Cunningham Lake (a human-built reservoir) is one such water body with a mussel invasion. Nebraska Game and Parks decided to drain the lake to expose the shallow-growing mussels during the winter and freeze them out. It was a good idea but caused an unintended enforcement problem.

The game fish in the lake congregated around the spillway, and some local foreigners could not resist the buffet of fish before them. One officer said the scene was "like watching a herd of pelicans." Groups of forty to fifty people would show up, form a line across the spillway and wade through the water, herding the fish to others holding dip nets, cast nets, spears and anything else that could catch fish. They would even pour bleach into the water to force the fish to the surface. The fish were put into rice sacks and hauled away.

Officers had to patrol the spillway for two months while the water levels dropped. One group was charged with the poaching of over six hundred crappies. There really wasn't an easy solution. One well-intentioned idea to save fish likely resulted in unintentional harm to the native stocks. Nature is tough enough to work with without poachers.

It seems some of the dumbest stories come from turkey hunters. DNR officer Jeff Day of South Carolina had a couple of dandy ones. He was out driving when he rounded a bend to find a ground blind set up in the middle of the road. He asked the hunter what he was doing in the middle of the road. "Why, I'm turkey hunting!" the man answered matter-of-factly. (He might have said, "Because that's where my blind is.") It's obviously—or maybe not so obviously—extremely dangerous and illegal to hunt in the middle of a road.

In another incident, Officer Day was patrolling an area during turkey season. He happened upon a parked truck with some corn in the back. Corn is often used illegally for baiting turkeys, so Day got out of his vehicle and followed the trail into the woods. He heard a shot. A little farther along, he came across his prey. The poacher was standing by a bait pile and a dead hen turkey. Hens are not legal to shoot.

The poacher looked at Day and said, "I hope this is okay?" Day checked the shotgun and found a second live round in it. "Oh, that was to shoot that other turkey over there," said the poacher, pointing. Another hen turkey was nearby, this one alive. Some days there is just no limit to stupidity. Game wardens have to learn to tolerate and deal with these mindless actions. It's like dealing with a virus. Early in an officer's career, they are exposed to poachers and sort of develop an immunity to their actions. Then, just when they think they're over the worst, another variant comes along, worse than all the rest. And there is no vaccine.

OHIO SURPRISE

OHIO WILDLIFE OFFICERS DECIDED TO SET UP A DECOY DEER IN AN area where night hunters had been reported. They set the bedded buck decoy about forty metres from the road and positioned their vehicles out of sight, ready to pounce should a poacher show up.

They had just gotten their vehicles under cover when a call came over the radio: "We got one coming ... they're stopping ... passenger is on the road with a gun—be ready!" *Bang!* The sound of the .44 Magnum echoed through the valley. The foam-filled decoy had another hole in it.

The officers quickly surrounded the truck and were surprised to see that the shooter was a woman. They were even more surprised to see that others in the car were also women, drinking beer. The officers took the gun, dumped the beer and wrote some citations. The women began crying, probably because of the dumped beer more than anything.

The shooter appeared in court, paid her $1,500 in fines and costs, lost her hunting privileges for two years and was told she had to take a hunter education course. She approached one of the officers afterward and said, "Thanks, Nick." Like many men, he didn't quite understand the woman's sarcasm. He turned and said, "Okay, for what?" The woman sobbed as she said, "Now I can't go on my elk hunt in Colorado that I've been planning for two years!"

Nick finally found some words of his own. "You're welcome, but that's not because of me. I didn't make you shoot the deer. And don't forget to 'like' us on Facebook."

OLD SCHOOLHOUSE POACHER

GREENBRIER COUNTY IN WEST VIRGINIA IS A BUSY AREA FOR wildlife officers with the Department of Natural Resources (DNR). Officer Todd Petrunger took a complaint one day during hunting season regarding spotlights that had recently been seen in a rural area in his patrol district. He was familiar with the area from past years' experience, and he decided to have a look during daylight. The reported location was private property with an abandoned schoolhouse in the middle of a large, open grassy field. The area surrounding the school meadow was a national forest with mature timber that provided great cover for deer. But deer were attracted to the fields for feeding on the lush grass, making this an ideal hunting spot.

Petrunger learned that a group of hunters had made the schoolhouse their hunting camp during deer season. It might have been fine, except this group was believed to hunt at night. I guess you could call it a school for poachers. Petrunger also learned it was a fairly large group of guys who liked to party. Sometimes they'd choose to party all night, sometimes do a little spotlighting off the porch and sometimes do both.

With the help of a couple of other officers, Petrunger set up surveillance one night when the group was in the schoolhouse. Under the cover of darkness, the officers worked their way through the big timber with a deer decoy. They set the decoy up near a narrow draw. The idea was that an officer would be hunkered down in the low draw, out of danger of shooting and ready, if a shot was fired, to pull the decoy over using a long rope attached to its legs. If it fell over after

Officer Todd Petrunger and others took four years to catch a group of West Virginia nighttime poachers. *Photo: Todd Petrunger.*

the shot, the officers were pretty certain a group would come out to recover the deer, and then they'd arrest the entire group.

The ongoing party was in full swing when suddenly the lights in the schoolhouse went off. Two of the poachers came out on the deck with rifles and a spotlight. They lit up the field but not one of them spotted the deer decoy. Perhaps it was "alcohol vision." They scanned the field, passed their "used" beer over the rail deck, went back to drinking and never came out again. The dejected officers left the area without a catch. They were unable to return until the following year because other poaching reports kept them busy the rest of hunting season.

The next year, the determined officers again set up in the schoolhouse field one evening, but the group partied all night and didn't come out to spotlight at all. Again, other work commitments and tips kept them busy and they were unable to set up there for the rest of the season.

It would be two more years before the field was watched again. In the fourth year of the known activity, Petrunger kept an eye on the property until he noticed some people at the schoolhouse during a daytime patrol. He really wanted to catch these guys this season, and he persuaded his boss to let him spend an entire week watching the schoolhouse when the poachers showed up. That meant other officers would have to choose the most urgent calls and leave some complaints for later. That's a tough decision to make, but it has to be done when the calls outnumber the officers.

Petrunger, Sergeant Chris Lester and another officer worked the first night of the operation. They parked a safe distance away and worked their way through the big timber until they reached the edge of the field. As they drew closer, they turned their headlamps off and moved carefully through the trees with their deer decoy. The undergrowth was dry, and it was difficult to move without snapping the occasional twig. They kept checking the schoolhouse through their binoculars and determined there were only four students in this "night class." The officers expected more poachers to arrive later, based on their previous observations.

The officers had watched for several hours, during which they stealthily made their way to within fifty metres of the front porch, when the lights went off and the spotlight came out. Two of the occupants emerged onto the porch while the other two remained inside. Someone stepped on a twig, causing a loud snap. The officers froze in their tracks as the light scanned all around them. They were in camo but had to remain absolutely motionless. Then the spotlight went out and they could see a small amber light swinging back and forth in their direction. That got their hearts pumping. The light was the infrared night scope on a rifle swinging back and forth in front of them. But the two poachers never saw a target and they soon resumed their drinking.

A new plan was needed. With a break in action, Officer Petrunger called dispatch for local deputies and asked them to drive cautiously into the schoolhouse meadow. This would distract the poachers and allow the officers time to relocate around behind the schoolhouse. They stashed their decoy in some brush before moving. The deputies arrived as planned, distracting the poachers away from the field. A deputy was talking to some of them as the three officers approached the schoolhouse undetected and checked inside it. All four of the men were identified. The two seen spotlighting were arrested and placed in patrol vehicles. It was now safe for Sergeant Lester to walk over and pick up their hidden decoy. Lester found that corn had been put out for deer bait. The corn was located in the exact spot where the officers had stood when the poacher's rifle had scanned the area with the infrared scope. They had been very lucky.

Two were charged and later convicted of a number of violations including spotlighting and non-resident hunting violations. They lost their hunting privileges for a year in West Virginia and their guns were seized. The two guns seized were more suited for a Rambo movie, a 300 Blackout rifle with an ATN night scope and a Glock handgun, both equipped with silencers. The poachers had proper paperwork for the firearms with them, and state law allowed their return after the fines were paid.

In this case, it took four seasons to complete a file that had been launched by a public complaint. It's not uncommon to have multiple reports of suspected poaching at the same time. Officers have to choose. This can be difficult for the public to understand because people don't realize how busy the officers are, especially during hunting season when poachers can operate with less chance of being caught.

MILITARY POLICE— REVERSE BUST

KANSAS WILDLIFE OFFICERS BECAME SUSPICIOUS ABOUT A reported salvage permit held by a military police (MP) member for an elk. None of the officers had issued such a permit. (Salvage permits can be issued for roadkill animals.) The call coincided with a complaint about two spike bull elk being shot the night before and left near the military base.

As chance would have it, the officer who attended the military base was pulled over by an MP for speeding as he passed the gate. That stop had an ironic twist—the MP that stopped the officer was the poaching MP with the alleged permit. Imagine, he pulled a vehicle over and ended up being charged by the driver! He was interviewed about the salvage permit and admitted he didn't have one. He confessed that a group of them had been out driving around at night and shot the two elk with handguns from the vehicle using spotlights. They then hooked the animals to their vehicle and tried to drag them to a gate, but they couldn't find the gate. They broke off two of the antlers for souvenirs and bolted.

Two of the MPs admitted to shooting the elk and two others said they held the lights and assisted. They confessed to doing the same thing with two white-tailed deer. They showed the officers where they'd taken the deer carcasses. A total of forty-four charges were laid, with guilty pleas entered by the two main poachers involved. This was a shameful, cowardly act by the very people we rely on for freedom and security.

HUNTING FOR "THE ROCK"

TWO HUNTING FRIENDS FROM KENTUCKY GOT A MAJOR BREAK when they were invited to create a hunting television show. Mr. "Gills" and Mr. "Dumbkin" showed some footage of a few of their hunts to a major hunting channel at a Louisville trade show. Shortly afterward, a deal was struck and the two became full-time hunters, filming and producing twenty-six episodes a year. Their first episode of *Hunting with "Schmucks"* aired in October 2013.

The two were having a great time doing something they loved. It can be very challenging hunting some big-game species. It is extra challenging to capture the hunt on video without spooking the animals. Things were going well until they aired their big bull elk hunt episode in Wyoming. The two massive bulls they shot were impressive. However, one keen television viewer, a Wyoming Game and Fish Department (WGFD) employee, who was watching and listening to their story knew something wasn't right. The countryside and vegetation in the video didn't match the area they claimed to be hunting in. Mr. Gills, while referring to their elk hunt, stated on air that "we didn't know what we were getting into." That was an understatement.

The person who'd watched the show contacted a WGFD officer, who did some searching on the internet and found two still photos that Gills and Dumbkin had taken at the kill site. The officer sent the pictures to all the game wardens in eastern Wyoming to see whether they recognized the location in the pictures. One veteran officer, Rod Lebert, thought the picture looked like an area he was familiar with. There was a two-metre-high rock in the photo. He knew of several areas with a similar unusual rock feature.

Lebert and other officers began their search, looking for "the Rock" in Wyoming. Just the idea of trying to locate a single rock in all of Wyoming might turn most folks off unless they were passionate about their pursuit of poachers. The men visited four locations with similar rock structures. The first three were on public lands—the TV show hunters proclaimed they hunted only on public lands—but none was an exact match to the photos.

The last location Lebert knew of was on private property. They drove to the location and talked to the landowner, showing him the picture of the hunters beside the rock. "Those guys paid a trespass fee to hunt mule deer on my property," said the landowner, and he proceeded to show the officers the exact spot in the photo. They took the time to pose for a picture of their own. They were going to claim their trophy too—two poachers! The location was many kilometres from the area where the show hosts claimed to have taken the elk. This private area was known for having large bull elk and was only hunted every other year through an extremely difficult draw. They were getting warm.

The officers put their information together and, armed with search warrants, headed for Kentucky along with USFWS and Kentucky officers. Remarking on the homes and countryside in the rural area they were passing through, one of the Wyoming officers said, "The only thing missing is a guy sitting on the porch playing a banjo." (A reference to the movie *Deliverance*.) They formed two teams and simultaneously knocked on the doors of Gills and Dumbkin. One of them still lived with his mommy.

When the officers sat down with them to ask questions, they denied anything had been done wrong. But after they were shown the picture of them and then the officers' picture of the same spot, they confessed and told the truth. Gills admitted that the two poached elk were at his uncle's place getting mounted. He took the officers to his trophy room to show off his impressive collection of taxidermy mounts. One officer pointed out a lovely banjo on a stand, and they all broke out laughing. Officers seized computers and other electronics to search for other violations. Later analysis found evidence that one of them had shot an antelope and left it. They'd also shot other small game animals without a licence. These guys were getting great ratings on television for being a couple of poachers.

The officers visited the uncle and seized the two elk heads. The uncle said, "When you're done with those, I'd appreciate getting them back so I can finish them off." That wasn't going to happen. The officers then went to see the show's promoter and producer, who had not been on the trips. Just then, the producer's phone rang; it was Gills calling with a rant about the mean wardens who had torn his house apart. The producer said, "I'm standing with those boys right now." Gills kept ranting, not realizing he'd meant the officers. The producer put the phone on speaker and said, "Hang on, I'm with the boys, the officers who were at your house—they're listening." The phone went silent and Gills hung up. Sometimes being a wildlife officer is more than entertaining.

Gills was fined $13,700 (including court costs and restitution for the elk). Dumbkin paid $17,740 in fines (including restitution and court costs). Both elk were forfeited. Both men were given a fifteen-year hunting ban in forty-eight states that participate in a national wildlife violator list (soon to be all fifty). They later admitted they had just gotten greedy. Their following had grown to over 340,000 fans and they were likely destined for bigger things—or so they'd thought.

You can't get much lower on the poacher's scale than these two. The TV show owners stopped the show and issued a statement claiming the two had acted on their own and were not supported by the network. They had bilked money from the television company and their sponsors to film themselves poaching and had done it more than once. If there's a wall of shame for poachers, these two should appear on the outhouse wall.

GOOD DOG!

ENVIRONMENT CANADA WILDLIFE OFFICER KIP DIRKS WAS PATROL-
ling the countryside in Alberta one fall day, checking for duck hunters.
After hearing shots, he happened upon a large, round cornfield with
a pivot irrigation system. The shots were coming from within the
cornfield, but he couldn't see anything because the corn was two
metres high and very thick.

Officer Dirks drove around the perimeter of the field, looking for
options, and found a couple of parked trucks. One was recognizable
as belonging to a poacher he had been after before. A muddy trail led
into the cornfield, but it would be dangerous and a dead giveaway
walking in, so he climbed a giant poplar tree growing along the canal
nearby. It was a bit dangerous climbing the flimsy tree, but it made a
perfect vantage point with his binoculars.

He could see four hunters with a hunting dog having a great old
duck shoot by the large pond in the middle of the field where the
irrigation had been leaking. The ducks were lured into the ankle
deep pool by decoys and duck calls. Dirks was able to identify the
hunters through his binoculars, but he felt a little strange hanging
on twelve metres up a tree, hoping no one would see him. Eventually,
the hunters packed up and headed toward their trucks. Just then,
Dirks's target hunter launched a dead duck over his shoulder into the
cornfield, never to be found again. Aha!

Officer Dirks scrambled down the tree and stood nonchalantly
by the trucks, waiting until the hunters arrived. Just as he expected,
they had exactly the right amount of birds for their limit. The poacher
proudly claimed, "We got our limit!" When questioned about the
thrown duck, the poacher claimed he was just training his dog to
retrieve the bird. "Well, then you wouldn't mind me borrowing your

dog to have a sniff around?" said Dirks. The poacher agreed to go with him back into the field with his dog.

Dirks stopped near where he had seen the duck thrown and sent the dog. Thirty seconds later the proud dog pranced out of the corn and took the over-limit duck to the feet of his owner.

"For #$%@#!'s sake, you stupid dog!" the poacher barked. Busted—by his very own hunting dog!

LOUISIANA HOME DELIVERY

LIEUTENANT KENNY BALKOM IS A TWENTY-YEAR VETERAN OF THE Louisiana Department of Wildlife and Fisheries. All officers have some memorable events throughout their career, but Lieutenant Balkom had one for the ages.

Balkom and his wife had finished watching television for the evening on a cold January 1. They had just crawled into bed when Balkom heard a noise. His wife said, "Oh, that's just someone with leftover firecrackers." Most officers tend to become suspicious of unusual noises and Balkom was no different, but his wife persuaded him to relax.

He was just about asleep when he heard another shot and the sound of an ATV. He jumped out of bed and ran to the front door, from where he could see someone spotlighting in his field across the road right where he fed his cows. "They shot one of my cows!" he yelled. "Honey, get my gun belt." Balkom ran to get his uniform on while his wife brought him his gun belt, but without the keeper straps that hold the belt in place. There wasn't time for details—this was not a uniform inspection.

He ran out and hopped into his patrol vehicle while keeping an eye on the ATV and the spotlights scanning the fields. They swept by in one direction, then turned and headed back. His plan was to wait until the perpetrators drove past, then stop them from behind. His heart was racing as the ATV went by and he pulled out behind them. The two-seater side-by-side quad held five people in it with gun barrels sticking out everywhere. One guy was standing in the back with a shotgun. Balkom said later that he thought he was stopping the Taliban!

Quickly, he called the local deputy for backup and reported his stop. He jumped out in the cold January air with a loose gun belt but without a jacket or shoes—there'd been no time to grab those either. After racing to the quad, he grabbed all five guns as fast as he could and the quad keys at the same time. Sometimes the best approach when alone is to act a bit unstable. Certainly, standing in bare feet holding an armload of guns could leave that impression. It didn't hurt that the poachers were stunned and drunk, and thus fairly compliant.

"What are you doing shooting my cows?" he yelled at them. "Oh no, sir, we're hunting rabbits," one replied. "Well, did you get any?" The man held up three freshly killed rabbits. "Well, that's illegal," said Balkom. His adrenaline subsided now that it seemed they had not shot one of his cows. His bare feet and lack of jacket were now telling him he'd better take care of himself first. Ordering the poachers to stay by the quad, he got into his truck with his new gun collection.

It took forty-five minutes for the deputy to arrive. Balkom told him to stay with the group while he ran to his house. "What? Where is that?" said the deputy. "Right over there," Balkom said, pointing across the road.

Balkom walked the thirty metres to his house and asked his wife to get him some sweet tea because it was going to be a long night. He returned to the ATV, now wearing shoes and a jacket, and told the group they were all going to jail. The first guy was put in the back of the deputy's car, but as he exited the ATV they saw him stuffing something under the seat. It turned out to be some marijuana. They'd also all been drinking. Their charges included hunting from a moving vehicle, open alcohol, hunting during illegal hours, hunting from a public road, driving an ATV on a public road and possession of marijuana. Unfortunately, there is no law against stupid.

The night cost each man about $1,000, plus loss of hunting privileges for a year. The group consisted of a bunch of men who lived in the city and were having a bachelor party that night of the rabbit hunt. They will have one of the best bachelor party stories ever and so will Lieutenant Balkom. There are not many officers who find poachers right outside their front doorstep.

HUNTING FOR DUMMIES

Fishery officer Stu Cartwright of the DFO in Kamloops received information about two guys fishing for chinook salmon in a stream that was open only for trout fishing. It was common for fishers to claim they were trout fishing even if they were using the heavy, stiff rods designed for salmon fishing. Cartwright and another officer decided to pose as a couple of fishermen and try catching the two bandits.

Dressed in plain clothes, they drove to the river in an unmarked vehicle and jumped out with their trout fishing rods. They hiked down to the riverbank and started fishing beside the two reported poachers.

It didn't take long for the conversation to get interesting. Cartwright asked why they used such big rods for trout fishing. One of the two, whose intelligence was likely outmatched by the fish he was trying to catch, turned to Cartwright and said, "Uh, we're fishing for chinook salmon. If we get checked we just say we're fishing for trout." Cartwright replied, "Well, guess what? Sometimes I dress up and say I'm just a fisherman and I'm actually a fishery officer." The two were relieved of their fishing rods and issued a ticket.

INDIANA'S COLD CASE

THIS DEER-POACHING CASE STARTED WITH A CALL FROM AN observant person on social media. The wife of Mr. "Fin" posted a picture on Facebook of Fin with a giant white-tailed buck, and the caller said the picture just didn't look right. Indiana conservation officer Jon Watkins checked out the picture and agreed the deer in the photo did not look like a normal freshly killed deer. The eyes were sunken and the coat looked strange. After some very detailed investigative work and involvement of expert witnesses, officers had enough evidence to obtain a search warrant for Fin's place. The online pictures were only the beginning of many steps taken to get the warrant.

Officer Watkins and another officer showed up at Fin's house and talked to him. They seized his phone and the big white-tailed buck hanging on his wall. His wife wasn't home at the time, and Fin had a story that just didn't seem to match all the evidence. His wife arrived home around the time the interview with Fin was ending, and Watkins took her aside. They learned she knew her way around the legal system. After a few minutes of chatting, they reminded her that the truth usually works out better when things get to court. She asked, "Can I go talk to my husband?" She was allowed to talk him and Fin returned shortly thereafter.

With a much clearer, more accurate memory, Fin said, "Can we just start over?" He described how he'd been hunting the previous year and shot another buck just as the monster buck stepped out of the trees, but he had no chance at it before it retreated. He reported the first buck, as required by state laws. He didn't need a tag to take a deer on his own property but was required to report it. A couple of days later, he returned to the same location where he'd seen the big buck. No doubt he felt safe because he was hunting on his own

The wife of the poacher who shot this deer in 2016 proudly posted it on Facebook in 2017. Oops! Indiana officers now own it. Isn't social media great? *Photo: Indiana Department of Natural Resources.*

property, where no one else would notice. He ended up calling in the big deer again and shot it. He took the head and put it in a deep freeze at his place, telling no one except his wife. The next year, he simply pulled the monster buck from his freezer and reported it as his deer off his property for that year. What a great story in his own mind— he'd scored a record buck and never fired a shot that year.

Afterward, Fin's wife was so proud of her poaching husband that she posted his picture of the deer on social media. That seems like a rather strange thing to do, but perhaps he had other shortcomings and this made her feel better about her husband. They would finally be able to score and showcase his two-hundred-class buck. But that was when things quickly went down the drain.

Other factors were in play as well. Most often, giant bucks are spotted on game cameras if they hang around a specific area for long. Other real hunters know they're out there. In this case, there were unconfirmed reports of the big buck having been captured on a trail camera the year before. No one reported it being taken and no one saw it the next year. True hunters are one of the best weapons against poachers.

Fin was convicted and given one hundred hours of community service, eighteen months' probation, a $741 fine and a two-year suspension of hunting privileges. But even after the case was over, Fin believed that he somehow had the right to own the massive deer. He figured because he didn't shoot another deer the following year, he should get this one back. Perhaps he'd spent too much time in the deep freeze admiring his deer and froze a few too many brain cells. He would have two more years to thaw those brain cells and then think about hunting.

BISON POACHERS

NO, THIS IS NOT A STORY FROM THE 1800S. THIS EVENT HAPPENED in 2018, but before I recount it, a bit of bison history. The bison herd in Yellowstone Park is believed to be the only pure, original plains bison herd that wasn't wiped out in the 1800s. The herd was at a low of twenty-three animals before strict protection measures allowed it to grow to over five thousand today. But this success story has not been without issues.

Bison are strictly controlled and contained within Yellowstone Park because they carry brucellosis, and ranchers surrounding the park have legitimate concerns that the disease could spread into their herds of cattle. Control measures had to be implemented as the bison herd grew and roamed outside the park boundaries. The first attempts were called hunts; however, hunters lined up at the park boundary as if it was a shooting gallery, and many felt this wasn't ethical. It's not legal to hunt within the Yellowstone Park boundaries. Currently, limited-entry licences are issued outside the park boundaries. The restrictions in place make for a well-managed hunt and control the threat to livestock. In the past, the park has also provided live animals to areas wanting to reintroduce bison.

These bison management practices have drawn scrutiny from some "do good" protesters over the years. They have protested management practices, insisting the bison should be allowed to wander anywhere they want outside the park. During my career, I've encountered protesters who don't have a clue about the issue they are protesting. They are even sometimes paid by companies, organizations or people who usually have ulterior motives.

On two occasions, the park has experienced vandalism to bison corrals, resulting in herds being released. The net effect of these thoughtless acts could be more detrimental than helpful. If bison roamed outside the park, they would have to be dealt with, sort of like Jimmy Hoffa. Fortunately, the bison returned to the park, where they knew the feed was more plentiful. Protesters have gone so far as to chain themselves to the squeeze gates where bison were held and tested. The chain gang was arrested and held in jail until taken before a judge, who banned them from the park for five years. If there were a species classification key for these protesters, it would probably be a subspecies of poachers. Their thoughtless actions can be just as detrimental to the resource as poaching.

Now, we'll get into the poaching story. It all started with a tip from the public about some shots heard in an area near Yellowstone National Park. No hunting seasons were open at the time except for coyotes. The complaint was logged and noted. Two days later, a wolf specialist with Montana Fish, Wildlife and Parks was out tracking some collared wolves and came across the carcasses of three large bull bison. The heads were gone and no meat had been taken. She called the local warden to report the incident. She also took some photos and marked the site on her GPS. After that, with two to three tonnes of fresh meat on the ground and the chance of encountering bears, she decided it would be best to leave the area for the day. Even though there was some snow on the ground, bears could still be at large and looking for a free meal.

At the same time, local wardens were helping to monitor tribal bison hunts in another area. Two of them visited the kill site reported by the wolf specialist, along with their new agency partner, Kikka, the German shepherd. They took a National Parks ranger with them for the job. Six centimetres of fresh snow lay on the ground, but that didn't stop Kikka from finding the skinned heads of three bison hidden in some brush nearby, presumably left for the poachers to pick up later. Kikka also found an odd .26-calibre Nosler casing under the snow. The heads and shell casing would likely not have been found without Kikka's nose.

In 2018, Kikka the German shepherd helped sniff out evidence of some bison poachers near Yellowstone National Park. *Photo: Coy Kline.*

Meanwhile, a keen-eyed National Parks service ranger reported he'd seen a vehicle parked in the area of the bison kill the same day the shots had been heard. He'd recorded the licence number even though nothing was suspicious at the time.

Strangely, a lone "hiker" happened to appear at the kill site while Kikka and the wardens were still there. This may not have been unusual except there were no trails anywhere near the site and it was several kilometres away from roads. The hiker, later determined to be one of the poachers, was surprised but tried to play dumb (not that hard for a poacher). "I'm just out here for a hike," he said. "I always wanted to be a warden." He really was a lot closer to a warden than his frightened clean underwear thought he should be. He identified himself to the officers and was let go at the time.

The wardens then called up another local warden who worked around the small community of Livingston to pass on the bits of evidence they had gathered. The community is one of those places where poaching has been passed on for generations by more than a few of the locals. The new warden knew one poaching family who had a .26 Nosler rifle. We're getting warm!

Next, a friend of the hiker-poacher was interviewed, and he spilled the beans on himself and his two friends. Apparently, they'd gone horseback riding and come across the three large bull bison. They did what many poachers would do—they shot them all, cut the heads off, skinned them and left everything. They had intended to return for the bison skulls when other animals had cleaned them off.

Meanwhile, wardens returned to the crime scene and did a complete forensic analysis of the bison. They found bullets in the bison carcass heads that were later analyzed and matched to all three guns the poachers had used.

The poachers, including the "hiker," were convicted and fined $2,605 each, had their rifles forfeited, were given eighteen months' probation, lost all hunting privileges for four and a half years and were ordered to take remedial hunter education.

In summary, a public complaint plus a biologist's discovery, a park ranger recording a licence number, a dog's nose, a carcass analysis, a local warden's knowledge and great investigative skills led to a conviction. This group should be commended for great teamwork and attention to detail.

DEAR FRIENDS
POACH DEER

A YOUNG MICHIGAN MAN WAS ATTENDING A CHIROPRACTOR COL-
lege in Iowa where he met an Iowa farmer's daughter. This is not a
joke. The Michigan man learned from the daughter that the Iowa
farmer had some great deer-hunting property. Out-of-state hunters
require a special licence, but hey, he knew the farmer's daughter, so
who needs a licence? After graduation, the young man returned to
Michigan to crunch bones. His dad and brother were also interested
in hunting (poaching, that is), so the three of them began travelling
to Iowa annually.

Over the next sixteen years, the trio of poachers continued their
yearly Iowa trip to hunt deer on the farmer's property. The poachers'
wall of shame grew to quite a collection of deer trophies, and still
no one knew about their poaching but them. When the Michigan
crew hunted on the farm in Iowa, they hid their Michigan-plated
vehicle in or behind the barn to avoid having any snoopy neighbours
question their presence each fall. Over the years, they became more
sporting-minded poachers, turning to muzzleloader and bow-hunting seasons to take advantage of the earlier hunt and focus on bigger
deer. They arranged for the farmer and his wife to buy local tags to
cover the deer they shot. In exchange, the Michigan poachers offered
food, accommodations and some guidance for fishing trips the Iowa
family took in Michigan.

It was a wonderful, hushed relationship—until 2017. A huge
white-tailed deer was known to be in the area of the farm, and all
the locals knew about it. A neighbour a few kilometres away had a
special interest in the large buck. He also had a DNR badge—he was

Iowa DNR officer Eric Wright. The hunting season came and went but no large buck was reported, even though other locals hadn't spotted the deer for a while. The officer checked with locals, then he checked Facebook and other social media looking for the large buck, but nothing surfaced.

Wright went on to other investigations and duties. He was checking through the landowner/tenant tags (special tags just for property owners/residents) related to another matter when a couple of names captured his attention. Mr. and Mrs. "Farmer" had purchased tags for over fifteen years, yet he'd never seen them hunting and never heard of them shooting deer. The officer had also heard through some church gossip that some Michigan folks hunted in the area. After a bit more work he decided to check with the Farmers.

When Wright drove into their yard, he noticed the elderly Mrs. Farmer in the garden. He stopped and chatted, saying casually, "How's hunting?" "Oh, I don't hunt!" she replied. "So why do you buy tags and then not use them?" The woman must have seen clouds building, and the fear of lightning caused her to say, "You better talk to my husband." The conversation went much the same with Mr. Farmer. He didn't hunt either, he said, and explained that the Michigan group were friends who came every year to hunt. Lightning never hit them, but the poachers were toast.

Searches at the Michigan residences resulted in the seizure and eventual forfeiture of nineteen deer (seventeen buck head mounts), two compound bows and a crossbow. The Farmers, who purchased the tags and allowed the poaching, paid a $780 fine. The trio of poachers paid $51,000 in fines and lost their hunting privileges for three years. I expect the tithes given at their church were reduced for a while because of these three bandits.

THE GALL OF POACHERS

BEAR GALL BLADDERS AND BEAR PAWS HAVE BEEN POACHED IN nearly every jurisdiction in North America where bears live. The driver of this appalling poaching is the Asian market. It had been primarily a Korean market, but wealth in China has caused prices to skyrocket into thousands of dollars paid per gall by the end buyer. The poacher will get a fraction of that, with each level of the market increasing the price.

There is some scientific proof that bear bile contains more ursodeoxycholic acid than the bile of other animals. The acid is known to dissolve gallstones and help with liver disease. I'll drink to that. There are synthetic alternatives; however, traditions over thousands of years are difficult to change. The claims of curing heart issues, epilepsy and hemorrhoids are not proven. Some might laugh at the suggestion that gall bile could cure a case of hemorrhoids. I laughed until I remembered a painful case I had years ago. In retrospect, I'd have paid a lot for a cure. I wouldn't try the bile, though.

Some Asian countries allow and support bear farms to harvest bile. Vietnam and South Korea have banned their bear farms, but China still allows them. They keep the bears in pens and place fixed tubes in their gall bladders to extract the bile. The goal of bear farms was to reduce the pressures of poaching around the world. Unfortunately, traditionalists prefer wild bear gall, and demands have increased and driven market prices even higher.

Bear paws are a delicacy for bear paw soup in the same Asian market. The bear claws are often removed to feed an entirely different illegal market. Poachers will usually leave the rest of the bear carcass to rot.

The demand drives the poaching. Some legal bear outfitters take the gall from bears their customers shoot legally, but taking the gall to sell is illegal. Many undercover operations have taken place over the years with the same disgusting discoveries. Dozens and sometimes hundreds of bears are taken by poaching rings. One such case occurred in Quebec, where over one hundred bears were taken. The three-year-long investigation resulted in 121 charges and sixteen search warrants. Many traditional Asian medical practitioners in North America have been convicted of purchasing bear galls for use in their businesses. They are usually given fines in the thousands of dollars. That won't stop the trade.

Activists against bear hunting will claim stopping bear hunting will eliminate the problem. Not a chance. It would only take the legal bear hunters out of the wilderness and leave fewer eyes watching to catch and report the poaching. It's one of the wildlife conservation challenges that has no easy solution. I won't point the finger at the Asian traditions and place the blame on them. We all know North America is guilty of its own decimation of many species throughout history. The best solution would be to work with Asian countries' leaders and design a mutual solution. Until then, the concerned public and wildlife officers have to continue to work together to reduce the poaching with whatever legal methods are available.

CONNECTICUT—
GONE TO THE DOGS

MANY NORTH AMERICAN FISH AND WILDLIFE AGENCIES HAVE learned the value and importance of a canine section to assist with their work. Connecticut environmental conservation enforcement officers decided to start a canine program with four officers and four dogs. One of the first officers with the program was Sergeant William (Bill) Logiodice. His father had been a long-time member of the Connecticut State Police and had instructed its canine program for a number of years. His dad retired before Bill joined the agency but he had the honour of presenting Bill's badge when he graduated from training.

Bill's dog, Ruger, was initially trained to search for cadavers. Later, Bill requested to have the dog trained for fish and game detection. His request was granted, which led to the formation of the fish and wildlife dog section. All of Connecticut's fish and wildlife dogs are now trained to detect, locate and signal when they find fish, deer, waterfowl and turkeys. Bill's dog was trained to sit when he located a target.

Bill was just pulling into his driveway at the end his shift in March of 2016 when he received a call about some illegal striped bass fishermen. It was well after dark when the call came in. Bill had been an officer for about eight years at the time, and he recognized the area of the reported violations as being a hot spot for people who poached striped bass. Bill took Ruger, met with another officer and drove to the area of interest.

They had just started down the trail to the fishing site when a fisherman emerged. The man was legal but reported a group of four guys fishing nearby who seemed to be catching a lot of fish. The two officers and Ruger carried on down the trail and located the group of four, who each had coolers nearby. Ruger immediately sat beside the coolers, indicating there were fish inside. The fishermen openly admitted to catching and keeping two fish each even though the limit had changed to one the previous year. The coolers all checked out with two fish each; however, all were below the minimum legal size of twenty-eight inches.

Meanwhile, Ruger was up and scurrying around, searching more of the area. Bill noticed that the dog was excited and kept circling one particular area nearby. He went to Ruger, now seated beside a black plastic bag full of wiggling fish. The two fish each that the men had claimed turned into a total of thirty-eight striped bass ranging from eleven to twenty-four inches—all illegal. Two of the poachers had licences and the other two hadn't bothered to get them. All four had exceeded their daily limit and possessed undersized fish, and two didn't even have a licence. Even a dog can count better than these guys.

This bust was a landmark case in persuading the agency and some skeptical officers to go to the dogs. It's common for some people to resist change until an event happens to prove the change is worthwhile. Many agencies have learned the value of dogs for a variety of fish and wildlife tasks. Dogs are especially good in locating hidden fish or wildlife in the dark or in hidden compartments on vessels or vehicles. Another big advantage is that dogs never complain about working long days or whom they work with. Dogs just love to work and, generally, dog handlers enjoy the job as much as they do.

ALL IN THE FAMILY

MUCH LIKE A DRUG ADDICT, SOME POACHERS BECOME ADDICTED to poaching. They start slowly, just giving it a try, and before they know it they are hooked and willing to do anything for a fix. Mr. "Bear" of Missouri is one of those serious poaching addicts, just like his father and two brothers. This charming group of men had bragged to friends. It was proven that Bear and his family had killed over one hundred deer over a three-year period before they were caught and sentenced in 2015. Some feel they have likely killed thousands of deer, turkeys and other wildlife. This disgusting quartet (plus ten other accused) would just drive around and shoot whatever deer they saw. They'd cut the heads off and leave the meat behind. Occasionally, they'd remove the back straps.

Missouri officer Andrew Barnes was one of over a hundred officers from the United States and Canada that helped in the investigation. He and others spent countless hours on the case, to the point where Barnes's wife grew tired of hearing about the story as it grew and grew—a not uncommon response from many fish and wildlife officers' spouses. The massive effort brought the poachers' escapades to a temporary end in 2015. The investigation grew until there were over twenty search warrants at numerous locations. The first warrant served on Mr. Bear yielded over fifty deer heads. Who knows how many animals disappeared after Bear alerted his crooked associates of that first warrant?

Bear's mode and reasons for his serial-killing of wildlife were incomprehensible. He held a full-time job and was presumably a good worker. His after hours and weekend time too were different from many other poachers. He wasn't known to have a drug habit or a drinking problem. He was polite and co-operative when arrested.

161

While some poachers struggle to tie their shoes, this guy was aware of all the legal lingo, the officers' authority and his legal personal rights when officers arrived to search his place. He had a wildlife-killing addiction unlike almost any other.

He'd often head out after work at dark with his dad, a brother or some friends for an all-night killing spree across the state of Missouri. The group would use spotlights to locate deer, shoot them, take pictures or videos, cut the heads off and hide them until their return trip in daylight. They often travelled to northern Missouri, where deer hunting was better. They drove across the entire state some nights, covering over four hundred kilometres before retracing their tracks at dawn to retrieve the heads they wanted from the carnage they'd left behind. They would then stop for a photo shoot on a property they frequented for "legal" photos. This would make them appear as real hunters shooting deer in legal locations and times. Bear went so far as to send his videos and pictures to outdoor businesses and television shows in the hopes of landing a gig on a hunting channel or selling some of the videos.

And his addiction wasn't just for deer. He and his cohorts would kill anything in the wild, including turkeys and fish. Sometimes they'd set illegal trotlines for catfish* and check them on their drive home. Bear knew he would probably be caught someday, and I doubt he cared at all.

Missouri's statute of limitations limits officers to violations occurring only within the last year. Bear's phone was full of pictures and data that depicted over two thousand violations in the previous 365 days. Officers chose only the best three hundred charges to take to court. Their charges included hunting at night with lights, hunting out of season, shooting from the road and using illegal weapons.

---

* A trotline is a heavy line strung across a creek or placed in a river, with many short lines with baited hooks attached to the main line.

Bear and his father received lifetime bans for hunting and trapping. His two brothers and a fifth person involved lost hunting privileges for five to eighteen years. The combined total of their fines was $51,000. That might sound like a good fine; however, if their claims were accurate, that's just $42.50 per deer.

Bear did as everyone expected and continued his addiction. He was caught again in late 2018. He received a one-year sentence in jail. The judge then surprised everyone in the courtroom with a signature sentence no one had heard of before. Mr. Bear was ordered to watch the 1942 Disney movie *Bambi* once a month during his entire stay in jail. The defence lawyer was not happy because that wasn't part of the plea bargain. Maybe the lawyer should have had to watch the movie too!

These types of poachers rarely change their ways. If Bear ever decides to head north to Canada for some hunting, he will likely be arrested. Apparently, he and a friend had gone all the way north to Saskatchewan in 2016 under the guise of a duck-hunting trip (this was likely not Bear's first hunting trip to Canada). They'd driven around to film themselves killing a few deer and other animals before heading home. At the time of Bear's Missouri arrest, Missouri officers called Saskatchewan officers and notified them about his latest violations. Mr. Bear faces eight charges in Canada and his friend faces fourteen counts for various hunting infractions including shooting deer, an antelope, a coyote and a badger. Bear could maybe use some training in duck identification too. Canada doesn't want these guys either—sorry!

PENNSYLVANIA POACHER

ON NOVEMBER 11, 2016, PENNSYLVANIA GAME COMMISSION WILD-life conservation officer Richard Macklem II decided to patrol an area where night hunters had been reported. Macklem thought about his late co-worker before he went on patrol. It was exactly six years earlier to the day that his fellow officer, David Groves, had been shot and killed by a deer poacher.

Macklem was positioned in a location with a clear vantage point to watch some large fields that deer tended to frequent at night. Christmas carols, anyone? "While shepherds watched their flocks by night ..."

About 10:00 p.m. Macklem noticed a vehicle driving slowly and scanning the field with a spotlight. He heard the tires skid to a stop on the gravel road before a small-calibre rifle shot rang out. The vehicle turned into the field as Macklem started his drive toward it. He would meet the vehicle on a small one-lane bridge, a perfect spot to prevent a getaway. He turned his emergency lights on and pointed his spotlight at the driver.

He was reaching for the door handle to exit his vehicle when the driver of the poacher's pickup turned his headlights on bright, revved up the truck engine and drove straight into Macklem's patrol truck. The poacher was able to push the patrol truck over and squeeze by. Broken glass was flying inside the cab of Macklem's truck. The poacher side-swiped him and carried on by.

Macklem, thankfully not injured seriously, was able to get his vehicle turned around to give chase. Reaching an intersection, he wrongly guessed the poacher had turned right when in fact he'd turned left. He called on the radio for backup, at first unaware that the radio antenna had been ripped off and his radio wasn't working.

Once he realized this, he called on his portable radio. Other officers and the state police converged on the area, but no one was able to locate the suspect's vehicle. Another officer did locate the dead deer. Unknown to the officers at that time, the poacher had driven through a deep ditch, hitting it with such force that the deer had bounced out of the pickup.

Over the next several days, officers canvassed the neighbourhood, searching for clues. A tip led them to an address and an interview with a passenger in the poacher's truck who co-operated and confessed. A search warrant was written that later led them to the house of the poacher, "Garfield." He wasn't home, and they ended up at Garfield's cousin's place. The cousin must have told him the wardens were on his tail, because Garfield succumbed to the heat and called himself in to authorities. He told the officers where the truck was. He had already spray-painted it black and had purchased an old wrecked vehicle for parts to fix it. He'd damaged it when he drove through the ditch. His paint job and repairs were an attempt to hide the evidence.

Garfield's case was to be heard by a jury. Shortly before the trial, he decided to plead guilty. He was given eighteen months in jail and seven years' probation to be served after his time in jail. He was also given fines of over $2,000 for prosecution costs.

Wildlife officers aren't always dealing with dangerous poachers. They frequently have to deal with dangerous four-legged animals too. Rick Macklem II is a second-generation conservation officer. He remembers riding along with his father when he was an officer with the Game Commission. A black bear had wandered into an urban area near Philadelphia. Dad was fairly new on the job and eagerly attended the complaint. He located the bear, tranquilized it, loaded it up and headed for the country.

Young Rick kept looking back to check on the sleeping bear. All was well until Dad looked in the mirror and saw the bear staring back at him. He didn't want the bear to jump onto the highway and managed to pull into a business where fences on three sides would restrict the bear's movement. Things were going well. Then Dad stuck the bear again with the tranquilizing stick, and when he pulled it out he somehow managed to embed the needle in his finger. At least the tranquilizing fluid was in the bear, not him! Dad was taken to the hospital. Another officer showed up to load the sleeping bear and took him to freedom. Dad recovered from the physical injury a lot quicker than from his injured pride.

MANGLED MOOSE

VERMONT FISH AND WILDLIFE DEPARTMENT OFFICER JASON Dukette responded to a call about a dead moose found in the ditch. He drove to the site expecting to find a roadkill moose. What he found was a moose carcass that was barely identifiable—the animal had been dragged down the road for many kilometres. He started backtracking the bloody trail and called another officer, Mike Scott, to come and help locate the kill site. The trail was harder to see as they got closer to the origin of the drag site. Early in the drag, the moose still had its hide attached and there wasn't much sign of blood.

Eighteen kilometres later, Dukette and Scott found the kill site in a hayfield off a dirt road. They noted truck tracks throughout the hayfield. They walked the entire field looking for clues and plotting the tracks. Near the kill site, they found an empty brass from a .30-06 rifle and a Bud Light beer can, the beer of choice for many poachers. They returned to the moose carcass, conducted a necropsy and recovered a bullet.

Public outrage was understandable. Numerous leads were received and followed up on, but the poacher wasn't located. Later that same day, the officers stopped at the county clerk's office. They had learned there was a security camera on the front of the building and went in and asked to view it. Sure enough, on the same day that the moose was first reported, the video showed a truck dragging something down the road at 2:00 a.m. with sparks flying off the chain attached to it.

Dukette knew a local poacher, a young man he'd dealt with numerous times over the years. He'd always dealt with the young poacher fairly, and the kid was usually co-operative. He had been raised in a foster home with poaching parents. At thirteen, "Don" would ride in the back of the truck at night while his parents drove around spotlighting for game. Don would be told what to shoot.

The video evidence from the camera and other clues led them to Don's doorstep. Dukette and Scott had prepared a search warrant and served it on him. When interviewed, Don told the whole story. He said he was at a party with some friends and decided to go night hunting (just like he'd been taught). They shot the moose and intended to take it to a friend's place to deal with it. In their poaching (or poached?) brains, clouded with some alcohol, they decided to drag the moose. Their friend wasn't home so they just kept driving and dragging the animal for eighteen kilometres before ditching the mangled mass of moose meat.

Upon conviction Don was ordered to pay a fine of $2,000, serve sixty days of working in a state work crew, seek alcohol counselling, forfeit his firearm and lose his hunting privileges for three years. As part of the conviction and subsequent sentencing, Don was ordered to go before the local restorative justice group. Citizens, hunters, a schoolteacher and others each took turns talking to the young man. He eventually broke down and cried. There might be a chance for this young man. For the sake of him and the wildlife, let's hope so.

OPERATION THUNDERSTORM

IN THIS BOOK, I HAVE FOCUSED ON NORTH AMERICAN POACHING. There were numerous connections to North America with Operation Thunderstorm, a co-ordinated international effort against wildlife crime involving ninety-two countries and resulting in millions of dollars' worth of seizures. The operation, led by Interpol, included police and wildlife agencies from all ninety-two participating countries.

The one-month operation in 2016 brought 1,974 seizures and identified about 1,400 suspects worldwide. Resulting investigations will go on for years. The seizures included:

- 43 tonnes of wild meat, including bear, elephant, crocodile, whale and zebra
- 1.3 tonnes of processed elephant ivory
- 27,000 reptiles—alligators, turtles, snakes and crocodiles
- 4,000 birds
- 3 tonnes of wood and timber
- 48 live primates
- 14 large cats—tigers, lions, leopards and jaguars
- 7 bear carcasses, including two polar bears
- 8 tonnes of pangolin scales

Remember, the best estimates indicate that 1 per cent of poachers get caught. The above seizures were from a one-month operation!

During the operation, two flight attendants were caught smuggling live turtles in their luggage. A man was arrested in Israel after pictures he posted on social media led officers to his home and a seizure of foxes, jackals and mongooses. Canadian authorities seized a container with eighteen tonnes of frozen eel meat. The entire operation certainly confirmed the magnitude and organization of criminal activity in the wildlife trade.

Operation Thunderball, a similar one-month operation involving 109 countries, followed the one above. This operation identified six hundred suspects with:

- 23 live primates
- 30 big cats and parts
- 440 pieces of elephant ivory
- 5 rhino horns
- 4,300 birds
- 1,500 reptiles, plus ten thousand live turtles
- 7,700 wildlife parts
- 74 truckloads of timber
- 2,600 plants
- 10,000 marine items, including dolphins
- a half tonne of pangolin parts

Houston, we have a poaching problem.

INTERNATIONAL WILDLIFE CRIMESTOPPERS

INTERNATIONAL WILDLIFE CRIMESTOPPERS (IWC) IS A NON-PROFIT organization that has been around since 1998. It was founded by a group of dedicated wildlife officers with formative meetings in 1987, and eleven years later it was incorporated. The group's goal is to help stop poaching of North America's fish and wildlife resources. Eighty per cent of the fish and wildlife agencies from Canada and the United States participate in IWC. It holds an annual meeting to discuss the latest success stories and challenges, and to discuss new techniques to help everyone reduce the amount of poaching. It is supportive of legal hunting and fishing.

In addition, the organization promotes public education in the differences between sustainable harvest and poaching practices, and it encourages public involvement in catching poachers. It helps wildlife enforcement agencies interact to share information, helps fund agencies with specialized equipment and supports cash reward programs. The board of directors includes outdoor users, enforcement officers and some environmental enthusiasts. The head office is based in Blairsville, Georgia.

IWC relies on donations from generous contributors such as Bass Pro, Cabelas and the National Wild Turkey Federation. Many hunters, fishers and members of the general public also contribute to this worthwhile cause.

There have been very few actual studies of poaching numbers. A study in New Mexico in 1977 and one in Alberta in 1987 both showed that 99 per cent of poaching goes undetected. It's really scary to think that the amount of poaching described in this book alone is much less than 1 percent.

It is important that agencies and the public recognize the value of this organization. It becomes even more important as poachers continue to expand and pilfer our increasingly limited fish and wildlife stocks. Everyone can be a part of the solution by keeping their eyes open, recording suspicious behaviours and reporting these activities in a timely manner. Almost everyone carries a phone. Use it to gather information but do not try apprehend poachers. You should report any poaching to your local authorities as soon as possible to avoid delays. You can also go to www.wildlifecrimestoppers.com to report suspicious activity in any US state or Canadian province.

SAY WHAT?

"EXCUSE ME, SIR. I'D LIKE TO SEE YOUR *DUDLEYA*." THOSE ARE words that few have heard from a game warden—unless they've visited the coast of California. The *Dudleya farinosa* is commonly called bluff lettuce. It's a succulent plant found on the rocky, craggy coastline of California. It's not endangered yet; however, the rate of removal is causing concern for the California Department of Fish and Wildlife. North Americans like the cactus-like plant because it's small, attractive and requires very little attention, sort of like a cat but it doesn't vocalize.

A few years ago, California game warden Pat Freeling fielded a call from a disgruntled post office patron. She had waited in line behind a guy with dozens of large cardboard boxes he was shipping to China. She was anxious and tired of the long wait, and eventually asked what was in the boxes. The man pointed to the ocean and said they contained something valuable. The woman thought the boxes might contain abalone and she was concerned enough to report it.

Officer Freeling phoned the postal inspector to ask permission to use his detection canine to do a search for abalone. The inspector said he would have the boxes x-rayed by Customs and Border Protection. The postal inspector emailed him three weeks later, stating the boxes contained dozens of *Dudleya* plants. He also said they had a security video of the guy who mailed the plants. The sender of the packages was long gone. Freeling took the information and disseminated it to other offices. He also kept the information and the file open.

About a month later, he took a call regarding two Asian males climbing down a cliff with a backpack, with one of the men acting as a lookout. Freeling believed the call to be about abalone poachers. He immediately went to the location and found a man with a backpack

Officer Patrick Freeling of California snapped this selfie with eight hundred *Dudleya* plants seized from two Korean poachers in 2018. The plants would fetch thousands of dollars in Asia. *Photo: Patrick Freeling.*

containing about fifty *Dudleya* plants. The man claimed they were for his garden. Freeling told him bluntly, "I watched you on video from post office surveillance cameras shipping this plant species out of the country." The man eventually confessed that he was selling them to a buyer in Korea and getting between $10 and $50 per plant. The trip to court cost him $5,000, three years' probation and 240 hours of community service.

This seemingly rare occurrence was followed by another incident. Freeling was patrolling a secluded spot on the coast and came upon a van parked in an obscure location. The van was a rental and appeared to be packed with boxes. He crawled out on the bluff and caught the two men taking *Dudleyas* and putting them into backpacks. Escorting the two Korean men to their rented van, Freeling found it packed with over eight hundred plants destined for Korea and China. The two were charged with felonies, fined $10,000 each and given a two-year suspended prison sentence. The judge stated, "If you return here for committing any violation you will serve two years in jail."

These types of sentences are usually the result of a good investigator with agency support presenting facts to a good attorney who conveys the right message to a concerned, informed judge. Any successful prosecution requires every link along the way to be solid and united. Over a period of six months, the CDFW charged five different groups, seizing thousands of plants valued in the millions. Fortunately, most of these hardy plants were replanted with the assistance of volunteers.

Shortly after this California incident, one of these Korean poachers was captured in South Africa poaching another rare, sought-after succulent. He and his new partner were caught with over sixty thousand plants. They had flown to South Africa on a tourist visa, rented a car, driven into a remote region of Africa and stripped areas of the ancient plants. Plants were from 200 to 350 years old. The two poachers were fined 2.5 million rand each (about US$140,000), and each was given a six-year suspended sentence. South Africa had four convictions over a five-month period in 2019. Two Czech citizens and several Koreans were caught at different times. The one Korean is awaiting extradition to the United States to answer to his charges in California in the case above.

The continued survival of rare plants depends on the public being vigilant and willing to report suspected violators because so few poachers get caught. Nations have to work together and develop global laws whereby a conviction in one country is deemed a conviction in another, similar to the United States Wildlife Violator Compact. Countries could also remove passports from people like this fellow, who travels the world to poach. We need to try some new tools to keep up with the poachers. The current resources available to fish and wildlife agencies won't get the job done. Country leaders need to take notice and support their agencies through action and resources, not just words.

HUNTING FOR DUMMIES

Officer Brian Anthony of the AZGFD was patrolling the backcountry for the Arizona Forest Service to notify outdoor users about an impending fire closure. He stopped his vehicle when he heard some automatic weapon gunfire. That's not legal in Arizona, so he drove to where he'd heard the noise to investigate.

Three young men told Anthony they had been shooting guns with their buddy "Pyro." Pyro had placed an old tube television on the ground. He then put 3.6 kilograms of pyrotechnic explosives in a bucket on top of the television. The three Pyro wannabes stood back as Pyro approached the setup, stopped at about eighteen metres from it and fired a shot. The explosion ripped the side of his face off. The exploding shrapnel from the television even hit the three standing farther back.

If you're interested, Pyro survived. I had no idea my mother was right when she said, "Getting too close to the television can ruin your eyes."

A GOOD CRAPPIE DAY

MINNESOTA CONSERVATION OFFICER DUSTIN MILLER RECEIVED A TIP (Turn In Poachers) call from someone who had been fishing for crappies. The caller and his fishing partner had caught thirteen crappies between the two of them for the day (the legal limit is ten each), but they had seen another group catch more than one hundred fish. A vehicle description and licence number were also provided.

Officer Miller, along with another wildlife officer and a police officer, knocked on the door of the residence of the registered vehicle reported to them. They had noticed fishing gear in the car as they approached the house. The couple living there allowed the officers to enter and admitted they had fish in their freezers. They consented to a search and also admitted they knew the limit for crappies. A copy of the fishing synopsis was lying on their table. Maybe they knew the legal limit, but they certainly didn't know how to count. Officers found 253 crappies in the two freezers in the house. They also got a surprise when they opened a small bucket. The stench of rotting fish inside would have gagged a maggot. Apparently, the bucket contained some yellow bass that were being allowed to "ferment" for up to a year before making them into soup. The officers didn't ask to stay for lunch.

The couple were charged and fined $1,500, about half of the potential fine they could have been given. They were also allowed to keep their limit of crappies and their soup base.

POACHING TRAPPERS CAUGHT

HUMANE TRAPPING IS A REASONABLE USE OF OUR WILDLIFE resources, as much as fishing or hunting. Many may disagree with that, but fur has long been a valuable renewable resource. The fur trade is what opened up many parts of North America. Trappers who don't use the proper trapping methods, however, are just another type of poacher.

In 2014, Minnesota Department of Natural Resources game warden Kipp Duncan received a complaint about a wolf caught in a snare. It's unlawful to snare or sell wolves in that state. Trappers setting snares can avoid catching wolves and other larger animals through proper size and placement of the snare. Duncan checked the location and found the wolf in the snare still alive; it had been caught for several days and had been chewing on its leg. Taking out his newly acquired piece of technology, a cellphone, Duncan snapped his first-ever selfie with the wolf in the background. The date, time and place of the picture would become evidence. He then had to kill the wolf because its leg was too badly damaged. He looked around the immediate area and found ten or twelve other snares set. None of the snares conformed to state law, and he disabled them all. He decided to set up some surveillance of the area and see whether he could snare these poachers.

The next day, Duncan returned to the snare site with a USFWS officer and sat the entire day, waiting for the poacher to return. A real trapper is legally required to check snares daily. Duncan applied another piece of technology and put out a game camera. Calling the person who found the snared wolf, he promised, "I'll catch this guy. It might not be this week or next week, but I will catch him." He spent several days patrolling and walking the area near the snares looking for others, disabling each one as he found it but leaving them all out. He found another series of snares set up and put a camera on one snare at that location too. Weeks passed and the poacher never returned. The cameras and snares were pulled out at the end of the season.

The next year, another complaint came in about a similar snare setup eight kilometres from the first location. Cameras were set up on that site as well. Another game warden 160 kilometres away encountered yet another similar setup and this time captured a photo of the poacher on his camera. They took the poacher's photo to trappers and local events, but no one recognized him. Refusing to give up, they sent the picture to other officers in that region of the state. One warden responded that he'd found a snare setup similar to the others, but still no one came across the poacher (or poachers).

Two years later, a citizen reported finding a fox in a snare. Duncan checked it out and found the same type of setups. After putting out cameras, he eventually captured the licence number and got a picture of the poacher. To his surprise, Duncan recognized the thug. Thirteen years earlier, he had been caught in another investigation 160 kilometres away.

Armed with all the evidence, Duncan was able to acquire a tracking warrant to place a tracking device on the poacher's vehicle. On Christmas Eve in 2016, he went to the poacher's house to attach the tracker. I doubt Santa Claus wanted anything to do with this house. To attach the tracker, Duncan crawled under the vehicle, which was parked on a pile of stinky animal carcasses. A warden's work is not always rosy. The vehicle didn't move for two weeks. Duncan was working on another case when his tracker signalled that the poacher was on the move.

The tracking device revealed a much bigger problem than had first been identified. Two older guys, I'll call them "Statler" and

"Waldorf" (the grumpy old Muppet men in the balcony), had several snare routes set out. Officers traced their movements and located over six hundred snares in total! No one could possibly check six hundred snares daily, especially two old guys. The officers now had enough information and evidence to obtain search warrants for the two poachers. They also had enough evidence to search the facilities of a taxidermist who was likely laundering the furs.

With the evidence they seized during execution of the warrants, officers assembled a crew of thirty-one to locate and pull 632 snares. Warden Kipp Duncan had the pleasure of searching Waldorf's house, where he'd been with a search warrant in 2003 for similar trapping offences. When the officers knocked on the door, Waldorf yelled, "Get the #$%@#! away from my house, Duncan!" "I'll leave when I'm done," Kipp retorted. "I'll just keep catching you unless you stop." Duncan had caught the poacher twice and his father had caught him about thirty years earlier when he was a USFWS officer. Some poachers are so bad they will only stop if they get too old or die.

Thirty-one officers were brought in to clear all the snares as quickly as possible and finally put an end to their crimes. The GPS unit they seized had all the snare locations on it. Some animals had been eaten and nothing but bones were left. In the end, a total of eighteen foxes, five snowshoe hares, two fishers (fur-bearing animals smaller than an otter), two wolves and a deer were seized from the snares. Officers also released a couple of dogs caught in the snares.

Waldorf had previous trapping-related convictions from 2004, 2007 and 2013. Statler and Waldorf were given a fine of $2,585 each, plus a one-year revocation of their trapping licence. That seems a bit light for a third-time offence. No one knows how many animals these two clowns took with over six hundred snares over the years. The taxidermist received a $250 fine and a two-year loss of trapping privileges. It is highly likely the two were using the taxidermist to avoid detection of their illegal fur.

Some cases take a lot of luck to solve. I believe the more you work, the luckier you get. In this case the luck increased because of Warden Duncan's dogged determination to keep digging deeper, trying new technology and bringing the problem to other officers' attention.

HUNTING FOR DUMMIES

Wisconsin officer John W. Buss patrolled the local sturgeon fishery often. Some Russian immigrants loved to catch sturgeon just about as much as they loved their vodka. Fishing sturgeon is legal in Wisconsin, but you must not leave your line unattended. Buss came across a fishing line in the water that led into a tent on the beach. He pulled on the line. He pulled harder, dragging the passed-out drunk from the tent before the man even woke up. There really was a jerk on the end of the line.

In another incident, Buss came upon a passed-out fisherman with his line in the water. An empty vodka bottle was lying beside the man. Buss shook him to wake the man up. The drunken man finally jumped to his feet and, with a total reflex reaction, took a swing at Buss with his fist. Buss ducked away as the man spun around, losing what little balance he might have had, and fell into the river. Buss pulled the dunked drunk from the water and had a good laugh.

NIGHT RIDER

IN 2018 WILDLIFE OFFICER JEFF DAY WAS PATROLLING FOR deer-hunting activity near a heritage preserve in South Carolina. The 2.6 square kilometres of reserve is primarily for wood storks, but other birds and animals such as deer frequent it too. The area also has a bow-hunting season for deer. Poachers have been known to wander into the preserve, then slip onto adjoining private property belonging to hunting clubs, or to hunt at night within the reserve.

It was a Monday evening when Officer Day noticed a truck he was familiar with. He saw hunting gear and an empty bow case inside the cab. He waited until legal light had ended (one hour after sunset in South Carolina) before deciding to look for "Buddy" in the reserve. It was a bright, moonlit night. He walked about a kilometre before he found a bike hidden in some bushes. In the distance he could see a light up in the trees. Wood storks aren't known to carry spotlights, so he quietly worked his way closer to it, then switched on his flashlight. The spotlight immediately went off.

Day yelled for the guy to turn his light back on, adding, "I can sit here all night if you want!" The light came on and a voice said, "I'm so sorry, sir." A polite poacher is an uncommon thing. The man slithered down the tree with his crossbow. Day seized the bow, the spotlight, a battery pack, a deer stand (a metal ladder and chair attached to a tree) and other hunting equipment. He also found a razor blade in his search. The poacher said it was for his prescription drugs. He had amphetamine pills that he cut up, crushed and snorted up his nose. This, along with a bunch of Red Bull, was used to help him stay awake all night to hunt. His bow was equipped with a red light activated by a switch near the trigger of his crossbow. This was not Buddy's first rodeo. He was charged and put in jail.

Day continued to check the parking lot regularly. A week later he happened upon the same truck just as dusk fell. He followed the same trail but ended up much farther into the reserve. Buddy had hung his empty Red Bull cans in trees to mark the trail. He was like Hansel and Gretel with a trail of tin cans instead of crumbs. Using night goggles to find his way along the trail, Officer Day caught a red glow in the distance and quietly walked up to Buddy, who was fiddling with his bow. Day stood right under the tree stand and turned on his flashlight, and Buddy muttered, "Oh, #$%@#!" Day said, "Are we really doing this again?" Strike two for Buddy! Another bow, spotlight, battery pack, tree stand and gear were seized. Buddy was fired from his job when the boss found out he was using the company truck for poaching the second time.

A few weeks later, Officer Day decided to take his newly acquired patrol vehicle into the park. He had recently been given a Pedego electric bicycle with fat off-road tires for patrol work. The bike is capable of going thirty kilometres an hour and covering one hundred kilometres on a single battery charge, and is so quiet that Day has driven right past deer before they noticed him. He took the bike into the area where he'd caught Buddy to look for signs of activity. He found some Red Bull cans and figured the poacher might still be active.

It had been about a month since Buddy was caught the first time. Day donned his night goggles, hopped on the electric bike and started down the trail. He continued down the path past where he'd caught Buddy the two previous times, moving slowly and scanning the bushes for signs of his quarry. He spotted some Red Bull cans. He was getting warm. Glimpsing a red glow in the distance, he dismounted and moved slowly toward Buddy. But the poacher was a bit wiser this time. He wasn't in a tree stand, possibly because he didn't want to lose another one. Instead, he was walking the trail and scanning the bushes for deer. Day turned on his flashlight, and Buddy froze like the proverbial deer in the headlights. How fitting! Buddy, like most poachers, wasn't as bright as the flashlight he carried.

Officer Day walked up and arrested him for the third time in a month. Buddy was also hunting on private property this time, without permission. Day seized his third bow, another spotlight, battery pack and hunting gear.

Buddy had been convicted once before for using bait for turkey hunting. His excuse? "I didn't know the bait was there." This time, Buddy will have to face the judge in "big boy" court. He will likely get a most deserved time-out from hunting. He might even be in line for some frequent flyer points from the judge.

HUNTING FOR DUMMIES

After a Michigan bass poacher was reported to the state's DNR hotline, an officer drove to the area, but the culprit had vanished. Word went out on the radio, and an off-duty trooper spotted the getaway vehicle. How did he know it was the poacher? The fellow was riding a unicycle and carrying a backpack and fishing rod. The conservation officer caught up with the poacher a few blocks away, riding in the bicycle lane. The unicycle poacher did not try making a getaway. He admitted to not having a licence, fishing out of season and selling bass illegally. At least he was driving in the cycling lane.

THE GIFT THAT
KEEPS ON GIVING

THE EAST SLOPE OF THE CASCADE MOUNTAINS IN NORTH-CENTRAL Oregon is rich with wildlife resources. Many of the million people living ninety minutes away in the greater Portland area flock to this region during hunting season. They keep the Oregon state troopers hopping busy through fall hunting seasons lasting into early December. The troopers also have responsibility for river salmon fisheries including Treaty Tribal fisheries, allowing little time for patrolling outside of legal seasons to catch the worst poachers.

Senior trooper Craig Gunderson has worked in the area for years. Each fall, he finds or gets reports of headless deer found in the region after hunting season. He and fellow troopers tried a decoy operation and increased patrols, but the remoteness of the area made their success rate low. Then the Rocky Mountain Elk Foundation donated some much-needed new electronic surveillance equipment. It had been out for only three days when a headless deer was reported in the area of interest. A review of the equipment revealed evidence of a truck and poachers out spotlighting. They found still more evidence at another location near where a truck had stopped; a headless deer was lying a hundred metres away in the bush. Their suspects were from Washington, so Gunderson relayed this information to the Washington Department of Fish and Wildlife.

Gunderson had trooper Jason Walters, who was new to the fish and wildlife division, with him on this day. Shortly after finding the deer, they encountered the suspected vehicle on the road. They pulled the truck over and found guns, spotlights and deer hair inside it. When Gunderson interviewed the driver, "Billy" rolled over like a well-trained dog. The evidence presented to him caused a total admission of guilt for the headless deer. Billy even apologized!

Billy kept glancing at his phone, and Gunderson grew suspicious. He asked whether the poacher had a picture of the deer on his phone, but Billy at first denied it. He explained that he didn't want to hand his phone over to the trooper because he had pictures of his not-so-shy girlfriend on it. Finally, after more pressure from Gunderson, he admitted that he did have a picture. He showed Gunderson a photo of fourteen deer racks laid out on the floor and said, "It's the third one from the left." He claimed they were all his buddies' deer and he was doing Euro-mounts (skull only) for them.

From the size of all the antlers in the picture, Gunderson suspected that they all came from his patrol region and were not the Washington black-tailed deer that Billy claimed. (He believed that because his area has hybrid black-tailed/mule deer with larger antlers than those found in Washington.) Billy's phone started buzzing and Gunderson recognized the name on the call display as a known poacher from the Washington area. The phone kept buzzing and Billy kept silencing it. Gunderson also talked to another guy in the truck who had followed the same poaching pathways in life. "Bobby" squealed like slick tires on hot pavement. They both signed consent forms and gave up their phones.

Gunderson looked through the pictures to find a dead squirrel and numerous bear, deer, elk, bobcat and mountain lion kills. It was also evident from the pictures that these poachers were using hunting hounds for hunting bears and mountain lions (using hounds is legal only for bobcats in Oregon). He called the Washington officers and arranged to hand the poachers over to them that night, after which they could follow them home to seize the animals. The Washington officers did just that and came away with twenty-eight deer heads, an elk and the grey squirrel that evening alone.

Both Washington and Oregon officers did parallel investigations and worked together to discover the locations of violations, identify more suspects and determine which charges would be most suitable. It took several months to analyze all the data on the phones and prepare more warrants.

The big warrant swoop involved about fifty Washington wildlife enforcement officers and six Oregon fish and wildlife troopers for the simultaneous search of seven residences and two taxidermists' facilities. More wildlife and phones were seized. After the search, they had twenty-three suspects with about 130 animals seized. It would take another eighteen months to look at all the evidence and determine charges; ultimately, nearly two hundred charges were laid by Oregon officers and about the same number in Washington. The phones revealed some disturbing text messages between poachers about how they could "take out" one of the Washington officers who'd caught one of them with a bear violation earlier. One bright poacher had gotten rid of his old phone and just transferred his contacts onto the new one. He was clear!—except that he'd transferred a bunch of data unintentionally (he was no relation to Bill Gates).

The rats started ratting on each other too. One of the accused called an officer and asked whether they'd found the six animals that another of the accused, "Benny," had removed from his house and stored at "Jack's" house. The officers immediately went to investigate, and that tip resulted in another visit to Benny. "How about those six mounts you have stored over at Jack's house?" asked the officer. They went over to Jack's and filled another pickup.

Warrants and information kept branching off to unearth new poachers. Three officers decided to try a cold call on a taxidermist who was implicated in only a single text to Billy that said, "Your bear is ready." They knocked on the taxidermist's door and were greeted by "Jim." "It's about time you guys showed up," Jim said. "I guess you came for the elk?" The officers thought, *What elk?* but displayed no surprise, and one of them said smoothly, "Yes." Jim showed them five bull elk mounts, all taken illegally. "What about the bear for Billy?" an officer said. Jim replied, "Oh, I'll show you that too." He took them around back to see a chainsaw carving of a bear he'd made for Billy. It was a good day for the officers. They'd arrived to ask about one text that referenced a piece of carved wood and came away with another five poached elk. If Jim ever reads this book he might be a bit embarrassed. It's okay, Jim. If you read this entire book, you'll find you're much smarter than most poachers.

Officers inspected a sample of thirty of the hundreds of known kill sites, some over two years old. They recovered evidence from twenty-seven of those thirty sites, with items such as bones, hair, skulls, shell casings and more.

The main poachers received lifetime hunting bans, fines and restitution ranging from hundreds to thousands of dollars, plus up to a year in jail. All firearms, hound-hunting equipment, hound boxes, vehicles and anything related to the violations were seized for forfeiture. In addition, they were given immunity to further charges up to that date if they gave unconditional statements about any and all people related to the evidence the officers had. Those statements led to more seizures and arrests. A memorable seizure was a big buck on the bedroom wall of one of the poachers. His buddy had told the officers, "Take that one too—I was with him when he poached that one." A full-body mount of a mountain goat that was taken on a poacher's wife's tag was also seized. She'd never been hunting. The final total was about three hundred animals seized, all because of some donated surveillance equipment and some great investigative work by Oregon State Police and Washington DFW officers.

The poachers received more than the penalties above. They were vilified in local media all over the state. They even received death threats for their actions. Yet another case involving bobcats resulted in another seizure of three bobcats. The poacher's fable imploded when some witnesses turned on him. And thanks to the Rocky Mountain Elk Foundation, the electronics were truly the gift that keeps on giving.

RHODE ISLAND TAUTOG

THE TAUTOG IS A SALTWATER FISH FOUND ONLY ON THE EAST coast of North America. It's not a pretty fish but it tastes great. Historically, it was considered a "trash" species until the 1970s, when its popularity took off and created a whole new fishery. Over 90 per cent of the harvest was and still is a recreational fishery. As often happens with desirable species, the popularity rises, the stocks are targeted, the stocks are depleted, restrictions are implemented and game wardens are expected to save them from poachers.

The tautog populations in the Rhode Island and Massachusetts area are less than a third of what they once were. Once they became less available, the price rose—it's now over $22/kilo retail—and poaching increased because of the value of the fish. Atlantic States Marine Fisheries Commission records show a peak catch of 9.8 million kilos in 1986, before a fish management plan was implemented in 1996. Since then, the catch has dropped to 1.54 million kilos in 2018. The management plan and stock recovery will only be as good as the enforcement efforts to control the poaching.

Rhode Island Department of Environmental Management (DEM) officers often patrol the waters of Narragansett Bay, checking recreational tautog fishers. Fishers catch the tautog with rod and reel using bait such as green crab to fish the rock outcroppings in nine to eighteen metres of water. Once a vessel locates the right spot, the fish can be caught fairly easily. The DEM has implemented a unique boat limit to avoid a boatload of people fishing in one spot and catching too many fish. The daily limit is six fish per person; however, the vessel limit is ten fish, no matter how many people are on board.

In October of 2019, while officers were patrolling the known tautog area, they approached a vessel with four people on board fishing. When they climbed onto the boat, they could see tautogs on the deck, in buckets and in coolers. They gathered up all the fish and counted forty-six tautogs—thirty-six over the limit of ten. The minimum size limit was sixteen inches, and forty-one were undersized. This is a glaring example of people who just don't care about protecting the resource. They often have the singular mindset of "gotta get some before they're all gone." The master of the vessel was charged and sent to court. He paid $600 in fines.

Although the tautog is highly sought-after by high-end restaurants in places like New York, these particular fish were forfeited and given to Amos House, a homeless shelter in Providence. Hopefully, efforts to rebuild the tautog stocks, supported by adequate enforcement and a willing public, will continue.

WILD GINSENG

WILD GINSENG IS FOUND IN EASTERN NORTH AMERICA FROM Ontario down to Louisiana. Ginseng plants survive only in large colonies of 175 to 200 plants in undisturbed forests. If a poacher removes most of the plants, that patch will likely be gone forever. Urban development is another threat to wild ginseng when mature forests are levelled for development.

Ginseng has been used in traditional Asian medicine for centuries. Unlike things like rhino horn and tiger bone, ginseng has been proven to be effective in treating a number of ailments. It has been used to control metabolism to reduce obesity, help repair heart damage, control glucose levels, prevent kidney damage, serve as an anti-inflammatory and reduce aging. Asians have classified some varieties of ginseng as *hot* and *cool* ginseng. They believe the woody root of hot ginseng can even cure erectile dysfunction. The North American variety is classified as cool and does not help with erectile dysfunction. First Nations have also used the plant for centuries to fight headaches, earaches, bleeding, fevers, vomiting, tuberculosis and gonorrhea.

Ginseng was second only to the fur trade to the economy in early colonization of the future lands of Canada. Many settlers turned to harvesting ginseng and even started farming it in the 1800s. This cash crop expanded over the years, making Canada the largest exporter of cultivated ginseng in the world. Why, then, is the wild plant poached?

Despite many attempts to synthesize or cultivate wild plants (or animals), the market prefers the wild version. One reason is that cultivated ginseng is subjected to chemicals and fertilizers, just like most other farmed crops. Cultivated ginseng must be harvested within three or four years. If it's left in the ground longer than that, it is susceptible to disease and fungus. Wild ginseng is generally free of disease, fungus and fertilizers and can take many years to grow, giving it more twisted, gnarly roots that are more desirable. A ginseng root shaped like a person with arms and legs can be worth thousands. I shouldn't be critical, but that's just goofy—go buy some animal crackers. Asian cultures prefer Canadian wild ginseng because they believe the air, water and earth are cleaner than in the United States. They also claim it tastes better.

Ginseng used to be legal to harvest in Ontario. Laws changed in 2008 as ginseng patches were disappearing due to overharvesting and poaching. Harvesting ginseng on federal lands has been banned since 2002. As often happens, making something illegal just drives the price up and attracts the more serious criminals.

Environment and Climate Change Canada (ECCC) wildlife officers in the Ontario region and provincial partners on federal land were using a technique to mark the roots of wild ginseng plants with an ultraviolet dye. The dyed roots would make them identifiable if poachers were caught after taking the plants. ECCC officers once found evidence of illegal harvesting when they located holes in the ground where ginseng plants had been removed. The poachers had even plucked the top of the plant off and stuck it back in the ground, attempting to hide their poaching ways. The only clue in the area was an empty pack of DK cigarettes. ECCC and the Ministry of Natural Resources and Forestry, having a joint interest in the ginseng population, investigated together to catch the thieves. They set up motion-sensor cameras and patrolled the area regularly to try to catch the bandits.

One day, they located a truck parked in a wooded area. There on the seat of the truck sat a pack of DK cigarettes. They waited to see who showed up. Two poachers stumbled out of the forest, each carrying a backpack filled with a total of 253 wild ginseng roots worth thousands of dollars. They were convicted and fined $5,000 and $4,000 each and barred from going near the area for ten years. Unfortunately, that won't begin to stop the poaching. Poachers can pay those fines with a handful of plants. In another investigation they seized 587 ginseng roots along with $7,680 cash.

Wild ginseng is not protected in many states in the US. The plant populations are being decimated to the point where poachers are travelling into parks and protected areas to find them. This presents a challenge if officers encounter anyone with ginseng plants. Legitimate owners have to prove the plants came from a location where they are not protected.

It's difficult to convince some folks, including judges, how important it is to protect all endangered plants and animals. Officer Dubois of ECCC once stated, "This is our ivory. It's a plant. It doesn't bleed and it doesn't cry, but it's in danger of extinction here in Canada." Public education is key to the plant's survival. Who knows what future remedy the plant might hold? There is no excuse for allowing them to become extinct.

NORTHERN CANADIAN CARIBOU POACHED

HUNTING CARIBOU IN NORTHERN CANADA HAS LONG BEEN A sensitive topic that few are willing to discuss. Many herds are at a fraction of their historical levels. The Bathurst herd has dropped from 470,000 to 8,000 in the past thirty years. Many experts claim to have the answers. Climate change, exploration, mine development, roads, wolves, local hunters and outside hunters have all been blamed, and all have had a part in the caribou herd reductions.

The population decline isn't a new problem either. Woodland caribou herds in northern Saskatchewan and Manitoba were dwindling in the 1950s. The two provincial governments and the Canadian government conducted an ambitious plan to study the caribou herd. Six men were hired to follow the herd for an entire year. They followed the herd north into the Northwest Territories to the spring calving grounds and followed their return south the next fall. The team lived with the caribou. They travelled by plane, canoe, dogsled and on foot. These were not your average biologists or outdoorsmen. No conclusive reasons were found for the caribou population declines. Seventy years later, we still don't really know all the answers.

Today, there is poaching of caribou by residents of the North. It's not the only reason for their decline, but it has had an impact, and after all, this book is about poaching. In the 1950s a woodland caribou river crossing in northern Saskatchewan was known to have been the location of some horrendous caribou slaughters. Locals had been introduced to firearms capable of firing many successive rounds. It was reported that some indiscriminate "harvesters" shot at herds of caribou, cut the tongues out of the animals they hit and left the rest. In the spring, the beach was covered with caribou bones where the event had taken place.

Fast-forward to this century and we still find some large numbers of caribou taken by individuals from the North. I talked to an Indigenous person working for the Northwest Territories government in 2013, while I was vacationing there. He shared that he'd witnessed several indiscriminate harvests by locals and was appalled at some of the slaughters he observed. Some hunters would shoot into the herd, only stopping when their guns were too hot to continue shooting. Some wounded animals stumbled away because the person was too busy dealing with the thirty-plus animals he'd shot and killed. One person cannot properly process that number of animals and many were left to waste. People in the North have to solve this issue.

Environment and Natural Resources wildlife officers have a daunting task to patrol the vast open lands where caribou live. The Northwest Territories have an area of 1.346 million square kilometres. Ian Ellsworth spent over twenty years working in the North in all three northern territories, including the Yukon and Nunavut. He described some of the patrols they did.

On one patrol in April 2013, he and another local patrolman hopped on their snowmobiles for the seven-hour ride to join two more officers for a patrol. They stayed overnight, then embarked on a week-long journey checking for caribou hunters. There were no hotels, restaurants or gas stations along the way. The sleds pulled behind were filled with fuel, food and tents. In April it is still −20° Celsius overnight, so you'd better have a good sleeping bag.

During that patrol, they found about fifty caribou shot and left to decay. Some had hindquarters removed and some had been left whole. One area had thirty-five dead animals with most of the meat left behind. The only hunters up there were locals; this was not anyone from the outside world. Officers investigated and eventually charged a local chief and two others with twelve counts of wasting meat. They admitted to shooting the caribou but claimed they had met another group of three hunters and told them to take all the meat they wanted. The other three took only what they wanted and the rest was left to waste. A fine of $575 was paid by one of the individuals.

One of the most tragic parts about most of these incidents is that the wastage is not created by young hunters. It's often the older community members shooting and doing the wasting. Many hunters will just shoot into the herd and take what drops. In times when the caribou are plentiful, large numbers are shot and often only the hindquarters are taken. The poachers will sometimes dry the meat and sell it to other northerners.

Ellsworth and other officers have tried to work with the hunters to reduce the wastage. Officers have even tried to set up a gun range and provide free ammunition to teach hunters how to shoot accurately. It shouldn't have to come to that, but they are desperate to try something to stop the appalling waste.

In 2018 in Iqaluit, Nunavut, ten caribou were shot illegally after the quota was reached. The community as a whole was restricted to harvesting twenty-five caribou and had already reached that quota. The caribou herds in the area have decreased by 95 per cent since the 1990s. It's especially difficult for these remote residents who have lived off caribou for generations to see their main source of food dwindling away, yet it's partly due to their own wasteful hunting.

I talked to Earl Evans, a long-time Métis caribou hunter from Fort Smith, Northwest Territories. He's the chair of the Beverly Qamanirjuaq Caribou Management Board that was established in 1982 to co-manage the Beverly and Qamanirjuaq herds. It's a reputable board working hard to save the caribou.

Evans has seen the problems with wastage of caribou numerous times. He and some fellow hunters once set up a hunting camp, and a group of hunters from the Fort Ray area set up beside them. The other camp was elders and youth on a cultural training camp, teaching the youth how to hunt and prepare the animals for dry-ing. Evans found and followed some drag marks in the snow that led to two whole caribou with only the tongues removed. When he questioned an elder about the waste, he was told that the caribou were too skinny, so they'd set traps beside the two caribou carcasses. The elder explained that the other animals would feed on the cari-bou and return in future years. This traditional knowledge would have worked years ago, but the drastic reduction in caribou numbers means there is much work ahead to change traditions.

Evans witnessed another example of wastage while hunting along one of the new diamond mine roads that have opened up the North to vehicle traffic. An elder was drying caribou in a tent while a younger man was shooting and bringing the caribou back to camp. Evans found a pile of eight or ten caribou covered with snow behind the tent. The hunter said they didn't have enough fat on them to smoke so they were being left. It's important not to jump to the first conclusion and condemn these people, because they do care about the caribou. They are only doing what was acceptable long ago. It's up to everyone to work together to change the thinking. Earl Evans has certainly taken on the challenge. In this last example, he took the time to talk to the hunter and the elder to educate and offer a better way. The hunter and elder quit the practice after that. It's not always that easy, but it's people like Evans who offer hope.

Evans and another Métis hunter, Fred Hudson, suggested a video be made to show how to hunt properly and without waste. It was a great idea, and in 2002 they were the ones who eventually made the video. In it, they demonstrate how to sight in a gun, how to pick an animal to shoot, where to shoot to reduce the waste, and how to dress the animal and care for it. Evans had witnessed caribou being dragged for many kilometres in crusty snow where half the meat on the animal had been scraped off before getting back to camp. The video talks about proper sleighs to transport animals. The video was given out to every hunter for years and still is.

Some locals blamed the outside "southern" hunters for caribou poaching and declining numbers in one particular area. After those complaints, hunting was closed to outsiders and only locals could hunt. But Evans saw the wastage continue. He has spoken to many groups in the North and is often criticized for being outspoken about the subject. However, some elders approach him after his talks and thank him for raising the concerns and offering solutions. We need more Earl Evanses in the North.

Pressures for exploration, mine development and ship travel through the Northwest Passage will all be critical factors that impact the herd's future. Those working for wildlife agencies in the North have a daunting task ahead of them to work with locals to find solutions. If the caribou lose, everyone loses.

HUNTING SHOW BLUNDER

IN 2019, A POPULAR HUNTING SHOW HOST ON THE OUTDOOR Channel was convicted of serious hunting violations from 2013. Back then, Mr. "Black," who lived in Illinois, was filming a white-tailed deer hunt in Indiana and shot at a respectable-sized buck. All was good until a huge white-tail stepped out a few minutes later. The larger deer was also shot and dropped in its tracks.

What would he do? His cameraman put his own deer tag on the smaller buck. Many months later, Black decided to cover his dirty tracks. He told his cameraman and producer to hide the footage of his smaller buck.

In this case, Officer Steve Beltran of the Illinois Department of Natural Resources, a technical wizard, found some suspicious photos involving Black online. Officer Beltran subscribed to the Outdoor Channel and found more evidence against Black on the show's website. The statute of limitations had passed; however, an Illinois wildlife law states that it is illegal to possess wildlife that was taken during a violation. Since the TV show host had shot a deer in Indiana, Beltran called in the Indiana DNR.

Two years had passed since the deer had been shot. Just before charges were filed, Black told an employee to destroy the eight-point rack from the first deer he'd shot. He must have thought that would cover things off.

Officers from both state agencies and the USFWS visited Black at his residence. Black was reminded that lying to officers was a federal offence and Martha Stewart was used as an example. (I wonder whether Martha knows how to cook venison.) Black started turning white and fessed up to the crime. He left and returned shortly after with the large buck. The officers seized the buck and invited him to court. Black was sentenced to thirty months' probation, during which time he was not allowed to hunt anywhere in the world. He also paid a total of $30,000 in fines and restitution. His show was cancelled and his sponsors were let go.

In this case, I decided to try contacting the accused in the story. I have to give Mr. Black credit for even taking my call. Not many poachers would do that. His story was that when he'd shot at the first respectable deer, all the other deer had scattered from the field. He could then see none from his high point in the tree stand and assumed he'd missed. He did agree he'd made a mistake by not going down from the stand and checking the area for blood. Moments later, the larger deer stepped out. He shot it and it dropped where it stood. A day and a half later, he and the cameraman returned to finish filming in the area. The cameraman found a blood trail and followed it to a dead deer that happened to be the first deer Black had shot. The cameraman had his own tag, so the deer was tagged and taken. If that was truly what had happened and the two had reported the incident right away, the outcome might well have been different.

In Mr. Black's case, he felt he was targeted because of his celebrity status and being held to a higher standard. He said even the judge stated that. While that may have been true, the standard is the law. Mr. Black complained that his twenty-plus years of reputable hunting had been tarnished and thirty months' prohibition from hunting was excessive. He also felt the Lacey Act allows too much latitude for investigating officers to use old legislation designed for more serious cases. He was confident a certain president's son would change those laws that gave wardens too much power.

He argued that a better sentence would have been for him to use his celebrity status and his television show to talk about the importance of learning the laws in every jurisdiction people hunt in. He said he could have made a video in which he would publicly apologize for his bad decision. If this had been part of his sentence, he said, he could get the right message out and help enforcement officers by educating his viewers. It was a great suggestion, and there's nothing stopping him from doing that on his own if he truly believes it. Rather than claim the laws are too strict, he could embrace them and support the officers that enforce them. Now that would be worth watching.

HUNTING FOR DUMMIES

Arizona Game and Fish officers were watching a known snake poacher—known to capture wild snakes and breed them. They had records showing he'd sold nearly four hundred snakes of one species. He had made about $60,000 selling illegal reptiles. The officers on surveillance saw the man come out of the house with a blue tote, get in his car and drive around the neighbourhood three or four times. They thought he might be doing a "heat check" (looking for authorities). The officers had intended to do a search that evening anyway, so one of them approached the poacher and asked what he was doing. He said, "I'm taking my two Gila monsters for a drive to try to stimulate copulation." Apparently, it works! It would appear some reptiles are similar to humans—the drive to reproduce often occurs in the back seat of a car.

MONSTER BUCK
IN MINNESOTA

OFTEN, A POACHER'S TROPHY BECOMES A WILDLIFE OFFICER'S BIG-gest case. Lieutenant Tyler Quandt of Minnesota's Department of Natural Resources had one of those career cases in 2009. He'd been a conservation officer for eighteen years at the time. Tips began coming in about a monster white-tailed buck taken with a bow by Mr. "Rank," and the tipsters told a much different story from the poacher's claim.

A couple of days after the deer was reported, Quandt and a fellow officer showed up to question Mr. Rank. It didn't take many questions before Quandt's Pinocchio meter went off. Rank initially claimed he shot the deer with a bow during archery season. Then he claimed he found it. That wasn't entirely false. He probably found it right after he shot it with a rifle while spotlighting at night from his truck window. If he had taken it with a bow, the deer would have been a world record score for an eight-point typical buck. The officers had enough legal grounds to seize several deer from Rank that day.

Officers then visited the taxidermist who had the cape from the big deer. The hide was to be tanned for mounting. Upon inspection, the hide appeared to have an odd-looking arrow hole in it, and forensic analysis later revealed evidence of bullet fragments in it. Investigators concluded someone had shoved an arrow through the bullet hole to make it appear as if it had been shot with a bow. Rank's attempted trickery in the story turned into the officer's treat.

More tips and information and investigating resulted in two follow-up warrants being served. The officers were looking for any rifles Rank might have, plus his cellphone. At the time of the search, Rank did not have any firearms in the residence where he was staying, but they did take his cellphone. Other officers assisted with more interviews, completing the investigation. Charges were laid against Rank. He pled guilty to illegal possession of the large buck and for failing to register a doe he had also taken. He was sentenced to 245 days in jail, a five-year hunting ban, $2,158 in fines and restitution, plus forfeiture of a bow used on another deer. He actually had to serve the entire 245 days in jail.

After the ordeal, like many who plead guilty, Rank then went on saying how innocent he was. Stories told outside the courtroom are just that—stories. Prior to the conviction, he'd been on probation for domestic assault and could not possess a firearm, and he claimed he hadn't had a gun since then. He also claimed he found the deer and wanted to cash in on the sale of the antlers. His lies were an initial attempt to appear to have taken the buck legally. I guess his financial luck was worse than his hunting luck. This poaching incident has made Rank a disliked man among the majority of legal hunters following the rules.

The deer had a Boone and Crockett net score of 185 and grossed just over 190 points. It belongs to the state of Minnesota. Half a dozen replicas have been made. Large trophies like this often end up being part of a "wall of shame" in agency educational trailers.

KENTUCKY POACHING
DERBY

A 5,500-HECTARE HUNTING PRESERVE WAS LOCATED ALONG THE Ohio River in Kentucky and owned by a hunting firearm manufacturer at the time of this story, in 2006–07. The company operated the hunting preserve under the name "Poachers R Us" (PRUS). The previous owners had used a local draw system to manage the deer herd and allowed the harvest of does. The gun company had formerly leased the property but found the management style interfered with their filming of big buck hunts, so they purchased it, giving them total control. They managed the property with the advice of a game management firm, which required them to provide harvest information and jawbones of deer taken. The jawbones were sent away and analyzed as part of the management plan.

Ultimately, this data alerted authorities through the state's harvest information system. A state deer biologist had noticed numerous irregularities when he compared state deer harvest data (on a system called Telecheck) with the information PRUS provided to the management company. This information was brought to the attention of Kentucky conservation officer Randy Conway. The PRUS property straddled an adjoining county, so Officer Conway contacted his neighbouring officer to analyze data from his area for the same time period.

The two officers spent weeks analyzing hundreds of tags and related information. They cross-checked PRUS data with the social security numbers of guests and the dates they were in camp. The officers then contacted and interviewed dozens of people, then spent many more hours on computers checking *that* information. These types of investigations require a great deal of patience. The officers ultimately found people were taking over their limit of deer, supplying false information and illegally transporting deer across borders.

They uncovered that Poachers R Us and its manager were getting company workers, friends and family to use the social security numbers of PRUS's guests to acquire extra tags (without their knowledge) to shoot more does. Why? Because they wanted fewer does on the property but didn't want to open it up to a draw system. The wealthy owner could afford to be selfish and break the law. PRUS and the property manager were fined a total of $50,000.

The best news since this violation occurred is that the Kentucky Department of Wildlife and some partners purchased over half of the property and converted it into a wildlife management area that is now open to the public. Other private individuals purchased the rest of the property, also using it to operate a business of guiding hunters.

HUNTING FOR DUMMIES

Oregon State Police and wildlife authorities were searching a poacher's home by warrant when the poacher pulled into the driveway. The driver and his sixteen-year-old son were wearing camouflage clothing and had three rifles in the truck along with a bunch of hunting gear. That might not have been so bad, but driving with camouflage and hunting gear in February is like waving a red flag. They were charged for a handful of offences including taking deer out of season.

WRESTLING WISCONSIN CHEATERS

WISCONSIN HAS A STRONG HISTORY OF PRODUCING GOOD WREST-lers and big white-tailed deer. (There might be a connection between natural protein and strong wrestlers.) Mr. "Skippy" was a landowner with about eight hundred hectares of prime deer habitat. His sons had been high-level wrestlers coached by the father of Mr. "Lawless." Mr. Lawless was a young hunting outfitter with a successful business in illegal hunting. Lawless brought in the hunters and Skippy provided the great property to hunt on, like a tag team of crooks.

DNR officer Dave Youngquist had been getting bits and pieces of information about illegal hunting activity on Skippy's property, which was located in his patrol area. Fellow DNR officers Mike Nice and John Buss were veteran officers in the agency and knew something was up with the Lawless operation. Through discussions with Officer Youngquist, they determined that Lawless was using bait for deer, hunting at night and committing a host of other violations. He was hunting well back and away from any public roads, making it difficult to monitor his actions. They wrestled with how they would handle the case, finally decided they needed some help, and invited the USFWS and other agency officers to work on the case with them. This case was initiated in 2002 and ended in 2005. The actual under-cover operation was less than a year.

The investigators learned that Lawless attended Rocky Mountain Elk Foundation banquets with large deer head mounts to help attract a steady clientele of hunters interested in a chance at a big buck. Lawless didn't seem to care about the law much. He baited the deer with truckloads of corn. He baited at exactly the same time each day to condition the deer to feeding time. He could then put hunters in locations where he knew the deer would pass as they came for the bait. His guests also hunted at night with spotlights from a stand or from a vehicle. Legal hunting seasons didn't seem to be important to him and most of his customers. Tags were not always needed. He would operate for over two months after the season closed! He kept a lid on things by focusing primarily on out-of-state customers with deep pockets.

During their investigation, a rare concerned hunting guest of Lawless called Officer Buss of the DNR to report he'd shot a turkey illegally with Lawless and he didn't agree with the unlawful tactics used by this outfitter. Shortly after, a plan was implemented whereby an undercover officer was brought in to hunt with Lawless. He was encouraged to and did shoot his deer at midnight as directed by Lawless. The officer also witnessed multiple violations by other hunters. It was decided that they had more than enough evidence to charge a number of poaching guests and, of course, Lawless.

Rather than continue working directly on Lawless, officers decided to do simultaneous searches in eleven different states on over sixty people they had gathered evidence on, all related to the Lawless case. The dragnet included a sheriff (who lost his job after the bust), an attorney and doctors, to name a few. The searches resulted in over thirty head mounts being seized along with guns, bows, turkeys and a fully mounted large alligator. That was probably the first large alligator ever seized in Wisconsin! Lawless had illegally traded a Florida alligator hunt for a deer hunt. Both Lawless and the Florida poacher were charged.

Officers Nice and Buss had the pleasure of knocking on Lawless's door at 5:00 a.m. for the search. A bit bleary-eyed after a long night of partying, the man nonetheless quickly realized his goose was cooked and he talked and talked and talked. He made the officers breakfast and talked some more. The officers made lunch and they talked some more. Lawless had a phenomenal photographic memory.

The officers would mention a hunter's name and he would describe the person, when he had hunted, what he got and where he got it in absolute detail. He showed them his Rolodex file of all his guests. The officers continually relayed this information to other officers, who conducted searches at the other properties. Thirteen and a half hours later, they were done. Officer Buss had written forty-two pages during the interview.

Some might suggest that amount of time was too long and unfair for an interrogation. But the fact was that Lawless wanted to talk. The experienced officers obviously made him feel very comfortable and he kept going. It's important to treat the poacher with respect, no matter what they have done. But if the poacher acts like an idiot, the rules may change. The officers' great work was evidently appreciated by Lawless. Shortly before his court appearance, Lawless's father visited Officer Nice at his residence. Nice had never met the man but he too wanted to talk. He told Nice that his son wanted to see both officers before he went to prison. He felt no animosity toward the officers. He said his son had told him that "the officers couldn't have treated me any better." He wanted to thank them.

Most of the fifty people charged were convicted of their own crimes, and Lawless was sentenced to two years in jail, paid $63,300 in fines and restitution and was given a three-year ban on any hunting and fishing in any state after his release. Skippy, however, got off much lighter. Neighbours were unhappy that his probation did not exclude hunting, and he continued to bring in hunters from out of state after the convictions.

Well after the case ended, Officer Buss was at home and received a collect call from the federal prison in Minnesota. It was none other than Mr. Lawless, and he just wanted to thank John again for the way he'd been treated by the officers. Talking to both Nice and Buss, it became obvious to me that these two officers shared an amazing passion and skill for interviewing people. They'd worked together for years and knew each other's every move. And most importantly, they understood that everyone wants to tell their story, even the bad guys.

Years later, Officer Nice was on a river patrol when a fisherman on the shore waved him over. It was none other than Mr. Lawless. They talked for a long time. Lawless thanked him again. He said he had a full-time job and a full-time lady and had his life in order. He said he'd never get involved in such activity again. There's no doubt his fair treatment from the officers throughout the process had given the young man the right impression and may have influenced him to turn his life around and start making the right decisions. Those kinds of moments don't make it into the file or onto the stat sheet, but they should.

When the two officers were telling me their story, they both spoke of how absolutely exhausted they were while walking down the driveway after the thirteen-and-a-half-hour interview. They'd put everything into the case, especially that interview. They both remembered shedding some tears, knowing they'd finally completed the job. Hats off to Officers Nice and Buss and to everyone that was part of the biggest bust in Wisconsin's history.

AN OFFICER'S WORST NIGHTMARE

LIEUTENANT WAYNE SAUNDERS WAS A CONSERVATION OFFICER with the New Hampshire Fish and Game Department for twenty-three years before retiring in 2018. He encountered his first game warden when he was six years old, while hunting grouse with his father. Wayne called the officer "the cowboy in the woods." He wanted to be one of those cowboys someday, and he eventually became one.

As a conservation officer, he also became involved in search and rescue operations and provided backup for local and state police when needed. Lieutenant Saunders had been on the job for two years when he received an urgent call on the radio. An armed and dangerous suspect had stolen a police car and was in the area. When Saunders happened upon the stolen car, the suspect immediately turned around and Saunders was in hot pursuit. The car drove under a train bridge and suddenly stopped. Saunders was close behind and followed him. The suspect had stopped under the underpass and set up an ambush. He levelled an AR-15 rifle at Saunders and fired before the officer had a chance to move. The bullet ripped through his windshield, then ricocheted off his badge and passed through his shoulder. In a hail of bullets, Saunders reversed his car and crashed into the Connecticut River. The suspect took off and left Saunders in his car in the river.

Lieutenant Saunders later learned that the murderer had shot and killed two of his friends, troopers Scott Phillips and Leslie Lord. He had shot Leslie Lord before he'd even gotten out of his patrol car. He'd shot Scott Phillips beside his police cruiser, then stolen the cruiser and driven to the local judge's office. He had hunted down

Conservation officer Wayne Saunders's badge (on the left) saved his life in 1997 from a murderer who killed a judge and two officers before Saunders encountered him. *Photo: Wayne Saunders.*

Judge Vickie Bunnell and shot her in the back as she tried to run away. She died instantly. Judge Bunnell had often carried a gun in self-defence of the killer, whom she'd dealt with before. The editor of the local newspaper had seen the man shoot the judge. He had tried to tackle the six-foot-four madman but failed. He too was shot and killed.

The killer had driven to his residence in the stolen police car, set his own house on fire, then taken off before encountering Saunders. The man's killing spree ended when he drove to a remote, treed area and set up an ambush. He managed to wound three more officers before he was finally killed.

It took investigators several days to sift through the ashes and property of the killer. There were a number of booby traps, six rifles, eighty-six pipe bombs and casings from a grenade launcher. This animal was not a poacher and such an event is rare, but it can happen anywhere, especially in remote areas that poachers tend to frequent.

Saunders remembers the ride to the hospital and wanting to stop at a corner store for something to drink. Shock is an amazing painkiller. He had serious injuries but eventually made a full recovery after many months of painful physiotherapy. He worked for twenty years more as a conservation officer. He was in charge of the state's Air Boat Team and the Operation Game Thief program, and near the end of his career was on the board of the International Wildlife Crimestoppers program. Today, Saunders hosts a popular podcast called *Warden's Watch* in his home state of New Hampshire.

A BAG OF SNAKES
IN ARIZONA

ARIZONA'S UNIQUE ECOLOGY IS HOME TO MANY UNUSUAL, OFTEN dangerous animals. This list includes the Gila monster (the only venomous lizard in North America), thirteen species of rattlesnakes, thirty species of scorpions, tarantulas, black widow spiders, blister beetles and the Sonoran Desert toad, to name a few. That doesn't mean it's a bad place to live. Just look at all the Canadians who flock to Arizona in the wintertime. Retirement communities are everywhere and most of the wild creatures get their bad reputation from lore and television. You have a better chance of dying by falling in the bathtub and banging your head than dying from a venomous snakebite. Venomous snakes don't want to bite you; they'd rather save their venom for smaller animals they can eat. They will bite if they are threatened, which is when the reported bites normally happen.

Because of poaching, you are less likely to see many of these animals today than in the past. One Arizona Game and Fish Department (AZGFD) officer witnessed the near elimination of one fairly common snake in the area he worked over his thirty-year career. The main culprit was poaching. It can be especially difficult to catch snake poachers for a number of reasons: 1) it's legal to get a licence and harvest some snakes, 2) snakes are very easy to conceal compared with most larger animals, and 3) they can be transported live rather easily. To make it even more difficult, there is a whole community of snake enthusiasts called *herpers* who enjoy finding and photographing snakes, much like birdwatchers. This makes it especially easy for the poacher to pose as a herper and gather snakes undetected.

Snake poachers feed the growing interest in keeping live snakes as pets. For example, Germany has become a hotbed for snake-loving buyers. It can be especially difficult to enforce snake poaching because state laws vary dramatically. Some states like Arizona don't allow the sale of local snakes, while other states allow it. Utah recently changed from not allowing sales to allowing them after one individual with good political connections made it happen. While the politician may feel he earned a vote, he has unwittingly (or not) written off one of the best weapons in fighting snake poaching in that state.

AZGFD warden Brian Anthony spent thirty years in Arizona and became a subject expert on snakes and reptiles in Arizona. He has a wealth of interesting stories. One of his very first cases involved everything from humour to unbelievable craziness. The case started when Mr. "Rattler" called in to report a suspected snake dealer. It's legal to own and sell some imported snakes with a licence, but local snakes can't be sold or traded. Rattler said he'd advertised his personal pet boa constrictor for sale on Craigslist. When a young man contacted him offering to trade a rattlesnake for his boa, he told the guy that would be illegal. Undeterred by that comment, the young man, "Mule," asked whether Rattler knew where he could buy other snakes. Later, it would be discovered that Mule had a drug habit and would do whatever he needed to get enough money for his fix. Buying and then reselling wildlife for a profit would feed Mule's habit. They never agreed on a deal, and Rattler reported the incident to wildlife officials.

Officer Anthony located Mule's online ad to purchase snakes, and Rattler agreed to help the officer catch the addict. Undercover, Rattler learned from Mule that the buyer of Mule's snakes was a wealthy man who claimed to be a police officer (he was not). Mule gave Rattler a list of four snakes he wanted him to find for his buyer. Rattler set up a sale with snakes provided to him by Officer Anthony. A deal was struck, allowing officers to track Mule to the buyer of the snakes. Mule didn't have a driver's licence, so his girlfriend took him and the snakes to sell them to Mr. "Charmer." Officers were able to watch and film the entire transaction.

Charmer lived in a $6 million mansion with his wife, who was a doctor—a seemingly unusual couple to be in the snake buying and selling business. Now the officers knew who Charmer was and where he lived. Using Charmer's ad on Craigslist, they had another officer contact him undercover, saying his friend had just moved out and left him with four pet snakes that he didn't want. He never offered them for sale, but still Charmer was interested. He was about to get bitten! Charmer offered and paid $50 each for the snakes. The transaction was made, providing more information for the search warrant officers would deliver the next day.

Officers showed up with the warrant and located the live snakes they'd sold to him, plus a bunch more. Anthony talked to Charmer, who claimed he'd been bitten by a rattlesnake once and almost lost his hand. The rattler that bit him was the one mounted and on display in his house. "After I was bitten," he said, "I became a brother of the snakes." If you find that creepy, there's more.

Charmer said he tried to buy more live snakes via the internet for his personal collection. He just couldn't find snake sellers, probably because he was offering three or four times the going rate, which drew suspicion from would-be sellers. He was adamant he was not selling them. Charmer claimed he'd caught all the snakes the officers wanted to seize. He wasn't prepared when Anthony pointed out to him that he'd just bought snakes from an undercover officer. He went quiet and slithered away.

The officers completed their search and seized a bunch of snakes and Charmer's computer. Along with snakes, Charmer apparently had a fetish for guns and knives as there were many visible and on display throughout the house. A female officer emerged from a room she was searching and said to Anthony, "You have to go in there." He went into the room and looked at the three-ring binders on the shelf she'd referenced. The officers had thought they might contain records of snake sales, but it was much worse.

Charmer had been corresponding with about twenty-five of America's most notorious living serial killers and criminals. I won't name them here, but if you can think of the worst ones you've heard of, he was likely writing to them. He was paying them to write back to him. He had developed a trust relationship with many of them. Why? He was curious to know what it felt like to kill someone. Some of the killers shared their thoughts and feelings. Police investigated this morbid behaviour, but he really hadn't broken any laws. Something inside his head perhaps needed some fixing, although he wasn't totally weird. He'd have a few friends over for poker nights occasionally. If he lost money, he'd get up from the table and come back with his next "buy-in," throwing a live rattlesnake on the table. I don't think he lost a hand after that. Okay, maybe he was totally weird.

Charmer was eventually charged with eight offences. Over the next four or five months a plea bargain was negotiated. During that time, Charmer did not stop his buying of venomous snakes. He would also buy snakes not found in Arizona, the deadlier the better, then release them into his neighbourhood! Remember, he was a "brother of snakes" and that's something a loving brother would do. Charmer even filmed himself feeding the snakes and releasing them. AZGFD fielded calls from Charmer's frightened neighbours regarding snakes during this period. I can imagine being his neighbour and saying, "I just don't feel like a hot tub tonight, dear." Charmer pled guilty to three counts and was fined $1,100.

Later, on a cold February day, Officer Anthony received a call from the police. Charmer was found lying dead in his theatre room. Anthony told them to get out because who knew what might have bitten him, then he went to the house and called the Phoenix Herpetological Society to come get the snakes. Charmer's wife had already made the call. She hated snakes.

It turned out Charmer had died of a heart attack. It's scary to think what might have happened with this man who was infatuated with guns, knives, venomous snakes and serial killers—what he might have done if he hadn't had a heart attack. Perhaps he was convicted in the highest court there is.

HUNTING FOR DUMMIES

Saskatchewan conservation officers were involved in a project to catch poachers who were using snowmobiles to chase down and shoot coyotes. Occasionally, the officers used a helicopter. On this particular helicopter patrol they spotted a snowmobile moving quickly across an open field. They were able to fly from behind and approach from the rear, getting right over top of the poacher, undetected. The officers could see a sawed-off shotgun slung over the guy's back with the barrel muzzle bouncing along, pointed right at the base of his head. When the noise of the helicopter above him eventually overtook that of his snowmobile, the driver came to a stop and turned his machine off. Surprise! A helicopter was hovering just above him. He was busted. The shotgun was loaded and it's likely his shorts were loaded too!

WHERE THE DEER AND
THE ANTELOPE LAY

NEBRASKA OFFERS A BROAD DIVERSITY OF WILDLIFE IN A VARIETY
of ecosystems throughout the state. Hunting and fishing are an
important part of most local residents' way of life. I and my wife,
Lorraine, witnessed this personally when we were invited to talk to a
group of Grade 5 students in the state. We were visiting our friends,
Officer Ray Dierking and his wife, Becky, in Broken Bow, Nebraska.
Becky, a schoolteacher, invited us to a show-and-tell period to talk
about living in Canada. During our talk, we showed some of that
colourful Canadian cash that's worth a bit more than Monopoly
money. It's always a joy to field questions from young people.

Many of their questions were good ones about hunting and fishing in Canada. When I asked how many hunted and fished, most
hands went up. Almost everyone had fished and most had hunted
by the age of eleven. Anti-hunters may cringe at that. In my experience, the vast majority of hunters understand conservation. Much
of the money hunters spend goes toward wildlife agencies to ensure
proper management and enforcement. In some jurisdictions, as I've
mentioned, less hunting equates to less money to check for violators.
Hunters are usually the ones observing and reporting the poachers
of the world. Poaching would be worse if observant, honest hunters
weren't out there. And it will become worse unless agencies keep hir-
ing enough officers and providing them with effective tools to fight
the poachers.

Unfortunately, an abundance of wildlife can attract an abundance of poaching activity, often from outside the local area.
Nebraska game laws allow locals to get special tags to shoot deer

on their own property, but these tags cannot be used by out-of-state hunters unless they are direct family. Nebraska also operates mandatory check-in stations for deer harvested during rifle season. (Deer harvested in other seasons can be reported by phoning in.)

In November of 2017, Nebraska conservation officers received two complaints that a local landowner was loaning his property tags to a group from out of state. The first complaint was from a keen observer at the check-in station. He'd seen a local landowner with a property tag who had shown up dressed in street clothes with some Louisiana hunters to check in "his" deer. Officer Matt Taylor took the complaint and decided to check out the property tag records at the check-in station.

Coincidentally, Officer Taylor just happened to arrive at the check-in station at the same time as a group of hunters from Louisiana arrived with another deer. Taylor was suspicious and devised a plan to gather information. He talked amiably to the proud hunters, and they agreed to let him take a picture of them with their deer. As he snapped their photo, he made sure to capture the licence plate of their truck in the frame. He later checked records and confirmed that the men were indeed from Louisiana. He and his partner decided to head to the property where the landowner tags had been issued and check things out.

On their way, Taylor took another call about a hunter shooting a deer from a main road. He tracked that violator down. The hunter claimed to have shot the deer while he was standing in the ditch and not from the road, but that really didn't change the resulting violation. (The law covers a no-shooting zone near highways for safety reasons.) Taylor issued a ticket, seized the deer, then met with the caller who'd reported the incident. The man suggested that Taylor head north to check things out by an abandoned school bus for some more violators.

Taylor and his partner drove to the abandoned bus, where they found, to their astonishment, the first group of Louisiana hunters they had set out to locate before all the interruptions. They found dead deer, deer racks and cut-up deer around the property. After sorting through the mess, they left the property with eight seized deer, plus a roadkill deer the group had picked up but not reported. Little did Taylor realize that his workday was not yet finished.

Officer Taylor again called the citizen who'd reported the road hunter and the second Louisiana group to thank him and advise him that he'd caught them both. During that call, the man suggested Taylor go check out yet another, different hunting camp set up a few kilometres away.

Taylor and his partner arrived at the local property to find a remarkably built "permanent" deer camp including sleeping quarters and a number of buildings. It turned out that this was yet another group from Louisiana that had been leasing this property for years. They were not familiar with the previous group from Louisiana that the officers had just dealt with. The camp was strewn with deer heads and other random deer parts, hanging carcasses, tubs of processed deer meat and a deep freeze full of more processed meat. The only thing missing was a sign reading LOUISIANA DEER MEATS. This was a bad day for Louisiana poachers in Nebraska.

Taylor woke two hunters who were sleeping in a nearby trailer while the rest of their group were out hunting for more deer. The two showed him around the property. One separate building contained all their hunting clothes so they could change in a scent-free environment before going hunting. One building contained a barbecue, a smoker, a deep fryer, a stove and cooking pots. These guys must have planned to eat the evidence. There were multiple violations for not cancelling tags and a vast array of other crimes to write up, so many that Taylor had his partner take over—he was getting writer's cramp. They seized four whole deer and other processed deer meat from the camp and left $9,000 worth of tickets.

Officer Taylor's day had begun at 6:00 a.m. By the time he and his partner had dealt with all the seized deer, it was 2:00 the next

It was all in a day's work for Officer Matt Taylor of Nebraska as he and his partner seized thirteen deer from twelve poachers in 2017. *Photo: Matt Taylor.*

morning. They had seized a total of thirteen deer and issued over $12,000 in fines to twelve poachers. Days like this are gratifying yet discouraging because you realize just how much poaching is going on.

If you had difficulty following the trail of phone calls and poaching complaints above, just imagine what Officer Taylor felt like. He had to keep reprioritizing the information coming at him from all directions, try to assess each situation's urgency, then deal with violators thoroughly and quickly before going on to the next most important one. He also had to weigh the validity of the complaint, as sometimes poachers will make false calls to draw attention away from their own poaching schemes. Once again, this story shows just how important information from the public is.

Game wardens are also constantly juggling complaints from some landowners about poachers on their property with complaints from other landowners about crop and fence damage from wildlife, yet they won't allow hunters on their property. Officers are caught in the middle, trying to catch poachers while appeasing both land-owners and real hunters.

Another major Nebraska poaching case, this time involving antelope, took place a couple of years earlier. Officer Sean McKeehan checked out a report of a dead antelope in a large field on a piece of private property. While driving around some irrigation pivots to get to the antelope, he found more dead antelope in the tall grass. Most of the animals were piled in bunches of three to five, including does, bucks and calves. A total of twenty-five dead antelope were found in the field, all apparently shot and abandoned.

Officer McKeehan and others set up surveillance for a couple of days, expecting that the poachers might return. Among the poached antelope was one large trophy, something rarely left behind by poachers. Ironically, in the past officers had set up a decoy deer only a quarter of a kilometre from the location of the antelope.

After the surveillance turned up nothing, the officers gathered up the twenty-five antelope carcasses. They also found and col-lected some spent rifle bullet casings in the field. They conducted full necropsies on half a dozen carcasses but found no bullets—they had passed through the antelope. The landowner wasn't very co-operative and offered no further information. Officers put out a $2,500 reward through the local Crimestoppers program, and the money was matched by a local wildlife agency. The $5,000 reward generated lots of interest and calls. Most callers only had suspicions; however, one caller's information resulted in locating two poachers.

The two men were arrested. They initially acted as if they'd just done a dumb thing (that was true) and had intended to shoot only one or two. They provided an open, recorded confession and never once tried to dispute the accusations against them. Over the course

Twenty-five antelope were shot and left in a Nebraska field in 2015. Suspiciously, the landowner didn't co-operate, but two poachers were eventually caught. *Photo: Nebraska Game and Parks.*

of two nights, they'd shot the twenty-five animals, but they offered no real reason for their crimes. If they'd been trophy hunting, they'd have taken the buck. If they'd been after meat, they would have taken some. They denied that the landowner was involved, yet the landowner did not consider them trespassers. There is a likely answer, but "likely" doesn't stand up in court.

TENNESSEE'S THREE STOOGES

FORT CAMPBELL, TENNESSEE, IS HOME TO THE ONLY AIR ASSAULT division in the world, the 101st Airborne Division. Strategically located on the Tennessee/Kentucky state line, the base serves the third-largest military community of the US Army, covering 420 square kilometres. Formed in 1942, the base covers prime white-tailed deer habitat and was accessible to the public for hunting for many years. But that changed after risk of unexploded ordnance was detected at two locations on the property. The two areas were called the large impact zone and the small ordnance impact zone. All was well until some scrap-metal collector started dismantling an unexploded bomb and almost became a rocket scientist. He lost an arm but survived. After that, the two impact areas were closed to the public.

Three local hunters had guided other hunters on the base for years. After the public was prohibited from using the two areas, these three treated them as their own private poaching preserve and continued to shoot deer there. Their impressive mounts of deer were the envy of many hunters—until 2010.

Military personnel had often reported finding headless deer carcasses on the base, but no one had been caught. In 2010, wildlife officers received information about three poachers on the base. Officers Jereme Odom and Dale Grandstaff, along with USFWS officers stationed on the base, located a suspect vehicle and searched the base property. They located "Larry" and "Curly" hunting on the base. Both were well-known poachers but had never been caught. Their buddy "Moe" was also drawn into the picture.

The officers prepared search warrants for the residences of the three poacher suspects and intended to serve them simultaneously with the help of Kentucky officers and the USFWS. Two of the men were at their homes, where the officers found over thirty deer mounts between the two places. It was a couple of days before they were able to connect with the third member of the group. By that time, he had hidden most of his deer. He'd even tried to hide a couple in the bushes on the property. It didn't stop the officers from seizing a total of forty-two head mounts (two were European mounts) of illegally taken bucks from the three poachers. All were fairly large mature bucks with Boone and Crockett scores ranging from 130 to 176. I'm sure the tears were real as the officers hauled them all away.

Officer Odom displayed a few pictures of some of the bucks on social media. This created a panic among the poaching community. Other poachers started hiding deer mounts and surreptitiously moving them around. These actions spurred other investigations that resulted in more charges against more poachers. At the time, this case was thought to be the biggest deer-poaching case in US history.

Larry, Curly and Moe each received lengthy hunting privilege bans of five to seven years, fines of $2,000 to $3,000 each, forfeiture of two firearms and the loss of the forty-two head mounts, worth thousands of dollars. They also received various sentences of house arrest and a lifetime ban from the military base. With all their experience, maybe these three could get a job as land-mine detectors.

BIG POACHER, SMALL MIND

SOME GAME WARDENS SPEND THEIR ENTIRE CAREER CHASING THE same guy over and over. Such was the case with Vermont game warden Dennis Amsden. If poaching convictions had frequent-user points, "Bub" the poacher would have had a get-out-of-jail-free pass after thirty-plus fish and wildlife convictions before the one in this story. Bub's sons have little chance of becoming anything but chronic poachers. Every single time Bub has been caught, he has had one or more of his sons with him. Bub was and still is the biggest poacher in state history.

Warden Amsden had been helping a local resident track down a wounded bear one day. He and a deputy game warden had their trusty deer decoy in the back of the truck. It was late in the day, so they decided to set out the decoy. Catching poachers is just like hunting or fishing. Knowing your quarry and having a good knowledge of animal behaviour and the right kind of bait often lead to success.

The wardens set up the decoy in a field in an area where night hunters had been caught in past years. Forty-five minutes after the decoy was set up, a vehicle came slowly driving by the field. It drove past the decoy, then returned from the other direction, coming to a stop right beside the decoy. A light came on and Amsden heard the distinct sound of a bowstring being released.

The officers gave chase and caught up to the vehicle after about a kilometre. The convertible had four occupants. Bub was a passenger in the front seat, and the driver was his sixteen-year-old son. Bub's youngest son was in the back seat with his oldest son, "Little Bub." Little Bub was the shooter who'd shot the deer—he had been raised to kill animals. Papa Bub would often catch live animals to bring home just so Little Bub could shoot them.

A trooper arrived on the scene after hearing the call on the radio. Approaching Amsden from the front of the vehicle, he asked whether he'd seen the hood on the car. Amsden shook his head, went to look, and saw what the trooper had seen—a Vermont Fish and Game magnetic sign! Someone had stolen the sign from a biologist's vehicle and put it on the car. That might be real funny to a person like Bub—until they get caught.

Bub refused to allow a search of the car, so it was seized. Arrows were visible on the dash and on the floor of the back seat. The next day, officers searched the area and found a bow and a rangefinder in the ditch.

Bub was fined $850 and given a two-year prison sentence, but only served thirty days. Perhaps my joke about a get-out-of-jail-free pass was not a joke? He was also given a three-year hunting prohibition. Little Bub was fined $250 and given a three-year hunting prohibition as well. The lenient sentences explain why someone could be caught thirty-plus times and still be poaching.

VIRGINIA ELK REBUILD

ELK THRIVED IN VIRGINIA, ESPECIALLY IN THE APPALACHIAN Mountains, until the mid- to late 1800s. Soldiers in need of food during the Civil War were hard on most wildlife, and this likely resulted in the demise of elk in the state of Virginia. Reintroducing elk was tried in the early 1900s and again in the 1920s and '30s without success. Virginia started again in 2012 by introducing seventy-five elk from Kentucky over a three-year period. Support from the Rocky Mountain Elk Foundation and joint efforts from Missouri, Virginia and Kentucky have grown the herd fourfold in the past eight years. Over $1 million has been invested in the program. Virginia may even consider a limited-entry hunt for licensed hunters in the near future—unless poachers beat them to it.

Early in 2016, Virginia Department of Game and Inland Fisheries conservation police officers responded to a call about a large, dead bull elk about fourteen metres off the road. It had been shot, the head was removed and the meat was left. The officers worked over seven months gathering information and evidence. They were able to prove that one person, Mr. "Looney," had poached animals on eight different occasions. He would drive around at night and shoot animals from his vehicle with a spotlight, using a .22-calibre rifle equipped with a laser light.

Looney was so proud of his poaching that he recorded many of the shootings on video. In one of them, he claimed his actions as being Poaching 101. In another very disturbing one, he shot a deer, transported it to a highway overpass and threw it from the upper bridge onto the road below, laughing all the while. There's a village somewhere in the world that is missing an idiot!

Looney was charged with poaching four elk, three deer, a black bear and a bobcat. After hearing the evidence, the judge commented, "There is no reason to kill animals in that nature [way]." He also described Looney's actions as cruel. I can think of a few more words. The judge took the poaching very seriously, and Looney was fined over $25,000, lost his hunting privileges for five years and was sentenced to nearly seven years in prison.

HUNTING FOR DUMMIES

A wildlife officer happened upon a seventy-five-year-old man wearing a long trench coat who appeared to be bass fishing. During their conversation, the officer noticed the chest pocket of the trench coat moving, yet the old man had his hands at his sides. Then he noticed a lower pocket on the other side twitching. There wasn't any wind that day either. The old man fessed up and pulled four live undersized bass from his pockets. The old man was so grateful for not being charged that he described another, more serious violation that the officer successfully followed up on.

NEWFOUNDLAND COMMERCIAL MOOSE POACHING

NEWFOUNDLAND, ON THE ATLANTIC COAST, IS CANADA'S MOST easterly island province. Four moose were introduced there in 1904 with the goal of attracting hunters and providing a source of business for remote communities. The success was astounding, and by the 1930s hunting seasons were opened. The population grew to well over 100,000 animals, giving Newfoundland the highest population density of moose in North America. Moose in Newfoundland have few natural predators, which means human activities are the main tools for managing the population.

Unfortunately, moose numbers have dropped in recent years and harvest rates have had to be lowered. Poaching is certainly a factor in the decline of moose numbers. Commercial poachers are an even greater threat.

Newfoundland's Department of Forest Resources and Agrifoods ran an undercover moose-poaching operation in 2006. Undercover conservation officer Roy Payne made himself known as a buyer of processed moose meat, and it wasn't hard for him to find those willing to sell to him. During the six-month operation, Payne gathered information that resulted in three different commercial businesses and ten individuals being caught and charged.

On a July day in 2006, over fifty conservation officers, RCMP and Royal Newfoundland Constabulary officers descended upon eight unsuspecting locations with search warrants. They seized hundreds of kilograms of processed moose meat, quarters of moose, migratory birds, three vehicles, three rifles and other hunting gear used in the various offences. There were over one hundred instances of illegal activity.

One commercial meat business, "Bogus Foods," hired a lawyer who told the judge his poor client was illiterate and didn't know all the rules. The lawyer claimed Mr. Bogus was honest and simply didn't understand he couldn't sell moose meat. Officer Payne testified that when he'd first contacted Bogus about purchasing moose meat, the man had readily offered to sell it to him, telling Payne to come over right away but not to tell anyone. If he was illiterate, he certainly knew the law. He was sentenced to three months in jail and fined $10,000. I hope he used his adult time-out to learn how to read. Perhaps his lawyer could spend some time with him and teach him.

Another meat store in a small community was also convicted of buying and selling moose meat. The owner was convicted of fifteen charges and received a total fine of $17,250. He didn't claim to be illiterate and didn't get any jail time. Several poachers who provided the moose were also convicted. One had poached ten moose. He was fined $10,000 and prohibited from owning a firearm for ten years.

In another, unrelated Newfoundland moose-poaching case, Mr. "Meatball" was caught conducting an illegal guiding operation. Meatball sold his resident moose licence to an undercover officer and flew him in to a remote lake in his Cessna 180 aircraft. Meatball was convicted of seventeen charges related to illegal guiding, hunting caribou without a licence and a range of other violations. The undercover officer gave evidence during the trial that during their trip, the accused had often referred to his rifle as his "poaching gun." The judge took special note of this fact. Meatball also owned a hotel where his poaching guests often stayed, making his illegal guiding business even more profitable. He avoided a stay in the Crowbar Hotel, but his Cessna 180 was forfeited and he paid fines of $6,000.

It can be especially difficult to catch and convict poachers such as these who live in small, tightly knit communities. People generally are either benefiting from the poaching or are scared to report poachers for fear of retaliation. I highly suspect a big reason for the decline in the moose population is poaching. It may not all be commercial poaching, but if enough people take a moose unlawfully, the cumulative impact can't help but cause the decline in numbers we see today. Ignoring a neighbour who took just one moose for meat is only adding to the problem. Until the residents of Newfoundland work together with conservation officers to stop the poaching, the legal hunters and the moose will be the ones who suffer most.

HUNTING FOR DUMMIES

In 2017, Department of Natural Resources officer Todd Petrunger in West Virginia received a complaint from a man stating he'd seen his neighbour shoot two deer fawns. Officer Petrunger made his way to the address and approached an elderly man in the driveway. When questioned, the old guy openly admitted to shooting the two young deer. The deer had committed the deadly crime of eating vegetables in his garden! Residents can legally obtain a permit to shoot a deer for crop damage, but the old guy had neglected to do that. Perhaps he felt the paperwork would take too long and his garden would be gone before he got the permit. Whatever his thinking was, it wasn't right to shoot two spotted fawns that were likely still nursing with their mother. Officer Petrunger seized the meat and hides from the two deer and issued a warning to the old fellow.

THE UNPAID WARDEN

THE MAJORITY OF FISH AND WILDLIFE OFFICERS HAVE VERY understanding and supportive partners and family members. Some of them go far beyond being supportive and actually gather information on suspected violators. This was the case years ago when a Washington wildlife officer's wife was in a beauty salon in the neighbouring state of Oregon. She noticed a business card with the name of a fishing guide offering trips in her home state. She recorded the business card information and gave it to her husband.

The information was passed on to Washington Department of Fisheries and Wildlife detective Charlie Pudwill. He checked the existing licences in the state and determined that the guide, "Witless," was not licensed to fish where he advertised his trips. Pudwill helped arrange a fishing trip with the guide and some undercover officers. Those guided fishing days revealed more problems for Witless. He boasted of guiding hunting trips in Idaho and salmon fishing trips on the Skeena River in British Columbia. Further record checks showed he was not licensed for either location.

As a result, two Idaho Department of Fish and Game (IDFG) investigators booked a guided fishing trip with Witless on the Columbia River in Washington to determine the extent of his guiding activities in their state. During that trip, Witless again bragged about guiding on the Skeena River in BC. The two IDFG investigators then made plans for a guided salmon fishing trip to BC. They asked Witless whether they could bring their "Canadian cousin" along and he agreed to it. What he didn't know was that the "cousin" was another undercover officer from British Columbia.

Witless towed his twenty-two-foot jet boat north and crossed the border. His boat was clearly marked with a large permanent logo,

COLUMBIA RIVER GUIDE SERVICE, on both sides and a decal identifying it as being licensed to fish on the Columbia River. Perhaps Witless thought his Columbia River licence meant he could fish in any river in British Columbia? He was questioned by Canadian Border Services and denied he was guiding in BC. He signed a sworn affidavit declaring those facts and was allowed to enter Canada.

Witless drove his two snickering guests the sixteen-hour drive from the US border to Terrace, BC, where they met up with the covert BC officer. Witless was so clueless about fishing on the Skeena River that he stopped in at a local tackle shop and asked how to catch salmon. That wasn't the funniest part, though—he did it in front of his three customers! Maybe he should have asked the BC officer for tips. Once the officers had obtained all the evidence they needed on the fishing trip, they arrested Witless and took him into custody.

Meanwhile, back in Washington and Idaho, officers were ready to co-ordinate with the covert BC officer to attend Witless's residence and the Idaho hunting camp with search warrants at the same time Witless was arrested. They also had search warrants for some other individuals, including Papa Witless. There was lots of additional evidence in the Washington and Idaho locations that added to the BC case as well as the Idaho investigation. Witless's soon-to-be ex-girlfriend was not impressed.

Witless was charged in BC and given a $24,000 fine. His diesel pickup, fishing tackle and jet boat were seized and forfeited. They were estimated to be worth $110,000 at the time. In true Canadian spirit, he was given a ride to the US border so he wouldn't have to hitchhike home. The word of the bust spread through northern BC, and surprisingly (or not), a number of American sport fishing groups suddenly left the Skeena River. Officers believe other illegal businesses had been operating and the bust had scared them off.

Witless returned home to more problems. He was fined $29,150 in Idaho and given a lifetime revocation of hunting privileges. Papa Witless was fined $9,750 and given a five-year hunting suspension.

Six others were charged and convicted of various fish and wildlife crimes. They got off lucky because the statute of limitations had passed for some of the evidence seized in the searches. Witless's girlfriend had had enough too and left him. He lost his fishing gear, his jet boat, his pickup and his woman. That sounds like the makings of a good country song. Witless didn't intend to stay single forever. Rumour has it that he posted a picture of himself with his favourite white-tailed buck on a singles website. That should get the ladies emailing!

Once again, as with most large fish and wildlife investigations, success comes from keen officers with the dedication and stamina to follow the evidence trail. In this case, it all started with the unpaid warden, an officer's wife.

HUNTING FOR DUMMIES

Two Washington undercover officers were out fishing on the Snake River with an unlicensed guide. They were having a good day with the guy and he really started to open up with them. He bragged about numerous violations he'd committed in the past, including some of interest to the police. Near the end of the day, the guide said, "I've told you guys about a lot of bad stuff I did in the past. The next thing that'll happen is you'll pull out a badge and tell me you're game wardens."

One of the officers quickly replied, "No, we'll wait until tomorrow to do that." True to his word, the undercover officer put on his uniform the next day and formed part of the arrest team.

YOU BE THE JUDGE

MY SEARCH FOR POACHING STORIES TURNED UP THIS ONE FROM many years ago in eastern Canada. A young, eager deputy conservation officer was hired in Ontario. His duties included aerial smoke patrols, stream surveys, duck banding, canoe route evaluation and, of course, checking hunters and fishers. Like most officers hired in the 1970s, he had very little training. One fall day, he checked on some moose hunters returning from a fly-in moose trip in northern Ontario. He heard their plane coming in and walked down to the dock to see the local judge getting off the plane and unloading his untagged moose. The officer seized it.

When he went into the office, proud of his big bust, his two superiors chastised him and would not support any kind of charges against the judge. The young officer put his badge and identification card on the desk and walked out. The next day, his boss called him and told him if he didn't report to the check-in station for enforcement work they'd get someone else and his job would be over.

Sadly, the young officer with high moral standards lost out to a system that didn't have them. He regrets his decision over forty years later. He obviously would have made a better officer than those who supervised him. Organizations that support their officers will always be the strongest and most productive, and serve the best interests of wildlife and the public overall. Short-sighted managers are too common and have ended or tarnished the careers of many good officers—it unfortunately happens more often than we care to know. If you want to save whales, deer, snakes or dicky-birds, support your local fish and wildlife officers.

OPERATION
SOMETHING BRUIN

BEAR HUNTING IN THE STATES OF GEORGIA AND NORTH CAROLINA has taken place for generations. Some locals feel it's their right rather than a privilege. Baiting of bears has also been a tradition for decades. Some have trained hounds to track down and tree the bear until the hunter arrives to shoot it. These methods are legal at times and in certain places. But many residents don't see eye to eye with the law and would just prefer to carry on as their forefathers did a hundred years ago. Life would be good except for those pesky laws that sometimes get in the way.

In 2008 and 2009, forest service staff in North Carolina noticed an increased amount of bear-hunting activity on federal forest lands. The baiting, use of vehicles, illegal use of bear-hunting guides and destruction of forest lands were at the point where they felt something had to be done. It wasn't just staff noticing the problem; citizens were complaining as well. At least, most of them were complaining. Bear poachers are citizens too, but they save their complaining for the media and politicians.

An interagency and interstate undercover project called Operation Something Bruin was developed to address the problem. The local poaching community was very tightly knit, and bear poachers were careful not to share too many trade secrets with the outside world. But when undercover officers sought out bear guides, they found that the guides were easy to track down, and so were the violations. They exposed hunts that were conducted on federal forest lands using bait and dogs, and a swath of other illegal acts. The operation ran for several years before the feces made contact with the air conditioner.

Co-ordinated search warrants and arrests were made in a five-agency raid of residences. Officers seized bears, vehicles, guns, computers and other items related to the charges. The accused of course insisted they had been entrapped. They claimed their houses were raided and their children terrorized by the mean, nasty SWAT teams that descended upon them. I would expect such a response. The loudest howls often come from the people with the most guilt. Initial agency claims of eighty people charged were incorrect. Each agency was counting its own violations and some of them were crossing over between them and being double counted. Thirty to forty people were eventually charged with multiple violations, with many resulting convictions.

Public support for the "victims" rained down. One of the accused's wives raged about their innocence even though her husband pled guilty (go figure). She was a good speaker and easily rallied the community about the poor entrapped souls. The truth was, her husband had illegally guided the undercover officer on a bear hunt on federal land using bait. He used his hounds to hunt at night and shot a bear because the undercover officers missed twice (on purpose). The bear fell from the tree but didn't die, and the dogs began fighting it. The poaching guide was out of bullets, so he tried poking a bullet hole with a stick to kill the bear. Then he tried stabbing the bear with a knife before the officer pulled a handgun from his pack and shot the creature. Yes, the poaching guide had been framed! Well, he should be framed—a framed picture on a wall of shame.

This same poaching guide later directed the officer to a container of corn he said was used for hunting deer, hogs and bear. And his defence for all these crimes? He said later that he couldn't remember poking or stabbing the bear. He claimed the officer had forced him to shoot the bear. He claimed he had learned how to bait bears from the undercover officers. He was angry at how the officers had infiltrated his family by attending their Bible study and praying with his family. I guess the poacher felt it was a sin for an officer to pray.

Similar stories emerged from those charged with other offences. They claimed they were lured into illegal activity they would never normally do, like accepting $1,500 to illegally guide a hunter or bait bears. One of these so-called first-time poachers called a bait site "one of the most active bait sites in the United States." It was a remarkably accurate assessment for a newbie first-time guide. He told the officer to not tell anyone where he'd shot his bear.

Another poacher had phone video of him training his hounds. A caged house cat was surrounded by hounds and released. The cat escaped before the dogs caught it. The poacher shot the cat to let his dogs play with it. A raccoon was also videoed in a cage trying to escape. Another cat in a tree was shot. Perhaps poacher is too kind a word for this particular "framed" poacher.

The media frenzy showed that support for the poachers was strong. This only added fuel to the fires already burning. In the end, about fifty people were charged with 150 violations, mostly in North Carolina. The poachers' supporters fed the media and the media ran with it. They emphasized the undercover officers' illegal shooting of the bears and took the position that those officers should be charged. Those kinds of statements can gain the support of some southern folks. The raids on homes with children present and the trauma that resulted was another poorly thought-out accusation by the poachers. No doubt it was unnerving for those being searched, but it was also unnerving for the officers. They had to be ever vigilant of potential danger, firearms, threats and who knows what else. If they'd dropped their guard, it might have cost a life.

The majority of the accused pled guilty to lesser charges, thereby avoiding lengthy jail terms. That's a common practice in any legal situation. Many of those charged openly admitted they pled guilty only to avoid the serious time. That was a wise choice, except that they and their supporters then cried foul and said they really were innocent. This is another common practice. They can say anything outside a courtroom and someone will believe it. Most pled guilty because they were—case closed.

Politicians heard the noise of unhappy voters, though, and formed the Committee of Oversight and Government Reform by the House of Representatives, attended by many powerful, connected people. Testimony was heard from lawyers and agencies about the operation. The media claimed that millions of dollars had been spent on the operation. Wildlife agencies provided proof of just over $100,000 in total among them all. (This figure was for all the additional project costs, not wages.)

The Georgia DNR officers had body cameras on during their arrest—something that all enforcement agencies should do for everyone's protection. The cameras showed a very controlled search with the accused and his wife calmly seated without handcuffs. The officers were later criticized for not following safety procedures and cuffing them during the search. The media managed to miss that one. The accused's attorney showed up during the search and complimented the officers on how they'd conducted the search and left things so neat. I don't think the media highlighted that either. The media can provide a great benefit by informing the public, as long as they seek to present both sides of the issue as accurately as possible. It's a difficult task. There's always pressure to make headlines. Truth does not always do that.

In the end, the goal of raising awareness of the problem was achieved. Unfortunately, bitterness remains strong for many of those involved. A few spent some time in jail. There are probably a few more happy bears and other wildlife in the national forests, but they don't say too much.

After the kerfuffle had calmed down, most things returned to normal. Then a call came in about a dead black bear in the ditch in the same area where the poachers lived. It had white letters painted on its forehead and front paws that read WHATS BRUIN. Rewards were offered but no one was charged. There wasn't much media attention given to that either.

A few people will continue to poach because they feel it's their right. Large-scale undercover operations usually draw public attention. Some people feel that our society doesn't warrant such scrutiny, that it impinges on their rights and freedoms, that it's just not fair. Using an unmarked police car to catch speeders isn't fair either, right? The public should always know where the enforcement officers are and they should always be in full uniform, right? Even for catching drug dealers, right? Wrong, but sadly, a few leaders might support those statements.

I'd like to compliment the agency leaders and politicians who did support this operation. Those who didn't support it should be ashamed. Poaching kills far too much wildlife and that's a bear fact.

HUNTING FOR DUMMIES

With a warrant, Wyoming officers were conducting a search of a residence when they happened upon a large deer in a shed in the yard. The poacher claimed he'd shot it in a legal open area. The keen officers doubted his story and examined the stomach contents of the deer, in which they found the chewed-up leaves of a type of tree not found within 320 kilometres. They paid the poacher another visit and gathered more evidence that led to convictions for him and two of his buddies. You can be sure their subsequent stomach aches were not from too much laughter.

VENUS FLYTRAP POACHERS

THE VENUS FLYTRAP IS A UNIQUE PLANT THAT IS GREATLY SOUGHT-after as a houseplant. (Have you ever wondered whether a vegetarian would own a carnivorous Venus flytrap plant?) The flytrap is found natively only in a one-hundred-kilometre radius in the Carolina states. A survey conducted by the North Carolina Natural Heritage Program in 2019 counted a total of 163,951 individual Venus flytrap plants and estimated a total population of 302,000 plants remaining in the wild. This represents a reduction of more than 93 per cent from a 1979 estimate of approximately 4.5 million plants. Poaching has been a big reason for the decline. Laws have improved, making the taking of the flytrap a felony crime. A poacher can actually be charged for two offences for the same plant, as the top of the plant and the bottom can be considered different charges.

It is legal to take the plant from private land with the owner's permission. This makes it especially difficult for enforcement officers; if they stop someone with plants and the person claims they got them from private property, there's not much officers can do. State wildlife officers rely on electronic surveillance and the public to battle the constant threat of plant poachers.

North Carolina state wildlife officer T. C. Stacy received a public complaint reporting a suspected flytrap poacher. Poachers are often spotted and reported when they head into the swamp with plastic totes to carry the plants out. They usually work in co-ordinated teams to hit several areas at once in order to avoid the risk of all getting caught. In this 2019 case, Officer Stacy was three and a half hours from the reported location when he received information about the potential poacher. He and another officer decided it was worth a try to catch to the guy before he left.

They arrived at the location to find the suspect's car just leaving the area. They pulled Mr. "Jughead" over to have a chat and found a bag in the back seat containing some flytrap plants. Jughead admitted to taking the plants. He told them he would sell them to a buyer for twenty-five cents a plant. The plants would then be sold in flea markets and online for $5 to $8 apiece. The car contained 216 flytrap plants, each one a felony crime.

Jughead appeared before a magistrate who levied a $750,000 bond. There weren't enough flytrap plants on the planet to pay for his release, so he spent about six months in jail until a plea bargain was reached. Officer Stacy and his partner took the plants to a remote location and replanted them.

Jughead would have been better off staying in jail. It turned out he got lost in the swamp only months after his release. Search teams and a helicopter were able to safely locate him. He was no doubt poaching more flytrap plants, just as he'd been taught by his grandmother decades before. The flytraps had served his family like a bank account. If they needed some money, they'd just go poach a few plants. Sadly, many consider that acceptable. Jughead is very familiar with the legal system and will likely continue his hikes into the swamp until he gets permanently lost or incarcerated, or the plants become extinct.

DELAWARE DECATHLON

A TWENTY-ONE-YEAR-OLD MARYLAND MAN, MR. "DIPSTICK," WENT out deer hunting with a sixteen-year-old boy in nearby Delaware. That might have been okay except it was well after shooting hours, which is against the law. When they spotted a deer, Dipstick pulled over and fired a shot. Apparently, he missed—his aim was worse than his ability to follow the rules.

A concerned local resident heard the shot. He jumped into his own vehicle to find out who was doing the shooting. Dipstick took off with the resident chasing him down the back roads near Harrington. The resident got close enough to get a licence number and description of Dipstick's vehicle, then stopped following the poacher and called the game wardens from the Delaware Fish and Wildlife Natural Resources Police.

The call was relayed to Lieutenant Gavin Davis, who had just dropped off his officer in training, Nathan Valenti, at the end of their day. Valenti was out of uniform and getting ready to go to the gym for his routine workout, but he heard and recorded the information being passed on to Davis on his radio. Valenti knew he was much closer to the reported incident than Davis was, so he called the senior officer and offered to help. He then headed to the caller's location while staying in constant contact with Davis. As Valenti neared the reported area, he recognized a vehicle he met as the likely one they were looking for. With Davis's approval he turned and followed at a safe speed. He got close enough to determine that the licence plate didn't match the reported poacher's.

Valenti headed back toward the caller's residence. He was talking to the caller on his phone and Davis on the radio when he encountered another vehicle matching the description. This time, Valenti knew he had Dipstick's vehicle and was told to follow it safely but not stop it (policies for any agency only allow fully trained officers to stop a vehicle alone). Meanwhile, Davis and another game warden were travelling to meet Valenti, who was giving them a play-by-play of his location as he chased Dipstick's car. The poacher was somehow eluding the officers, so they decided to meet each other at the location where the shot had been reported. They again talked to the person who had called the incident in.

They checked the neighbourhood and the address of Dipstick's vehicle, but no one was home. They cruised the area and returned. The third time around, a different vehicle was in the driveway. It took three knocks on the door before a young man answered. The man was nervous and wouldn't disclose much information. After about an hour of questioning, he revealed he'd recently sold his vehicle, which matched the description of the one they were looking for, to Dipstick. They were at the wrong house! They called an officer who worked in the Maryland area where Dipstick lived. The vehicle wasn't at that residence either. They also found out Dipstick had recently been arrested for shooting deer at night near his Maryland home.

It had been a long day and night for all the officers, but it was about to get longer. They had planned an early-morning bust for some duck hunters who were using bait illegally. They headed straight from the overnight surveillance to the duck ponds without any sleep, where they set up the next morning and successfully bagged a few duck poachers. Sleep is overrated, especially when there are poachers to catch.

Several days later, Valenti called Dipstick and invited him into the office for an interview. He came in to see Valenti and three other officers for a long, long chat. Dipstick claimed his tailgate had dropped open and that would have been the loud noise the caller had heard. That comment earned him a 7/10 for creativity but a 2/10 for honesty. His second attempted lie was a bit better, when he said the gunshot was just his truck backfiring. He finally revealed the name of the sixteen-year-old who had been with him. One of the officers knew the boy as someone he'd arrested two years earlier for the same type of offence. That officer immediately left the interview room. He drove to the boy's house and picked him up, along with his mother. The kid told the entire poaching story in every detail. Dipstick's plan had backfired, not his truck.

Dipstick was charged for ten offences including hunting in a closed season, hunting at nighttime, having an unlawfully loaded firearm, discharging a firearm within fifteen metres of a public road, conspiracy (with the boy), driving without a licence, failure to have vehicle insurance with him, expired tags and improper registration and vehicle plate. It was a poacher's decathlon! This happened because one concerned citizen heard one shot and did more than expected to get the licence number to report it.

TEXAS POACHING
MASSACRE

TEXAS PARKS AND WILDLIFE DEPARTMENT (TPWD) GAME WARDENS received a call in September of 2015 from a landowner who'd found a dead doe on his property. His wife had told him she'd heard a shot during the night. That's not unusual in Texas given they can hunt for feral hogs at night. At the same time, the Leon County sheriff's office received a complaint about property crimes in an area near the kill site. The two enforcement agencies working on the cases soon learned the two crimes were connected. TPWD game warden Oscar Hansen and another officer teamed up with a Leon County sheriff, and their teamwork uncovered the biggest poaching case in the state's history.

The criminals were a derelict gang of juveniles. Their alleged ringleader was seventeen-year-old "Bonehead," who was a fine young man, according to his mommy. Mommy relayed a sad tale of her son when he was sixteen. They'd moved into a rental property and Bonehead had permission to hunt it. The property had a crooked boundary without fencing, and it seemed Bonehead had wandered onto the adjacent property while out hunting. He was reported and questioned by game wardens. Poor boy was fined for the trespass, and the fine was paid. What a fine young man! The real story was that Bonehead had crawled through a barbed-wire fence and climbed into the neighbour's wife's deer stand on several occasions. On the last occasion, the neighbour hid in the stand until Bonehead snuck in, only to be grabbed and held by the neighbour until the game warden arrived. That version is just a bit different from Mommy's story. It's called the facts.

To be fair, Bonehead's childhood didn't give him much of a chance to be anything but a poacher. He met his first game warden when he was about ten years old. He had come home from school to find the game warden giving Mommy, Daddy and Uncle some invitations to court for all the deer hanging in the trees like Christmas lights on their property.

In Texas a seventeen-year-old is considered an adult, and at age seventeen, Bonehead decided to move out. He moved into a trailer with twenty-one-year-old "Bubbles," who had an extensive criminal record. The trailer was much like a drop-in centre for a group of wayward young men.

The group started a three-month rampage of killing, theft and property crimes that was absolutely appalling. Evidence suggested that Bonehead was the leader. They were proven to have killed at least sixty-eight white-tailed deer, a blue heron, a vulture, an egret, several domestic cats and six head of cattle. Mommy would still defend Bonehead's innocence even though evidence showed he shot a cow, and when the cow wasn't completely dead he attacked it with a machete. He then turned on the cow's calf and slaughtered it with the same machete.

Many of the deer were shot at night using spotlights in an area adjacent to a busy highway. The deer were usually left to rot. In addition to the indiscriminate animal slaughter, the group shot out the window of a business, destroyed mailboxes, shot at a parked truck, committed burglaries of hunting camps and shot up road signs. They missed the sign that read REPORT POACHING—CALL THE GAME WARDEN.

The events shocked everyone, including the game wardens. It's amazing that so much shooting and destruction could occur and no one reported it until the dead doe in the field was found. The group had shot hundreds of rounds, often within view of a major highway.

Game wardens moved in to arrest the group and question them. Bubbles knew his criminal past would get him in even deeper if he lied, so he co-operated. He admitted to killing twelve deer and burglarizing two properties. He fingered another in the group, who also admitted to shooting deer and two burglaries. One by one the poachers dropped.

They were charged with a total of 120 felonies and fifty-eight misdemeanours. Mommy's public defence of her son continued. She claimed that all the alleged stolen property the sheriff had seized— two pickups filled with items including fishing poles, ammunition, knives, hunting gear, deer blinds, chainsaws and bags of corn—were actually items she had purchased for her dear son. Not surprisingly, she could not produce a single receipt for anything she claimed and it remained with the state. Mommy felt it was so unfair that her son was the only one who served time in prison; after all, dear Bonehead had shown the officers which houses they'd broken into. She claimed the officers took her son for rides, purchased food and candy and Dr. Pepper for him, and acted like his best friend to get him to confess. But enough about Mommy. The point I'm making is that this kid had little chance of becoming anything but a criminal with the kind of direction and support shown by his mother. And it gets worse. The young man is also a father with sole custody of a child, and he's only seventeen. What chance will his child have?

Bonehead served a year in jail and was given five years of probation. He was fined $2,500 in restitution to one property owner. One of his associates later appeared before the courts to answer to more serious criminal charges, which resulted in a five-year jail sentence for the associate. The charges against the juveniles involved in the case were dropped. Three of the nine rifles seized were forfeited. One of the forfeited guns had a homemade silencer attached to it. Sadly, the young men in this group will likely become frequent users of the judicial system for many years to come.

NEVADA NITWITS

THREE RESIDENTS OF NEVADA PLANNED TO POACH A BLACK BEAR. They knew the location of the bear's den and planned for a year to kill it. This was not a hunt. There was no particular reason other than stupidity.

They approached the bear's den from three different angles with three rifles and shot the bear multiple times. Not only was this disgusting, it was also dangerous to be shooting across to where the other two were standing. The three had never owned a hunting licence of any kind. They were just senseless poachers.

Nevada Department of Wildlife officers seized four rifles, cell phones and the poached animal from the three. They recovered casings from the scene as well. The thugs were fined $5,000 each and are never allowed to own a firearm. If I were the judge, I would have suggested pricing out some artificial intelligence.

THE CLODFATHER

THE "CLODFATHER" HELD A FLEET OF FORTY FISHING VESSELS AND was one of the largest groundfish fishing operators in the United States. He was once featured in a prominent magazine article as an immigrant with the business know-how to easily climb up the ladder of wealth in the commercial fishery. He always spoke out loudly against regulators, wardens, fishers, environmentalists and anyone who got in his way.

Wealth does not always mean kindness—or sanity. The Clodfather was paranoid that everyone was out to get him. When talking about his 1980s conviction for tax evasion, he said, "That'll be a fight to the death. I'll have them doing somersaults up there. They're #$%@#!ing with the wrong guy because when I'm right, I'm right. I don't #$%@#! around." Little did he know at that time that life would provide some real justice in the future.

The Clodfather was worth millions until an undercover operation brought his crimes to a crashing halt. His indiscriminate activities not only affected some of the weaker stocks that he fished, they affected the fishers working for him as well. He would record valuable fish with restricted catch quotas as cheaper species when he sold them. These actions resulted in his workers getting paid less for their share, and the government quotas were overfished without detection.

Clodfather's fall from glory and wealth started when two undercover officers posing as Russian businessmen approached him with the stated intention of purchasing his fishing fleet. He shared all the tricks he'd used to circumvent those pesky fishing quotas and described in detail how he avoided the taxman. All the conversations were recorded. That must have been so much fun for those officers.

Clodfather was arrested early in 2016 and charged with a plethora of bookkeeping scams including falsifying fish sales tickets,
conspiracy, twenty-five counts of lying to fishing officials, smuggling cash to Portugal and tax evasion. One of his "mules" was caught
smuggling cash out of the United States and depositing the money
in a Portuguese bank account. Who would do such a thing, you ask?
Why, it was a local sheriff with a long background in immigration and
customs. He was fired immediately. He was sentenced to one year in
jail. And it turned out the sheriff wasn't alone. I guess he didn't have
big-enough pockets for smuggling all the cash, so a fellow sheriff
helped out. He too was charged.

Clodfather agreed to plead guilty for his slimy crimes. He forfeited thirteen of his large fishing vessels along with their lucrative
fishing permits. Right after his guilty plea, his lawyer started to
rationalize and plead to the judge. It's an old practice: say you're
guilty, then tell a tale of why you're not guilty to lessen the penalty.
Clodfather's lawyer read a statement for him that included the words
"was the stupidest thing I ever did." The judge didn't take the bait and
retorted, "This was not stupid. This was corrupt. This was a corrupt
course of action from start to finish." The judge was paying attention. Clodfather's lawyer asked for two years' probation. The poacher
was sentenced to forty-six months in jail, three years' probation, a
$200,000 fine and forfeiture of the thirteen vessels (an estimated $27
to $30 million value), and ordered not to participate in the commer-
cial fishery in any way during his sentence.

Before the assets were sold, Clodfather's dear wife came to the
rescue and pleaded to the courts that she was the owner of eleven of
the boats. She argued she had no knowledge of the illegal acts; therefore, they should not be auctioned off but returned to her. Meanwhile,
another fishing company made an offer of $93 million for the entire
fleet of twenty-eight boats and associated licences. Interestingly, the
offer came from a fellow fishing syndicate that many locals felt operated the same type of business as Clodfather. The sale would have

to be approved by the government. The syndicate never followed through on its offer. After Mrs. Clodfather's successful claim to boat ownership, only four boats were ordered forfeited, including Clod's share of $2.7 million. This was later reduced to two vessels after two were given to Clod's wife.

The government officially closed the catch area where Clodfather had pilfered the fish stocks. No doubt assessments of stocks had to be made after the overfishing antics of this short-sighted, greedy poacher. Some commercial fishers with licences in that area protested. They were caught up in the dragnet set for Clodfather but had not followed in his criminal tracks. Perhaps they should have spoken out sooner; they must have known what was going on. Politicians were brought in to save the local industry, including Senator Elizabeth Warren. Those legal fishers were eventually given alternate licences to participate in an adjoining area's fishery.

The seized fleet ended up being purchased by a company that intended on keeping the vessels in the local fishery. A previous offer was withdrawn after vessel inspections concluded that the hulls of some vessels were compromised with rust and not worth the price offered.

Still, the lineup of those wanting a piece of the fish-poaching king was not over. The Coast Guard settled pollution charges with over half a million dollars in penalties. It turned out Clodfather's vessels had discharged oily bilge water and his crews threw used oil filters overboard on a regular basis. The National Marine Fisheries Service also filed civil charges, seeking nearly $1 million in penalties and the revoking of thirty-eight commercial permits. The National Oceanic and Atmospheric Administration settled on a civil penalty of $3 million and forced Clod to relinquish his seafood dealer permit, sell all his limited-access fishing permits, sell all his vessels and cease all commercial fishing by March 31, 2020. (By April Fool's Day in 2020, his name would be gone from commercial fishing records.) He was sentenced to forty-six months in prison. He was transferred to community confinement on April 30, 2021, to serve the balance of his sentence. When you're that high up, you have a lot farther to fall.

Large busts like this one are rare; commercial fishing permits are very lucrative and most fishers follow the rules. But quota systems, which have become a management tool for many fisheries throughout North America, are not without problems such as this one, and they are extremely difficult to detect. It usually takes a law-abiding fish plant worker, crew member, captain or "Russian buyers" as in this case to get to the real criminals.

HUNTING FOR DUMMIES

Vermont game wardens knew a habitual poacher through public reports but had been unable to catch him. They decided to set up twenty-four-hour surveillance on his property. Warden Jason Dukette prepared for his nightlong shift. Just as he was walking into the trees behind the property, he heard a shot coming from the house he was heading toward. Next, a flashlight came out and scanned the bushes, followed by the sound of a quad in the area. Dukette returned the next day with a search warrant. It turned out the poacher had a small portal in his bedroom wall from which to shoot deer that he lured to a bait pile in the backyard. He had barrels of apples in his basement. His tales of bagging big bucks were over and I expect he ate a lot of apple pies instead of venison.

WASHINGTON SEA CUCUMBER BUST

SEA CUCUMBERS ARE UGLY BUT WORTH A LOT OF MONEY, SORT OF like a few people. They are shaped like a cucumber with very slimy, warty skin and come in a variety of colours, also like some people. They are found throughout the world living mainly in shallow coastal areas; however, some species can live at depths of over ten thousand metres.

They have always been used in ancient medicine, particularly in Asia. Some medical claims, including the cucumber as an effective cancer treatment, have not been proven scientifically, but a number of compounds they produce have proven to be effective in other applications. These include extracts that help with arthritis, fatty acids that may assist with tissue repair, a compound that has been shown to be helpful in reducing scarring in brain operations, and still other compounds that have proven effective at reducing the development of malaria.

Sea cucumbers have few predators because they emit paralyzing toxins when threatened. Some species discharge sticky, toxic filaments from an opening near their butt. Now let's discuss feeding the black market for those inclined to eat these creatures.

In 2015, Washington Department of Fish and Wildlife officers received a tip regarding a local seafood business operator. He was using false bookkeeping to hide the amount of sea cucumbers he was buying and selling. Washington has both a commercial and a parallel tribal fishery that legally sell them. This complicated fishery arrangement makes it difficult to track and control the illegal activity, especially for a product that can fetch up to $440 per kilogram when dried. And they are worth a lot more in Asia.

The Washington fishery is divided equally between tribal and regular commercial fishers. In the 2015 season, the twenty-five state-licensed boats had reached their quota in a month. The forty tribal boats never reached their quota. This fact drew some scrutiny from the local fish and wildlife agency. The tipster led the officers to Mr. "Wrong," who owned a seafood business with connections to foreign markets. The books looked okay at first glance. Receipts were in order. But cheques issued by the owner revealed a different story—non-conforming numbers were handwritten on the corner of many of them. When questioned about the numbers, Mr. Wrong said, "I don't know, just some numbers!" We all know it's common to write some extra numbers on a cheque, right? Wrong. Just kidding.

Officers returned with a warrant for the previous two years of bookkeeping information. A complicated recovery of cheques issued revealed that 766 cheques had no fish ticket (receipt) attached to them and 289 documented fewer fish than were actually sold. The officers found that 109,000 kilograms of undocumented sea cucumbers worth over $1.2 million wholesale had been bought and sold over the two-year period. They were also able to show that Mr. Wrong profited about $2.4 million from these slippery transactions.

During the investigation, Mr. Wrong admitted the tribal fishers sometimes wrote down less product on the fish ticket—to avoid reaching their quota—and sometimes they didn't even fill out a fish ticket. All of this under-reporting is a technique used in many fisheries to avoid reaching the quota and having the fishery closed. Fish managers and agencies have determined the stock size and allowable harvest for a good reason: any overharvest will be detrimental to the overall stock.

I've encountered many similar incidents of under-reporting of catches in British Columbia fisheries. Our agency, the DFO, hired catch monitors to record catches in some fisheries. In virtually every case where I had occasion to follow up on a reported catch, the fisher underestimated their catch, whether it was commercial, recreational or First Nations. In one example, I was told a fisher had caught three chinook salmon when I had secretly observed him land sixty-nine. In another example, our officers were doing surveillance on a suspected illegal seller in the First Nations fishery. We watched as a catch monitor approached the fisher, who stated that he had caught seventy-five sockeye. The catch monitor didn't have the authority to search the vehicle, so had to go on the word of the fisher. But after the exchange was over, our officers physically counted 255. I could go on; it's a common problem in many fisheries. Strangely, officers' observations are often disregarded by managers. I don't understand the reluctance to include the information, other than the fact that it may be a bit embarrassing and difficult to add into the models designed to estimate catch. That's a whole different story that could be debated for pages.

Meanwhile, back in Washington, Mr. Wrong eventually pled guilty to one count of conspiracy under the Lacey Act and was given a two-year prison sentence and fined $1.5 million. Four divers received thirty days of community service and fines of about $2,000 each. This problem isn't unique to Washington state. There are many examples of illegal sales of sea cucumber throughout North America. Although stocks are not considered threatened yet, they certainly will get there unless better enforcement controls are established. It's especially important to maintain a sustainable population of an animal such as this that shows so much promise in medicine.

THE YUKON POACHER

THE YUKON (FORMERLY CALLED YUKON TERRITORY) IS SLIGHTLY larger than the state of California but has a total population of only forty thousand people. Twenty-five thousand of these residents live in the capital city of Whitehorse. The Yukon was opened up with the Klondike gold rush in the late 1890s. Gold mining is still a big part of this remote region of northern Canada.

Although this book is about poaching, I wanted to include a great story about the current world-record moose that was legally taken by Heinz Naef of Dawson City in the Yukon. Heinz was out on a "meat hunt" with some friends. He was not concerned about shooting the biggest animal. But he happened upon a giant moose and walked to within thirty-five metres of it before shooting it with his .30-30 British Enfield rifle with open sights. When was the last time you saw anyone hunt with one of those? No major sponsors or fanfare, just the biggest moose ever shot in the world. He cut the antlers off with a chainsaw and nicked them but didn't damage them. You can buy T-shirts in the Yukon for the biggest Yukon-Alaska moose. The experts call them Alaska-Yukon moose, but until Alaska finds a bigger one, the Yukon T-shirts will be sold as they are.

Sadly, however, even remote regions like the Yukon have poachers. The Yukon is home to over three hundred thousand caribou, seventy thousand moose, twenty-two thousand Dall (thinhorn) sheep and fifteen hundred bison. That's equal to about ten big-game animals for every resident. The locals aren't alone, though—they compete for the big game with ten thousand black bears, seven thousand grizzly bears and five thousand wolves.

In 2015, a series of anonymous tips led Yukon conservation officers to the house of Mr. "Einstein." He wasn't home when the officers showed up. Officer Aaron Koss-Young got up early the next day, returned to the house and waited for Einstein to wake up. He watched him make coffee and get ready to leave in his truck. That was when the waiting team descended upon and surprised Einstein and arrested him. Officers searched the house and outbuildings and seized eighteen firearms, ammunition, electronics, a bison, an elk, two deer hides, caribou antlers, two Dall sheep hides, four grouse, six rabbits, a set of eagle feathers and a pair of sheep horns. Buckets of rotting meat were found in the shed. Their investigation also revealed that Einstein had taken a caribou and sheep illegally the year previously. He was under a court order to possess no firearms at the time, but court orders are meaningless to many poachers. He lied to officers about the bison that was taken in a closed area until they were able to prove otherwise. It's amazing how many poachers contract temporary memory loss.

Einstein was charged with a total of twenty-two violations. There were a number of aggravating facts in his case. He'd shot the bison and hung it to dry for four days in warm weather. During this time, he also went out and shot an elk. When he returned home, the bison meat had started to go mouldy in the heat. Einstein partially cut up the animals over the next three weeks, causing a lot of the meat to be wasted. None of the animals were taken legally or treated properly. He'd used hard-pointed ammunition that is also illegal.

Einstein had likely learned how to operate from another poacher. He used his cube van with his company logos on the sides to shoot animals from, then load them whole without leaving a trace. The commercial vehicle drew less attention and completely contained any animals he poached. He'd take some of the whole animals home and gut them in his shed. He had a complete change of clothes in a bag in his cube van to change out of his bloody clothes and avoid suspicion. This is another glaring example of how unlikely a poacher is to get caught without the public's help. Can you imagine an area bigger than California with only thirteen officers to police these criminals?

Einstein was convicted of eighteen of the twenty-two violations. The Crown lawyer asked for six months in jail and a $30,000 fine to be paid to the TIP (Turn In Poachers) fund. His seized eighteen rifles were all forfeited. Einstein was desperate to avoid jail and offered to pay $45,000 and accept a lifetime hunting ban if he didn't have to go to jail. It was a pointless offer on his part since he had never bothered getting a licence anyway. The judge decided on $20,000 and a six-month conditional sentence, with three months of house arrest except for work, followed by another three months of house arrest between 10:00 p.m. and 6:00 a.m. He was also given a twenty-year hunting ban and ordered to take a hunting and ethics course. In my next life, I want to be a judge. I believe poachers like Einstein don't deserve another chance to hunt, ever.

HUNTING FOR DUMMIES

Mr. "Weak" of Wyoming couldn't resist the urge to poach a very large mule deer buck. Like many poachers before him, it was his ego that caused his demise. He simply had to show off the taxidermy mount at the hunting show in Salt Lake City the next spring. One hunter took a particular interest in the mount. He had date-stamped game-camera photos of the giant buck Mr. Weak had poached, which were taken well after hunting season had closed. He willingly provided them to the Wyoming officer. Oops! Mr. Weak paid $19,000 in fines and spent ten days alone, and not in a tree stand.

HAWAII OPIHI

YOU MAY NOT HAVE HEARD OF THIS TASTY, MILD-FLAVOURED little shellfish. Opihi is highly sought-after by native Hawaiians, who will eat them fresh or with raw tuna or simply barbecue them whole. They also have a high-end restaurant market as appetizers or in a trendy drink called the New Wave Opihi Shooter. The drink comes in a glass mixed with spicy tomato and herbs. (That's a pet peeve of mine—people claim something tastes so great, but they mix it with a bunch of spices and swallow it without even chewing it! Why bother? Just put an ordinary piece of raw meat in the drink and leave the scarce opihi to the locals.)

No, these seven hundred opihi are not learning to surf in Hawaii. They were seized from two poachers in 2020. *Photo: Hawaii Department of Fish and Wildlife.*

Opihi are found on remote, rocky shorelines below the water. The locations have to be remote because if they aren't, the opihi disappear. They can be difficult and dangerous to harvest because of the steep, rocky shores and surf they are often associated with. There is a limited commercial fishery, and local people are allowed to pick them in open areas but not in the protected areas. They must be larger than one and a half inches across the shell. Surprisingly, there is no bag limit. Not surprisingly, they are becoming rather scarce on Oahu.

Some locals show little respect for the tiny shellfish. In 2020 two residents, "Ron" and "Ron," were caught picking opihi in the Pupukea Marine Life Conservation District. The area has been closed to opihi harvesting for years, and these locals had no excuse to be there. It's illegal to remove any marine life from the area. When Division of Conservation and Resources Enforcement officers caught these two Ronnies poaching, they counted 784 opihi. Their market value was about $300. (Not the Ronnies, the opihi. I expect the locals would value the Ronnies at much less than that.) This wasn't their first law-breaking experience either. We'll have to wait to see what the judge thinks their crime was worth.

KNOCKIN' ON
HEAVEN'S DOOR

IN 1880, THE FIRST ENFORCEMENT OFFICERS IN THE STATE OF NEW
York were called New York fish and game protectors. Today, New
York's conservation officers assist with all types of police activities
when called upon. During 9/11, they assisted the NYPD and all first
responders. Their proud history has been marred with fourteen
on-duty deaths over the years. It's a dangerous job anywhere, but
this state has had more than its share of tragic events.

James Davey was hired as a conservation officer with the New
York Department of Environmental Conservation in 2004. He'd been
working with the agency for twelve years when a regular night patrol
turned tragic.

Davey was working in a rural area, checking a property for hunters after receiving recurring trespass complaints from the property
owner. Watching through his binoculars, he noticed a truck parked
in a hedgerow on the property adjacent to the complainant's land.
Two men were in the truck and it was mid-afternoon. There were
ten to fifteen deer in an open field near them. Davey suspected the
two might be waiting until dark to shoot some deer. He left the area
to work on a pre-arranged decoy operation with Lieutenant Liza
Bobseine in another area. Lieutenant Bobseine is a third-generation
warden. Her grandfather was a game protector. Her younger brother
is also a warden.

It was getting dark, and after having no success with the decoy,
Davey suggested they try to locate the truck in the field he'd seen in
the afternoon. Coincidentally, just as they were arriving, the complainant from earlier called to report he'd just heard shots from the

field. The officers discreetly pulled into a parking spot near the field and got out. They couldn't see any vehicle lights.

It was raining and very dark as they crept across the 230 metres to the hedgerow. They found fresh vehicle tracks, presumably from the truck he'd spotted earlier. As they drew closer, Davey could see the silhouette of a truck. They stayed low and got to within forty metres of the truck. "Get down," he whispered. They crouched and listened. They could hear two voices by the truck. Bobseine heard another noise, later determined to be a bullet being chambered. They waited a while until Davey suggested they get up and approach the two poachers. They both stood, and Davey took one step forward as a shot rang out. He immediately dropped to the ground, having been struck by the bullet of a .30-30 rifle. The poacher later claimed he had thought it was a deer and fired at the dark outline he saw. His poaching friend did not fire his .30-06 because he was out of bullets.

Bobseine also thought the guy was shooting at a deer and did not immediately realize that Davey had been shot. The poachers did not shoot again. Davey told his partner he'd been shot, and Bobseine yelled at the poachers to drop their guns. She shone her light at them as they ran toward her. It was obvious they thought they'd shot a deer.

She grabbed their guns and threw the weapons into the darkness, yelling at one guy to call 911. She quickly dropped beside Davey and started treating the horrible wound in his hip and groin area. Blood was pumping out at an alarming rate that she later described as looking like milk pouring out of a jug. She pressed hard on the gushing wound and never let up the pressure.

Lieutenant Bobseine shared the twelve-minute recorded 911 call of the incident with me. It made the hair on my neck stand up. I felt sick. It's an amazing recording of an officer maintaining control of a nightmare situation. She's holding constant pressure on the wound while trying to direct the two poachers and answer the barrage of questions from the dispatcher. The shooter is holding the flashlight while she administers first aid. She sends the second poacher with his truck to meet the ambulance. Medevac is ordered but the weather doesn't allow them to fly. Bobseine constantly encourages Davey, reassuring him that he'll be okay. At one point he asks her to pass on word to his family. He knows he is in trouble.

The first on the scene was a volunteer firefighter and retired police officer. The latter encouraged Bobseine to keep doing what she was doing. Davey remembered giving the poachers orders, not knowing whether they would try shooting again. In fact, they ended up helping with the emergency evacuation. He would later learn the bullet ripped through his groin and hip, blowing his pelvis into three pieces. His major artery and vein to his leg were severed and he would have died within minutes if not for Bobseine's quick thinking. He was not out of danger for a long time, though.

The ambulance would take well over an hour from the initial call until they reached the hospital. Bobseine kept the pressure applied the entire time. Her hands were swollen to twice their size and had turned purple from the lack of circulation. Davey's blood pressure was dropping fast. She remembers how calm and determined he was through the entire ordeal. He was obviously aware of the magnitude of his injury.

An emergency operation through Davey's abdomen was performed to clamp off the major artery to his leg to control the bleeding. The main vein had been totally severed and the main artery was badly damaged. The surgeon noted that the artery had some clotting that likely saved him from certain death before he reached the hospital. Doctors took a piece of artery from his good leg to repair the missing artery in his other leg. During the entire procedure, Davey would need the equivalent of 1.5 times the blood a human holds. He remained in intensive care for two and a half weeks and was held in an induced coma for three weeks. Doctors had to open his leg muscles up from his knee to his hip three times to help reduce the swelling. Today, Davey has mostly recovered; however, he has long-term circulation problems with the leg. The vein never completely repaired itself and causes swelling, especially when he walks longer distances.

The poacher who shot James Davey was sentenced to a $20,000 fine and six months in prison. He will never own a firearm again in his life—not legally, that is. He was also ordered to do one hundred hours of community service including speaking to students about firearm safety. I thought that was light until James told me he'd prepared an impact statement for the judge. In it, he suggested a lighter prison term because he thought that the poacher had truly mistaken him for a deer and that the costs to society of a long prison term would be wrong. He felt a long-term probation period would be best. He also said he just wanted the incident to end. That's an admirable thing. I doubt many people could do that, especially so recently after the event. James was in extreme physical pain that lasted for many months. However, other pain was coming. His wife left him a month after he was out of the hospital. Two months later, his grandfather died.

When James told me the story, my palms were sweating. It's hard to imagine what he and Lieutenant Bobseine went through in the field that night. They would not have known for certain what the two poachers were thinking. The poachers could have panicked and decided to shoot them both. The officers could have shot the poachers too, when they ran toward them holding their rifles.

I am not one who knows the words to many songs, but when James finished telling me the story, for some unexplained reason I thought of the song "Knockin' on Heaven's Door" by Bob Dylan. I didn't know the words to this song either, so I later looked it up, and this is the first verse:

> Mama, take this badge off of me
> I can't use it anymore
> It's gettin' dark, too dark to see
> I feel I'm knockin' on heaven's door.

Fate has a way of popping up many times throughout life. The day before James Davey was shot, Lieutenant Bobseine had read an article about an elk hunter who'd been shot in the leg. The man saved himself through applying pressure to control the bleeding. She would have known how to treat the wound regardless, but the fresh reminder from the story stayed with her.

Dark humour often helps officers recover from traumatic situations. When Bobseine visited Davey after his three weeks in an induced coma, she told him, "I know there was a shit fight over who was going to get to use that decoy ... but you didn't have to become one!"

I talked to Davey in the spring of 2020. He had remarried and had a wonderful seven-month-old child whom he doted on. Liza Bobseine still proudly patrols the state of New York like the two generations before her.

COVID-19 COULD
SAVE WILDLIFE

THE WORLD CHANGED WHEN COVID-19 SWEPT ACROSS ITS NATIONS and instilled fear in every society. It will likely change the way we conduct our lives, travel and business in many ways, forever. Ironically, the disease that began with wildlife may have a positive impact on wildlife. Reduced travel for a few months improved water and air quality in many countries around the world—our beleaguered planet was able to take a breath of fresh air. Those changes are likely temporary; however, another change could have long-term benefits to wildlife.

On February 27, 2020, China banned the trade and consumption of wild animals within China. The live "wet" markets of Wuhan were the epicentre of the virus outbreak and were the most likely source. It's believed the disease was transferred from wild animals to humans. If that ban continues, it could be one of the most positive changes for wildlife in many years, especially if the ban includes all wildlife and parts. The ban also prohibits the hunting and breeding of wildlife except for selected, pre-approved purposes such as "scientific research, population regulation and monitoring of epidemic diseases." The *South China News* also reported that "Online trading platforms, commercial markets, agricultural markets and restaurants, as well as transport and logistics companies shall not supply venues or services for wildlife consumption."

Time will tell how serious China is about this ban, and whether it will actually follow through with it or whether it is just a smoke-and-mirror show. It's unknown whether the ban will apply to wild plants. I sent an email to the reporter who wrote the article, asking a few questions. It's been well over a year, but I don't expect to get a response. In any case, hopefully, other countries will follow suit and implement their own similar wildlife bans. It's interesting to think that a decision by China could turn out to be a significant conservation decision.

But it's more likely that a new wildlife threat will emerge as the world recovers from COVID-19. The virus has disrupted the worldwide food supply chain from growers to delivery. I expect people will turn to poaching wildlife as a food source and for money. The courts will probably take these actions lightly. I hope I'm wrong.

HUNTING FOR DUMMIES

Ohio officers were on patrol and happened upon a couple of dumb turkeys. The two were older gentlemen who were gathering up turkey decoys right beside a deer bait station (illegal) when the officers pulled up. The two, oblivious to hunting laws, didn't even try to cover anything up. Both had thick Russian accents. They admitted to shooting a turkey (illegal—it was youth-only season). Their two turkeys were a jake, which is an immature male, and a hen (both illegal). They had shot them both with a rifle (illegal). They were using an electronic caller (illegal). They hadn't checked the birds at a check-in station (illegal). At one point in the conversation, one of the guys asked, "How #$%!@#!ed am I?" If you're dumb enough to ask that question, you're likely smart enough to know the answer, and it ain't pretty. The officers got writer's cramp filling out tickets that totalled about $4,000 for the two turkeys. They had a violation for every turkey law in Ohio except using a live bird as a decoy.

THE NORTH AMERICAN WILDLIFE ENFORCEMENT OFFICERS ASSOCIATION

IF YOU'RE NOT A FISH AND WILDLIFE OFFICER, YOU MAY NEVER have heard of the North American Wildlife Enforcement Officers Association. (If you *are* a fish and wildlife officer and haven't heard of it, you should get out more.) The association was formed to promote professionalism in wildlife enforcement through training, networking and professional recognition. The organization also honours its fallen officers during the opening ceremonies at each conference. From 1980 to 2019, twenty-two Canadian and seventy-seven American fish and wildlife officers were killed in the line of duty. Funds are gathered to provide support to families of the deceased officers. Support for this fund is always welcome.

NAWEOA's vision is "unified international natural resources enforcement and protection." The need for a unified international approach to poaching has never been greater. The global trade of the world has opened up the global trade of poached and smuggled wildlife and plants. The stories contained in this book are but a small sample of what's going on throughout North America. And I haven't even touched on the big, known issues of poaching of African animals; I've purposely focused on our own large issues in North America.

The idea for NAWEOA was conceived in 1980 by a group of three Canadian officers, Rick Hoar of British Columbia, Lou Ramstead of Alberta and John Fallows of Alberta. They got together by phone and discussed the concept. They wanted a place where wildlife officers from all over North America could meet to discuss similar problems, share knowledge and form connections across borders. John Edwards from Saskatchewan was contacted and jumped at the chance to get involved. John Fallows contacted John Babcock in Montana, who agreed with pursuing the idea. On July 12, 1980, the first meeting was held in Great Falls, Montana. Sixteen representatives from western Canada and the north central United States made their way, at their own expense, to discuss and build the foundation for NAWEOA. They included:

Alberta: Lew Ramstead, Ponoka; John Fallows, Lethbridge; Syl Pompu, Vermilion.
British Columbia: Richard Hoar, Creston.
Idaho: Lee Frost, Hailey; Kit Christensen, Twin Falls; Terry Baltazor, Shoshone.
Montana: John Babcock, Shelby; Tom Bivins, Choteau; Ed Comly, Stanford; Stanley Peck, Cascade; Jack LaValley, Great Falls.
Saskatchewan: John Edwards, Glaslyn.
Wyoming: Dennis Almquist, Pinedale; Chuck Oakley, Kemmerer; Chuck Thornton, Big Piney.

The first paragraph of the first minutes of the first meeting read: "On July 12, 1980, an organizational meeting was held in Great Falls, Montana, to discuss the feasibility of, if deemed necessary, [establishing] the North American Wildlife Enforcement Officers Association. Delegates from Montana, Wyoming, Idaho, British Columbia, Saskatchewan and Alberta attended. All expenses associated with this meeting were at the officers' expense ..."

In the meeting, the officers discussed a number of great topics including training, equipment and communications. Wildlife officers are called game wardens, conservation officers, fish and wildlife officers, fishery officers, police, and other titles. They agreed on *enforcement officers* because that covered everything. (Of course, officers are used to being called a few other choice names not listed here.) Wyoming agreed to host the meeting the following year, in Cody. The first official convention was held in 1982 in Regina, Saskatchewan.

Some agencies frowned on the concept of this organization. There was paranoia and fear that officers were trying to create a North American union. Can you imagine how frightening that must have been? Giving wardens rights like those of so many other international unions—what a preposterous notion! I'm joking, of course, but it was no laughing matter. That was not their goal and never has been. Even today, there are some agencies that show little support for this important get-together held each year. But many agencies do understand and support the association. Wildlife officers from everywhere are grateful for that. Through training, they have seen the benefits of the organization and the success of interagency cases, as shown throughout this book.

The NAWEOA convention is held every year at a jurisdiction willing to support it. The gathering starts with a moving recognition of any officer(s) killed in the line of duty over the past year. There is always a chilling tribute, and this alone is enough reason for the conference to be held. The officers' families are often present and recognized by all in attendance. A five-kilometre torch run is also held that pays tribute to the same fallen officers. The meeting then switches to training, discussion about major cases and guest speakers, followed by evening social events. The interaction with officers across borders is a key element in keeping up with the bad guys.

NAWEOA encourages spouses and families to attend the conferences too. Officers' spouses get together and listen to speakers and mingle, sharing stories about being the partner of a game warden. Being the spouse of a wildlife officer is not your average relationship. It's not just the dangers of the job. Wardens' families must answer the phone at any hour, and are often called upon to care for some wounded, wild animal or to store a dead animal in their freezer. They never know what their spouse will drag home next.

The social highlight of the event is an afternoon of practising warden skills. Teams are formed from agencies or a mix of agencies that challenge each other in fun events such as wildlife identification, investigation techniques and other officer skills. Lifelong friendships are made. Retired officers are encouraged to attend. What other occupation holds an event that involves spouses, families and retired employees? NAWEOA is always seeking financial support to host its annual conference. If you'd like to help support this worthwhile organization, contact them at www.naweoa.org.

NAWEOA is also a supporter of the Game Warden Museum. The museum is located in the Peace Gardens along the international border between Manitoba and North Dakota. It includes a memorial to fallen officers and pays tribute to all officers who protect our fish and wildlife resources. The facility also serves as a public education platform and encourages public support.

THE LAST WORD

IN THE COURSE OF PUTTING THESE STORIES TOGETHER, I CON-
tacted and talked to hundreds of officers, agency staff and retired
officers. I enjoyed meeting all of them. Unfortunately, however, once
I began contacting officers, poaching stories were all too easy to find.
The plethora of material was great for writing a book, but frankly, I'd
rather have had a more difficult time finding poachers.

If you enjoy our fish and wildlife resources in North America,
please say thanks to your local fish and wildlife officers and their
staff. Please do your part to help save our wildlife, and support game
wardens by reporting poachers and suspicious activity. It's so important to be part of the solution. Poaching is a pandemic that needs
everyone's help to control. You have helped fish and wildlife officers
in a small way by purchasing this collection. I will be supporting the
Game Warden Museum with proceeds from this book.

I hope you enjoyed reading the book as much as I did writing it.

ACKNOWLEDGEMENTS

I AM DEEPLY INDEBTED TO THE FOLLOWING PEOPLE FOR THEIR stories and for their help in the preparation of this book. My ideas could not have been turned into a book without them.

Dennis Amsden, Brian Anthony, Ken Balkom, Andy Barnes, Al Barrus, Steve Beltran, Rick Berggren, Liza Bobseine, Greg Borne, Kerry Bradford, Al Breitkreutz, Donald Brown, Matthew Bryant, John W. Buss, Florian Büttner, Jim Carroll, Stu Cartwright, Randy Conway, Ernie Cooper, Jim Corbett, Phillip Cottrill, James Covell, Terry Damm, James Davey, Jeff Day, Kip Dirks, Jean-François Dubois, Jason Dukette, Kipp Duncan, John Edwards, Ian Ellsworth, Anthony Esposito, Earl Evans, Bob Farrell, Kevin Fitzsimmons, Patrick Foy, Pat Freeling, Joe Frost, Calvin Fulton, Alain Gauthier, Dave Gavin, Jesse Gehrt, Carlos Gomez, Dale Grandstaff, Craig Gunderson, Mike Hanson, Kallum Harrington, Tyler Harrison, Doug Hayes, Joe Haywood, Candy Henderson, Oscar Hensen, Jared Hill, Rick Hoar, Frank Huebert, Jeff Irwin, Mike Jones, David Kalb, Tom Kenway, Todd Kinnard, Coy Kline, Aaron Koss-Young, Jake Kreamer, Kyle Kroll, Richard Laboissiere, Rick Leach, Rod Lebert, Chris Lester, Bill Logiodice, Andy MacKay, Richard Macklem II, Chris Maier, Nando Mauldin, Sean McKeehan, Jeff McPartlin, Dustin Miller, Brooke Mitchell, Jonathan Moser, Scott Murdoch, Mike Nice, Jereme Odom, Ron Ollis, Ron Payne, Todd Petrunger, Ivan Phillips, Craig Porter II, Charlie Pudwill, Tyler Quandt, Les Sampson, Wayne Saunders, Cal Schommer, Mike Scott, Brian Shinn, Dustin Shorma, Sean Spencer, T. C. Stacy, Florian Stein, Brady Stevenson, Matt Taylor, Bob Timian, Nick Turner, Nathaniel Valenti, Jon Watkins, John Webb, Matt Wemple, Chad Williams, Eric Wright, Trevor Wyatt, Dave Youngquist, Ian Zieman, Jim Zimmerman.

Randy Nelson was born and raised in Saskatchewan and moved to the BC coast for a job as a fishery officer without ever having seen a salmon. In his thirty-five-year career, he became the most decorated fishery officer in the history of the province, having received multiple awards, including the international Pogue-Elms Award and the Queen's Jubilee Medal. Randy is an accomplished athlete, having raced in over two hundred competitions including ten marathons. He used that running ability to literally run down and catch hundreds of poachers. He has also curled over four thousand games and played in numerous national championships including the Brier, Seniors, Masters and Canadian Police Nationals. Randy is also the author of *Poachers, Polluters and Politics* (Harbour Publishing, 2014). He lives in Kamloops, BC.